IMAGES
of America

MORGAN COUNTY

On the Cover: Bob Atchison's construction crew is pictured here building thee Empire Reservoir dam around 1907. Clarence M. Work and Cree Work are included in the photograph. Empire Reservoir is part of the Bijou Irrigation District. (Courtesy of the Fort Morgan Museum.)

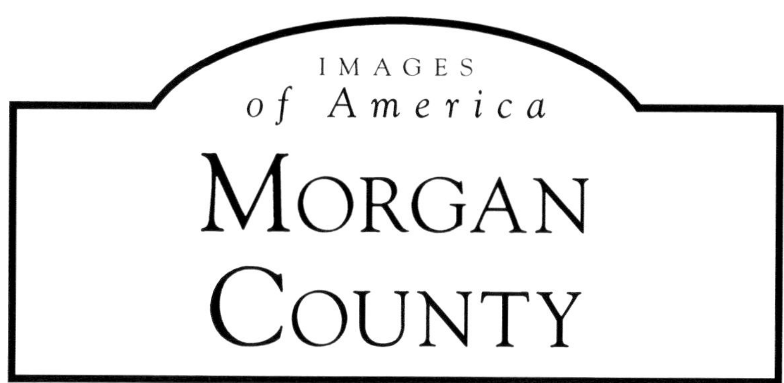

Brain Mack and Linda Midcap

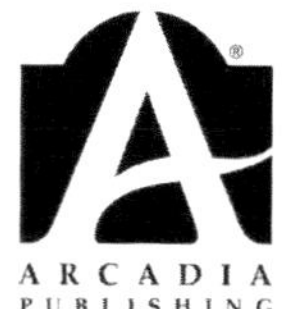

ISBN 978-1-4671-1565-0

Published by Arcadia Publishing
Charleston, South Carolina

Printed in the United States of America

Library of Congress Control Number: 2015947747

For all general information, please contact Arcadia Publishing:
Telephone 843-853-2070
Fax 843-853-0044
E-mail sales@arcadiapublishing.com
For customer service and orders:
Toll-Free 1-888-313-2665

Visit us on the Internet at www.arcadiapublishing.com

CONTENTS

Foreword

The Fort Morgan Heritage Foundation is pleased and proud to publish this pictorial history of Fort Morgan and Morgan County. This book includes many photographs of the lives and times of our forebears, who took part in the birth and growth of Fort Morgan and Morgan County. We can see in this book the changes in how things were in the past and how they are today. Our forebears were strong and courageous people with dreams, visions, and foresight who built a community that promised prosperity, safety, and security. We learn from the past to improve the ways of the present. It is a never-ending progression. The mission statement of the heritage foundation and the Fort Morgan Museum reads: "The Fort Morgan Museum deals primarily, but not exclusively, with the history and culture of the people of northeastern Colorado, through collecting, preserving, interpreting, researching, and exhibiting materials reflecting the diverse history and traditions of the area. We serve as a depository for historical items and records and act as the educational and informational center for the community."

The Fort Morgan Heritage Foundation is open to everyone. A governing board consisting of 17 volunteers meets monthly to assist the professional museum staff in charting the course of the museum programs, publications, and exhibits.

— Donald A. Ostwald Sr.
President, Fort Morgan Heritage Foundation

Acknowledgments

As a community, Morgan County has a fascinating history, and we are delighted to be able to shed a light on some of the people, places, businesses, and events that have made that history so rich. While this book contains only a shadow of everything that has made Morgan so special, we hope that readers are able to get a sense of the community we have long considered to be home. Compiling the photographs and information in this book was a rewarding work of intrigue, as we learned more about Morgan County than expected. This endeavor could not have been completed without the assistance of the following contributors: Walter Barrett, Merle and Margie Bristol, James Butler, Sara Canfield, City of Fort Morgan, Kay Coffin, Gerty Chapin, Jerry Cooper, Community History Writers, Sue Christensen, Bethany Crandell, Lyn Deal, Thelma Downing, Fort Morgan Museum, *Fort Morgan Times*, Timmy Fritzler, Jenni Grubbs, Jenese Hankins, Gail Hawkins, Heritage Foundation, Barb Keenan, Chandra McCoy, Maxzine Lorenzini, Viviane Lorenzini, Dave Luna, O.J. Metzger, Jo Ostwald, Anne Overturf, Lanny Page, Dave Roberts, Gerry Thiel, McKinley Thompson, and Kathy Wood.

Unless otherwise noted, all images are courtesy of the Fort Morgan Museum.

INTRODUCTION

Like the oceans, and mountain ranges, the enormity of the prairies was a natural barrier to Western settlement and possible enemy incursions. Until the last half of the 19th century, the inhospitable plains were dreaded as never-ending monotonous miles by those early European and American explorers and trappers who traveled them. To the Native Americans, primarily seminomadic Arapahoes and Cheyennes, the northeast Colorado area, which provided food, shelter, clothing, trading goods, religion, and culture, was their home. They hunted bison, antelope, deer, and other plains animals. Some wintered there, protected by bluffs in dry creeks such as the Wildcat and Bijou. They did not own the land but claimed the territory as theirs and would fight to keep their sovereignty over it.

The first explorers, mountain men, military men, and traders found little to entice them to settle. The vast, treeless, dry, seemingly endless landscape hid its potential under its sea of grass. They saw little beauty and found no riches in its vast horizon or in the subtle hues of the many grasses and plants, so they hunkered down and endured, getting through it as quickly as possible.

After the Louisiana Purchase, and the success of the Lewis and Clark expedition, Zebulon Pike led a military expedition of exploration, whose tasks were to assess, survey, and map the prairie territory in 1806. In 1820, Stephen Long, who led another expedition of exploration, followed the South Platte River until it reached the Rocky Mountains. Long wrote about an "orchard" after camping by a large cottonwood grove near the river, and later, traders named the spot Fremont's Orchard. Both Pike and Long described the high plains as "becoming, in time, as celebrated as the sandy deserts of Africa." Neither believed any form of agriculture would be successful. Both were wrong.

The discovery of gold in the Colorado mountains in 1858 created the impetus for growth in northeastern Colorado. First, stagecoach stops and pony express stops were created to facilitate mail and supplies as well as transportation for prospectors and others attracted by the promise of wealth.

In 1864, a fort was built on the bluffs overlooking the river and the natural ford at Muir Springs to protect wagon trains and act as a deterrent to Indian attacks. "Galvanized Yankees" (captured Confederate soldiers who volunteered to serve in the Union army, fighting Indians in the West rather than languish in prisoner-of-war camps) as well as Union troops manned the fort.

The fort, named for a popular Union officer who, ironically, never saw the fortress, only existed for four years because, by 1868, most of the Plains Indians had been forcibly removed to reservations, the bison were being systematically slaughtered, and there was no longer a need for protection for wagon and supply trains. Also, the Union Pacific Railroad had completed a line to Cheyenne, Wyoming, and settlers began to come by rail to claim land under the Homestead Act.

With the Native Americans and bison gone, the vast acres of lush buffalo grass offered fantastic opportunities to ranchers such as cattle kings John W. Iliff and Jared Brush, who grazed thousands of cattle in the eastern third of the state.

Their dominance was challenged by the successful creation of an irrigation canal (1882) in Weldon Valley, the brainchild of those who believed that water could turn the desert into an Eden, and soon homesteaders began to settle in the valley.

The popularity of the Homestead Act and Timber Act, as well as the disruption of the Civil War, led many men and women to envision a brighter, independent future in the West. Abner S. Baker, a Civil War veteran, joined Horace Greeley's Union Colony Number One. While hunting buffalo near Beaver Creek, he realized that the unplowed land could be fertile if water could be brought from the river by canal.

In 1884, Baker completed the Platte and Beaver Ditch and platted the townsite. Modestly, he named the new community after the fort. Many of our founding families came from Baraboo, Wisconsin, and were part of Baker's extended family; others came from Canada and eastern states. They shared common Protestant religious traditions, conservative Republican political views, and entrepreneurial ideals. They were old-stock Americans whose ancestral roots were predominately English, Scottish, and Scots Irish. They recruited settlers like themselves, advertising for thrifty, serious, wholesome families who would work hard and do their civic duty. They believed in temperance and believed that adversity and personal obstacles created opportunities for persistence, self-discipline, and faith.

They valued neighborliness, cooperation in working for the good of the community, good schools, music, moral literature and drama, sports, and organized civic, social, and cultural clubs and other activities, which were necessary components of a civilized, successful community.

The first school was opened in 1885 by J.H. Farnsworth, proprietor of the first hotel; later, he sold it for $400 to the newly formed school district. Prof. Sidney M. Prince taught the first class of 20 students in the spring of 1885. Even though the first church was not built until 1886, a Sunday school was started immediately for the religious education of the children.

The Farnsworth Hotel was the site of dances, plays, and musical evenings. In 1884, a brass band was formed; it gave concerts to raise money for music and instruments. Baseball teams were formed, horse races were held, and many women in town started the Fort Morgan Helpers, promoting religious, social, and musical improvements in the community.

In 1887, Morgan County was formed from Weld County; in 1889, Fort Morgan became the county seat. This designation, along with the routes of the Union Pacific and Burlington Railroads, ensured that growth might be slow but would be steady. Editorials in the *Fort Morgan Times* (begun in 1884) made it clear that Fort Morgan wanted only respectable, clean-living people as its citizens.

The most rapid growth, in the first decade of the 20th century, occurred because of the construction of more canals and reservoirs. Jackson Lake, the largest reservoir in northeastern Colorado, guaranteed there would be enough water to irrigate crops such as sugar beets and corn. Winter wheat also became an important crop.

In 1906, the Great Western Sugar Company built sugar factories in both Brush and Fort Morgan. By 1910, the city had purchased land for a downtown park, created a water-sewer system, and built an electric generation plant, which furnished free electricity for porch lights. Fort Morgan gained a national reputation as the "City of Lights." A public opera house was built, as were as a county courthouse and a city hall. There were nine churches and a Masonic lodge. The city gave tax incentives to those who planted trees. A small, dedicated group of ladies raised money to beautify the cemetery first, then began to raise money for a library.

However, the job opportunities created by building canals and reservoirs, growing sugar beets, and operating a sugar factory changed the homogeneous culture of the town into a more diverse one. Growing sugar beets required hand labor and knowledge of growing beets. Recruiters visited towns in Russia, inhabited by German Russians; because life in Russia was growing increasingly difficult, many German Russians signed contracts with the Great Western and immigrated to Nebraska and northeast Colorado. Sugar beet growing farmers would be allotted so many workers. Also, Great Western recruited Mexican families to work as beet labor. Since the growing season was from spring to autumn harvest, workers had to find other housing and jobs to support their families. Soon, Mexican colonies and German towns were created by Great Western to keep those hardworking families here year-round as a reliable labor group.

The introduction of groups of immigrants, brought to work into the Fort Morgan community, follows a familiar pattern: each group met with hostility, distrust, and prejudice. Their "foreignness" threatened established residents who feared them as the Other—a mind-set that increased mutual suspicions and tension. Often, groups who endured such persecution and hostility when they first arrived treated later newcomers with the same fear and distrust.

Because agricultural and ag-related jobs often attract new immigrants, and Fort Morgan's major industries are ag-related, the newest immigrant groups—from Africa, Central America, and rural Mexico—will continue to enrich our community as they begin to make Fort Morgan their home. Already, ethnic stores and restaurants offer a choice of cuisines and styles. Children of immigrants are participating in sports, graduating from Fort Morgan High School, and attending college.

As of this writing, Fort Morgan has a population of 12,000. It is surprisingly cosmopolitan, because it is firmly attached to many foreign countries through the global economy and social media. Its convenient location to the Front Range makes it an attractive place to live. Its wide, tree-lined streets, well-cared-for gardens and lawns, flourishing Main Street, and cultural and educational amenities are appealing and reflect on the deliberate farsighted choices made by earlier generations. Fort Morgan does offer a diversity of opportunities to a growingly diverse population, but at its core, the founders' belief in hard work, persistence, civic responsibility, and neighborliness still holds true.

This pictorial history proves that "a picture is worth a thousand words." Our compilation provides a snapshot of a time gone by, a window into our past, the foundation upon which our community is built.

— Barbara Keenan

One

Military Fort Morgan

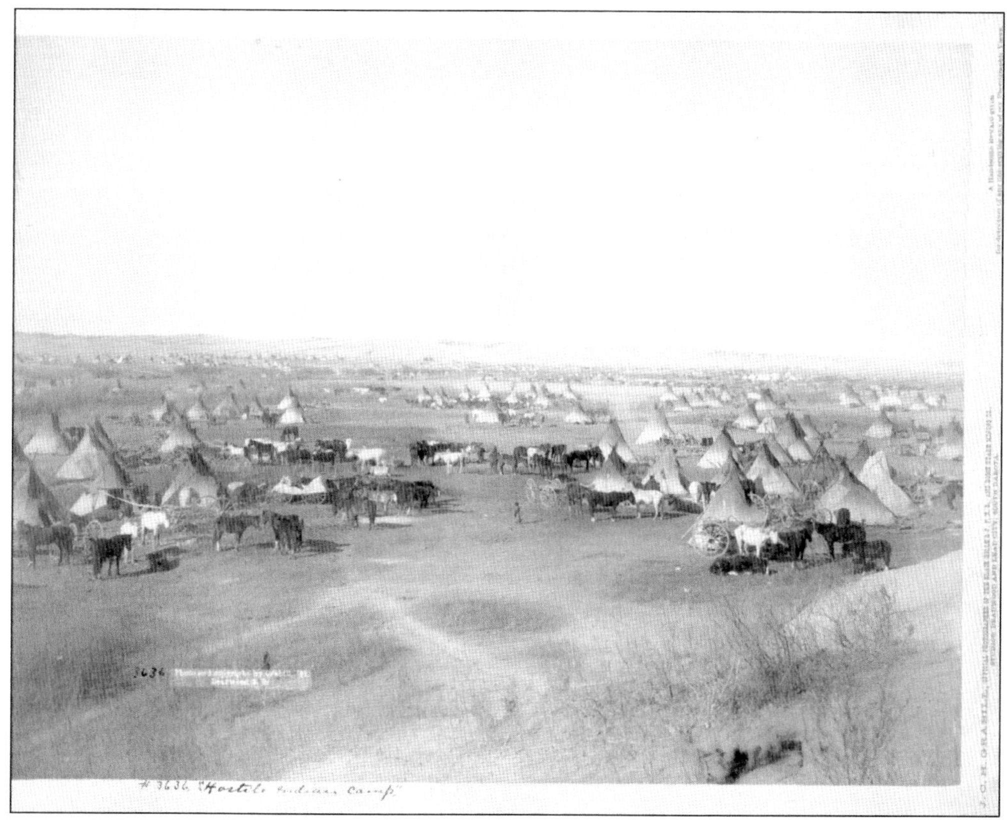

Before the time of westward expansion into northeastern Colorado, the land that would become Morgan County was hunting ground for the Arapahoes and the Cheyennes. (Courtesy of the Library of Congress.)

South Platte River Trail, Julesburg to Denver

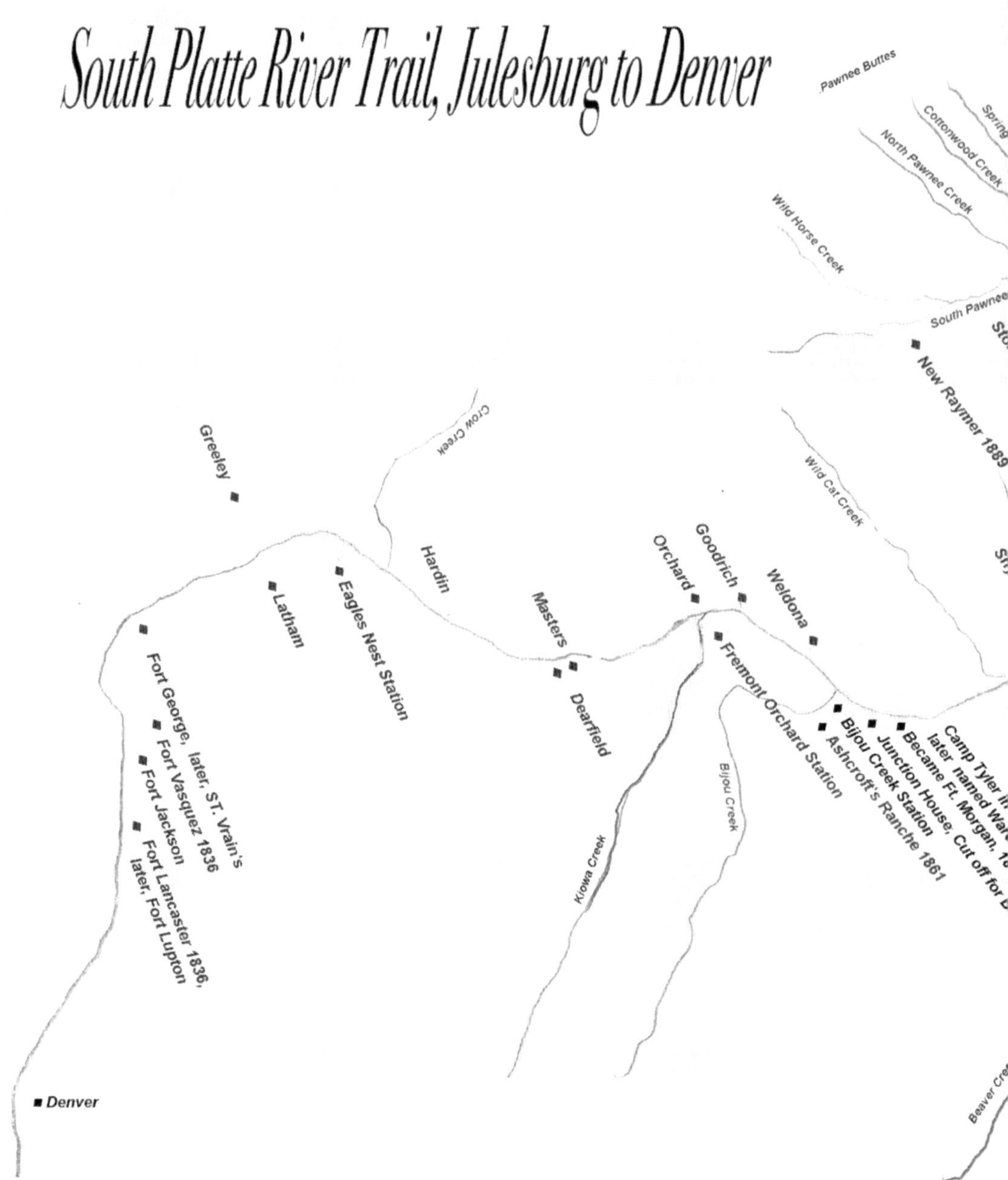

For centuries, Native American tribes used a trail along the south side of the South Platte River (later known as the Overland Trail, the South Platte River Trail/Road, and the Denver Trail/Road). Stephen H. Long used this same trail during his 1820 expedition, but he was only one of many explorers to do so. Following the discovery of gold in Denver in 1858 and then in the Rocky Mountains beyond, the South Platte River Trail, passing through what eventually became Fort Morgan, was the primary east-west road for stages, wagon trains, mail, telegraph, and eventually

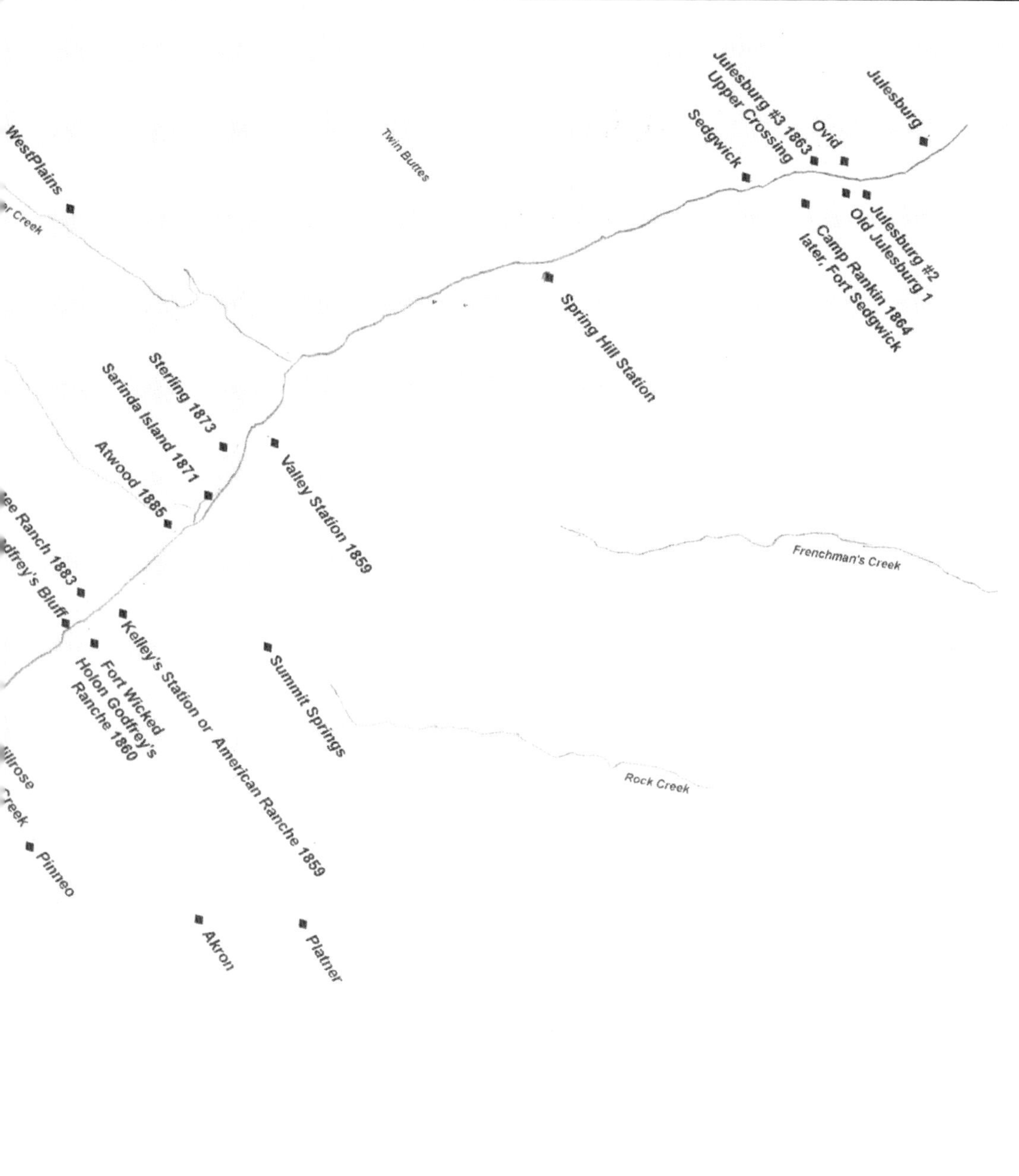

railroads. Along the trail, adobe and sod stations were located 20 or 30 miles apart. The stage stations were 10 or 12 miles apart, the horses being driven on the run and making the distance in about an hour. Some of these stops were actually ranches whose proprietors took advantage of the lucrative trade with the many travelers traversing the trail. Eventually, Fort Morgan, situated halfway between Fort Sedgwick and Denver, became the largest of the posts.

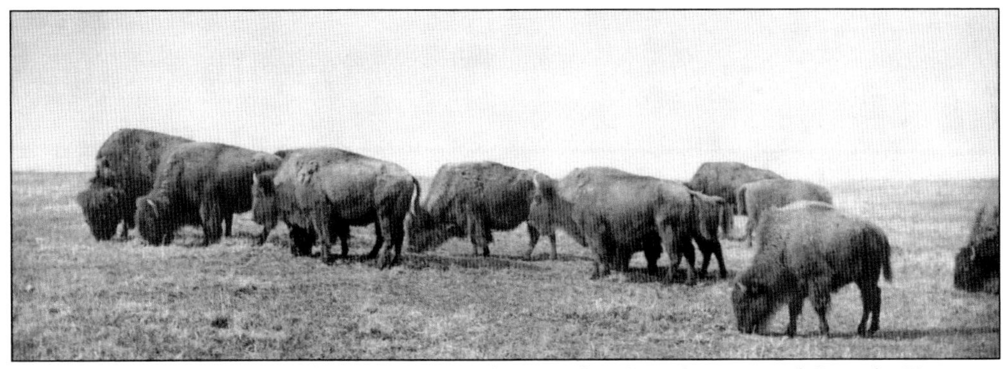

At one time, over 25 million bison were spread across the United States and Canada. However, by the late 1880s, the total number of bison in the United States had been reduced to fewer than 600 individuals. Most of these were herded onto private ranches, and the last known free-roaming population of bison consisted of less than 30 in the area that later became Yellowstone National Park. (Courtesy of the Library of Congress.)

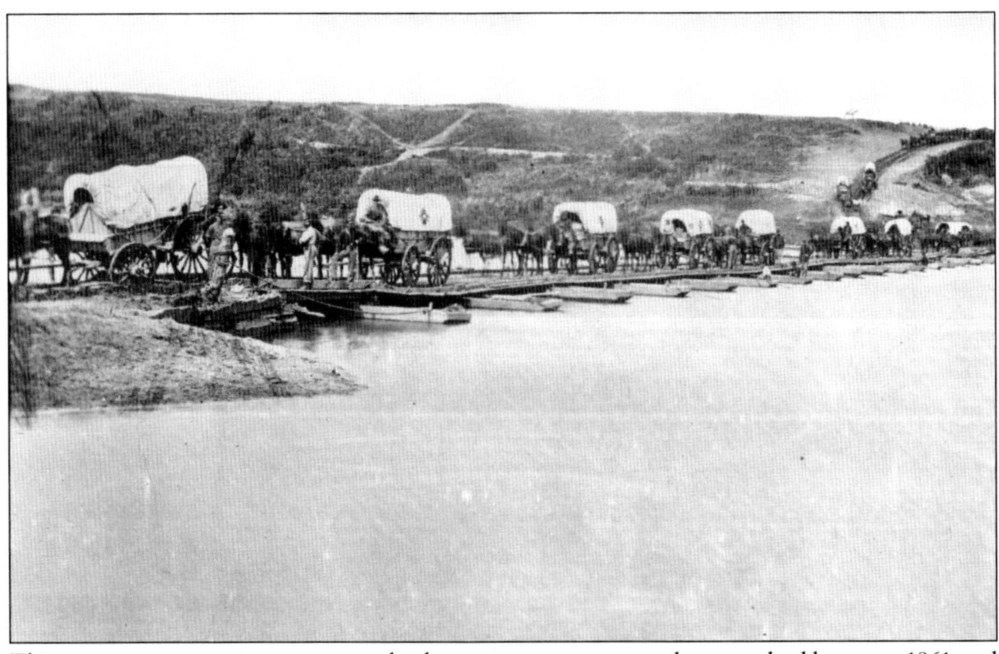

This wagon train crossing a pontoon bridge on its way west was photographed between 1861 and 1865. (Courtesy of the Library of Congress.)

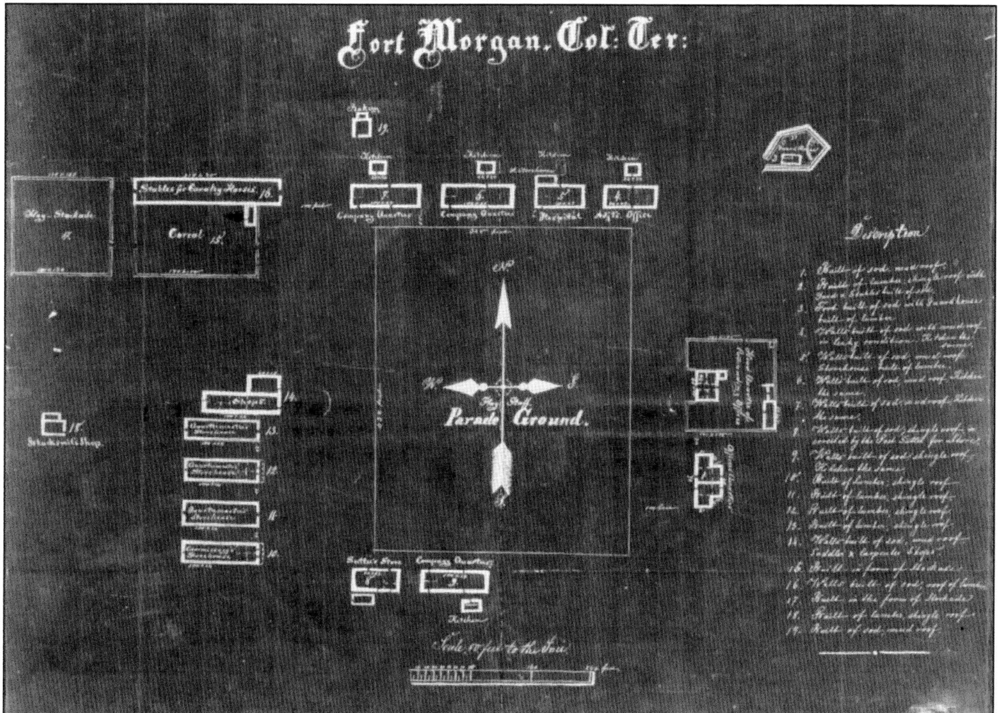

This plan (scale 1 inch = 50 feet) for Fort Morgan were obtained from the National Archives in Washington, DC. It is believed to have been produced in 1866 by the US Army. The map shows the locations of the camp buildings, which are in a square with a parade ground in the center. In the upper right corner is written "Plan of Camp Wardwell"—Wardwell became Fort Morgan in June 1866.

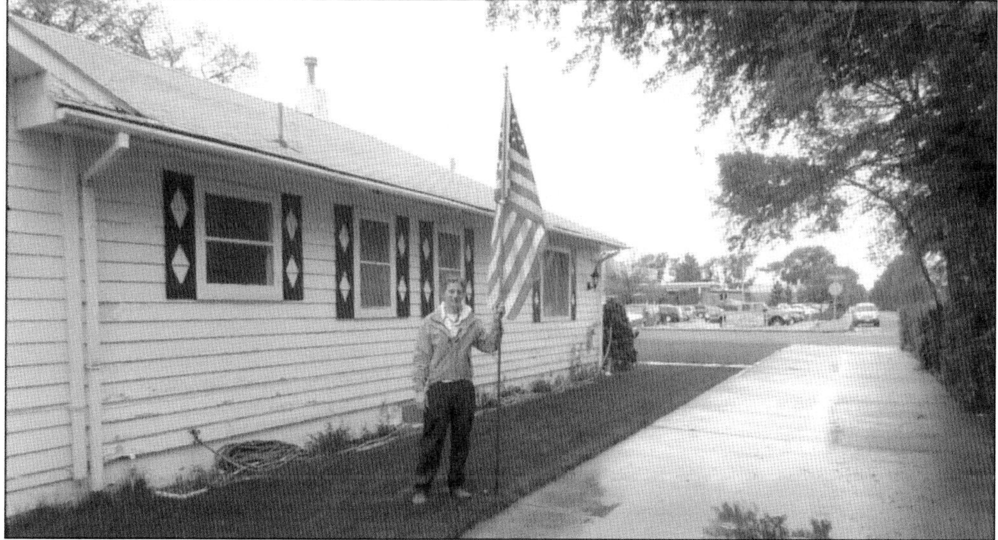

In 2015, the Fort Morgan Museum took on a project to locate the fort. The flag pictured here marks the spot where the original flagpole stood. The area is currently home to Fort Morgan's hospital, high school, and several residential homes. Officers quarters would have once stood at the intersection of Riverview Avenue and Grant Street.

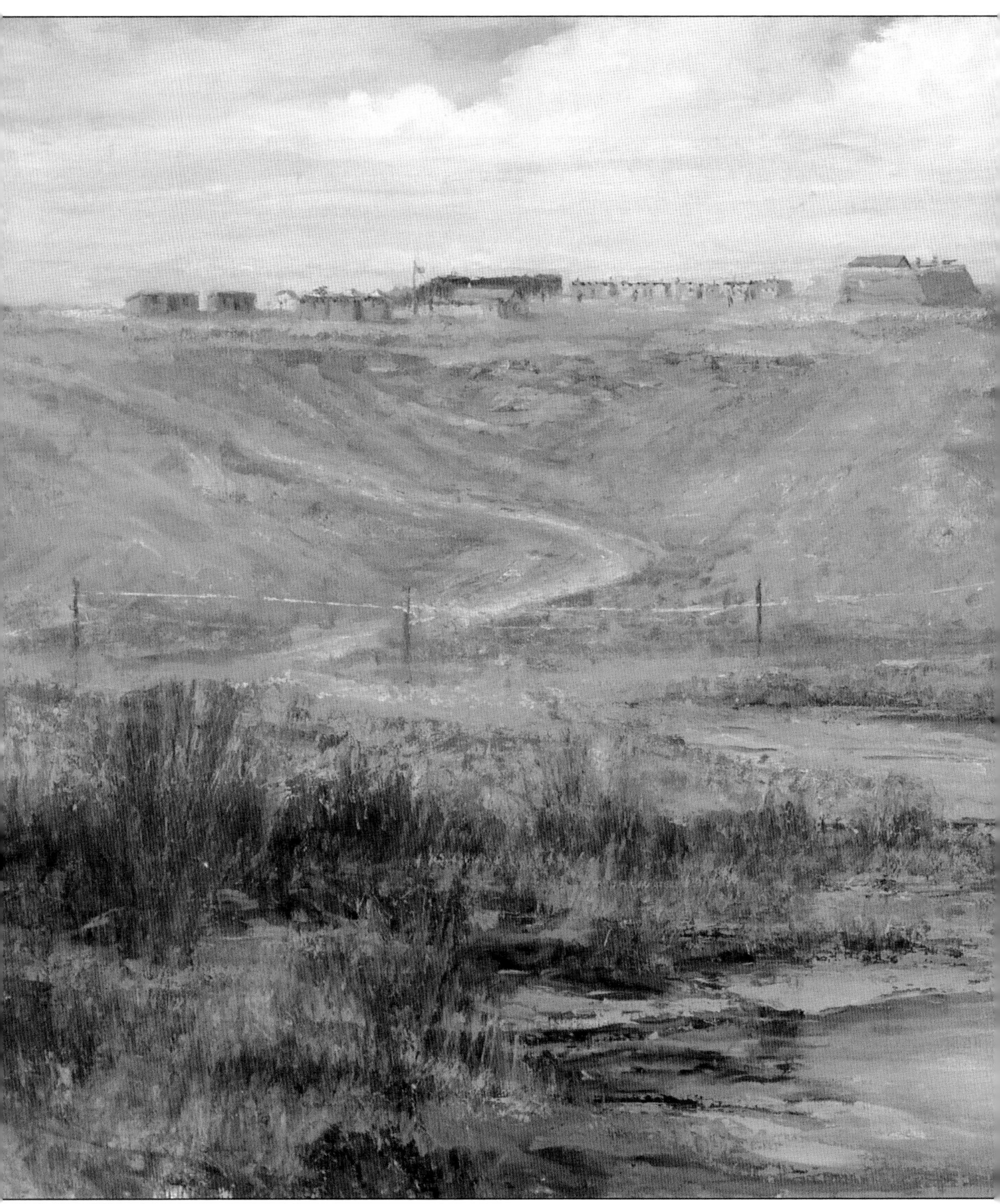

The fort eventually grew to be a large collection of solid sod buildings enclosed within a stockade calculated to hold 200 wagons or serve as a drill ground. The site selected for the fort was on the brow of a prominent plateau 60 feet above the South Platte River. In addition to its natural advantages of water and forage for the fort's animals, it proved to be a strategic location for a wide-open view of the prairie and any advancing attacks of the Cheyenne or Arapaho warriors. Trains of six to 20 wagons each were held at the fort until the collection grew to at least 100 wagons.

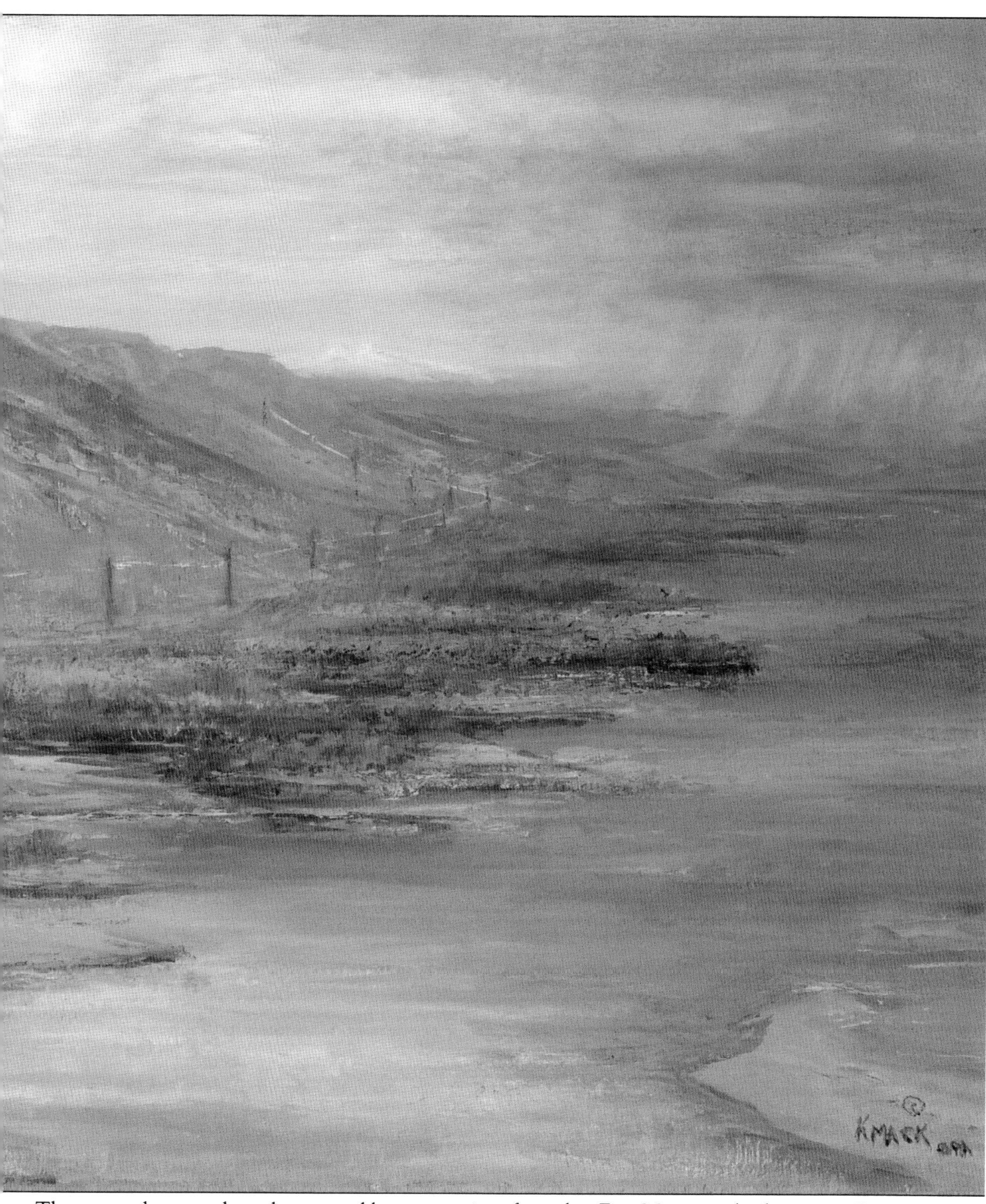

They were then conducted westward by companies of cavalry. Fort Morgan, also known as Post Junction, Camp Tyler, and Camp Wardwell, was in existence from 1864 to 1868. Located along the South Platte Trail, the fort was active—19 different companies from 11 regiments represented both cavalry and infantry—with an estimated 1,200 to 1,400 soldiers were stationed at the fort. (Courtesy of Karol Mack.)

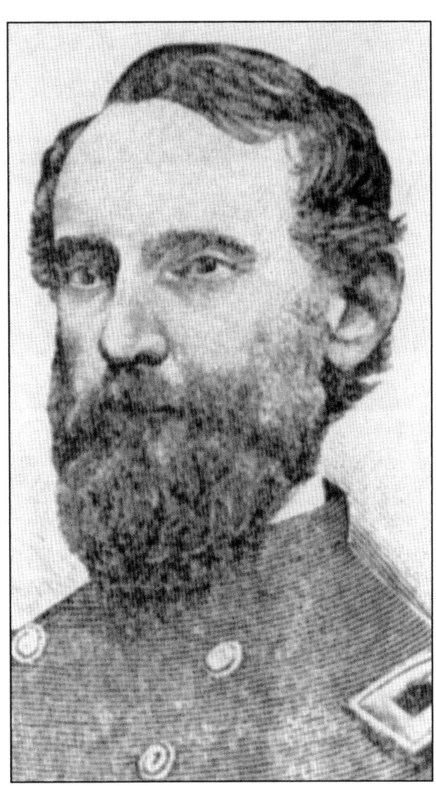

On June 23, 1866, Gen. John Pope, commander of the district, ordered Fort Wardwell's name be changed to Fort Morgan in memory of his recently deceased aide-de-camp, Col. Christopher A. Morgan, who died a tragic death of asphyxiation from a gas leak in the general's home.

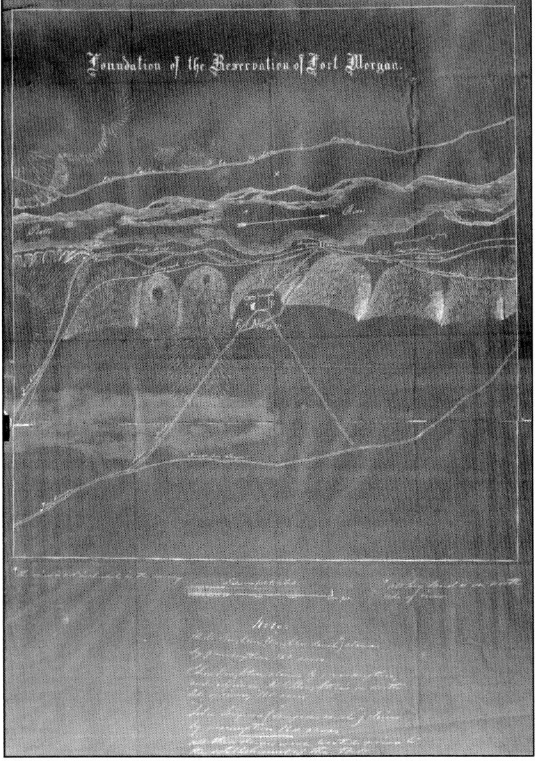

This map of Fort Morgan shows the location of the fort with buildings, the trails or roads, telegraph lines, and ranches. In the legend, the following is written: "M.O. Boughton (Boughtons Ranch) claims by preemption, 160 acres. Boughton claims by preemption and M.O. Boughton's on the north-side of the river, 160 acres. John Simpson (Simpsons Ranch) claims by preemption 160 acres. All claims were created previous to the establishment of the post."

The marker for Fort Wicked can be seen just over the Morgan County line. The illustration appears in the October 13, 1866, *Harper's Weekly*. The article states, "Fort Wicked, Colorado noted as the ranch where a brave man named Godfrey, and his wife held over two hundred attackers at bay for two days during the troubles last year — killing many and wounding others, and finally driving them off."

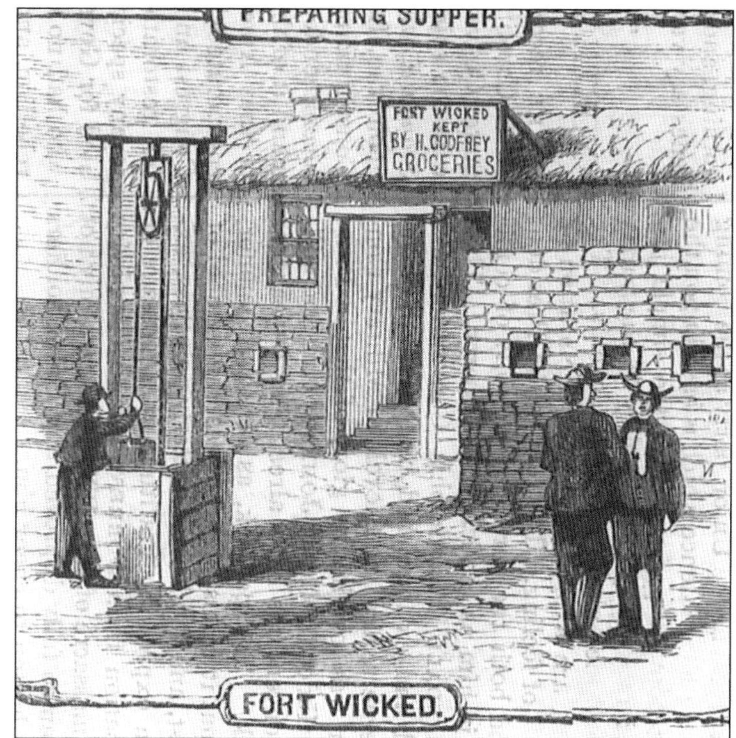

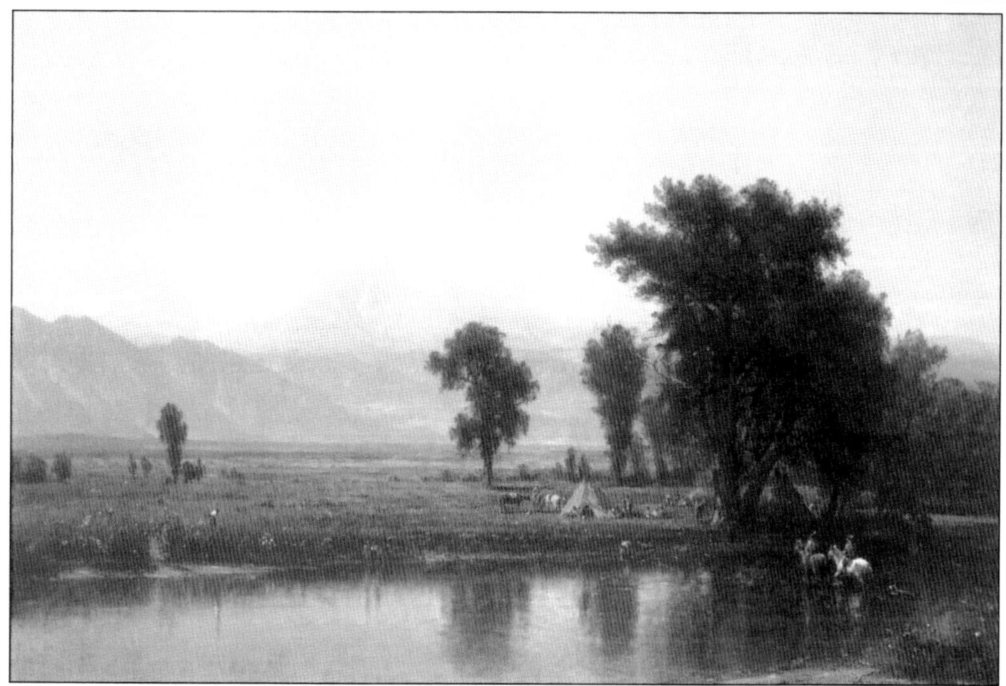

Worthington Whittredge completed *Crossing the River Platte* in 1871; it is now displayed in the White House's Roosevelt Room. Whittredge journeyed across the Great Plains to the Rocky Mountains in 1865 with Sanford Gifford and John Frederick Kensett. The trip resulted in some of Whittredge's most important works.

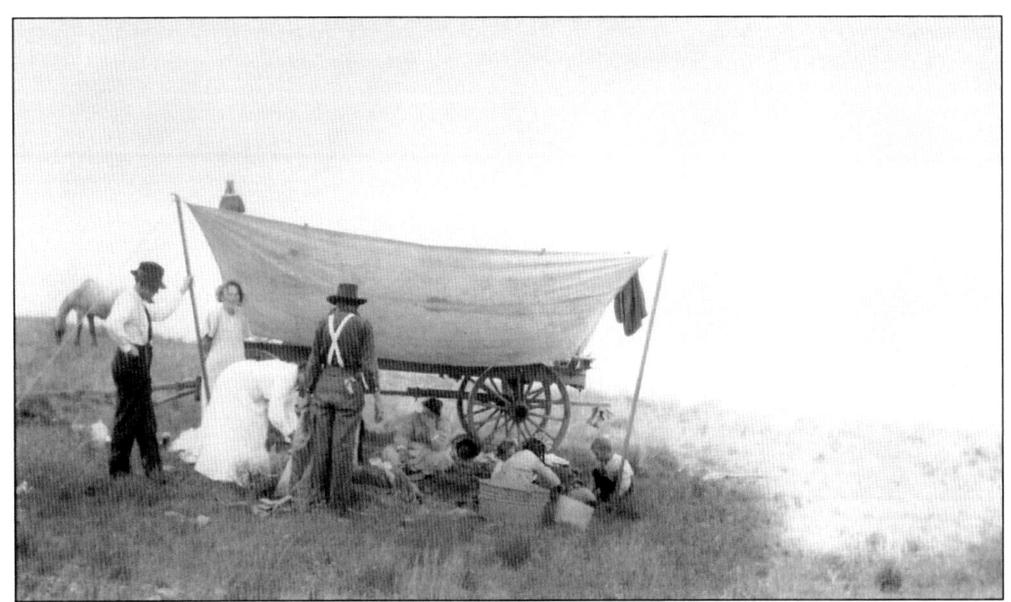

The discovery of gold at Cherry Creek, Colorado, and later in the Rocky Mountains, resulted in a great migration of people following the South Platte River Trail. Families made camp nightly, and in instances of inclement weather or injury, camp was set up for several days or more.

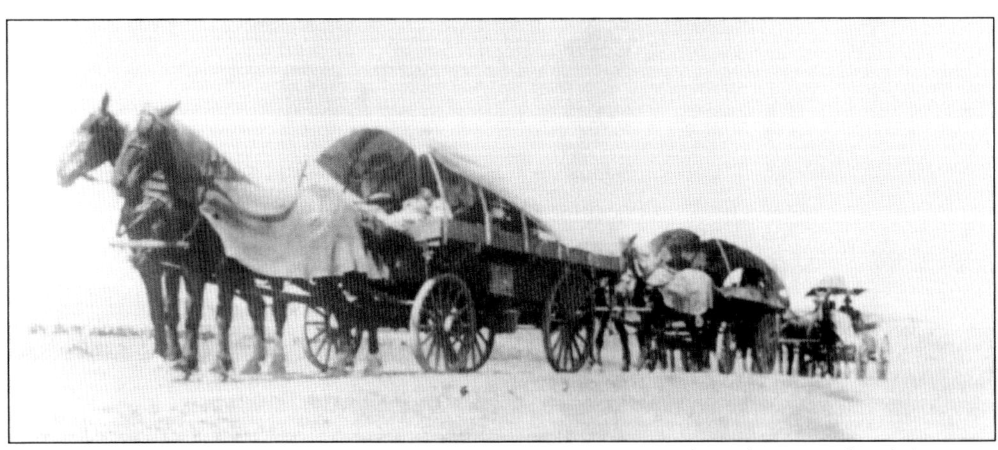

Wagon trains were still arriving as late as 1914, as seen in this photograph of the Lem Welever family.

Two

Ranching and Agriculture

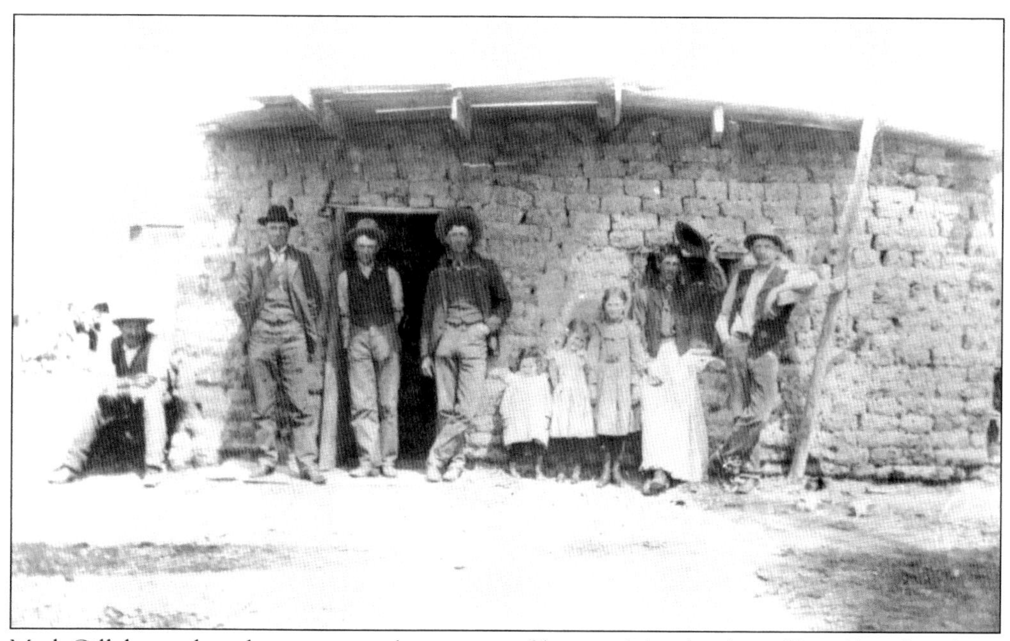

Mark Gill, located on the extreme right, is pictured here with his family and hired hands in front of a sod bunkhouse built in 1871 on the 22 Ranch. (Courtesy of Denver Public Library.)

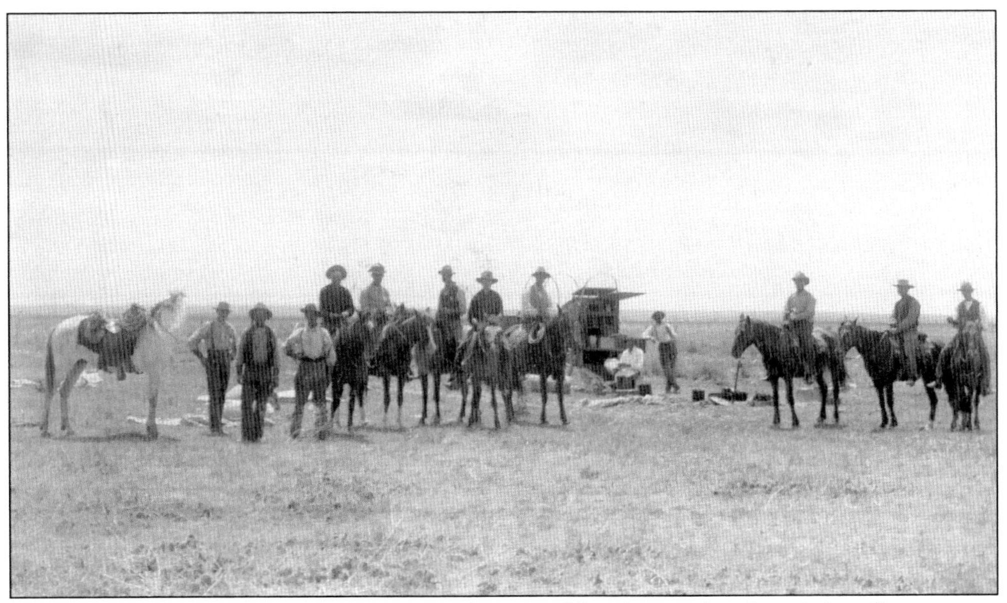

Working cattle on the wide-open plains was only successful with many hands and a lot of horsepower. The chuck wagon accompanied the roundup, feeding the men three meals a day. John Samples took this photograph in 1885 but gives no indication where the roundup took place.

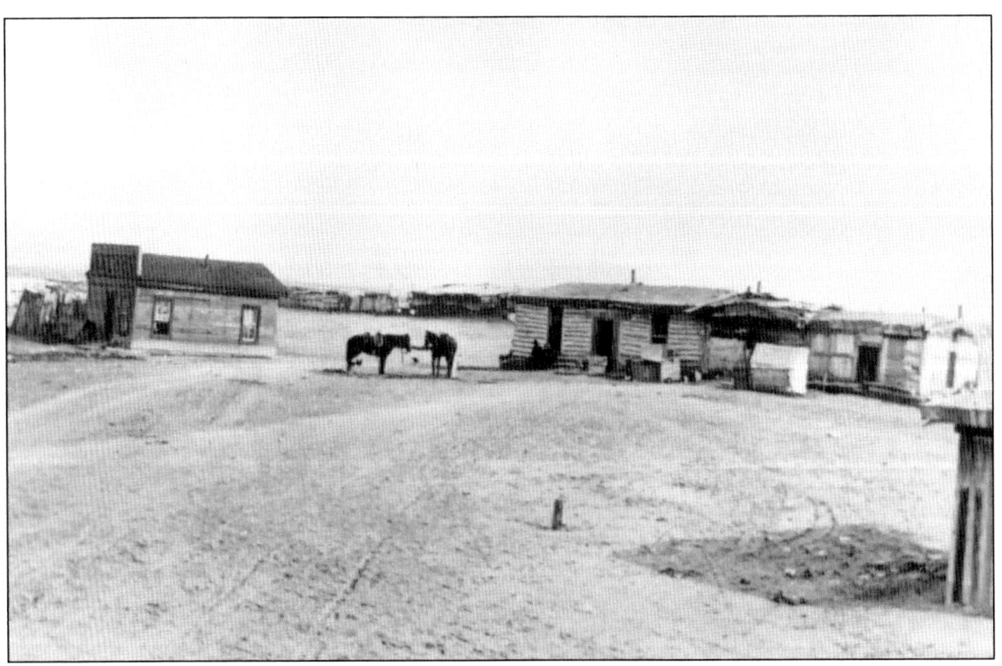

The first home of the Abner S. Baker family is pictured here around 1885. Baker is recognized as the town's founder. Robert W. Atchison's family lived at this location from 1892 to 1899. Louis Kinkel lived here from 1900 to 1906, and his slaughterhouse was here for many years.

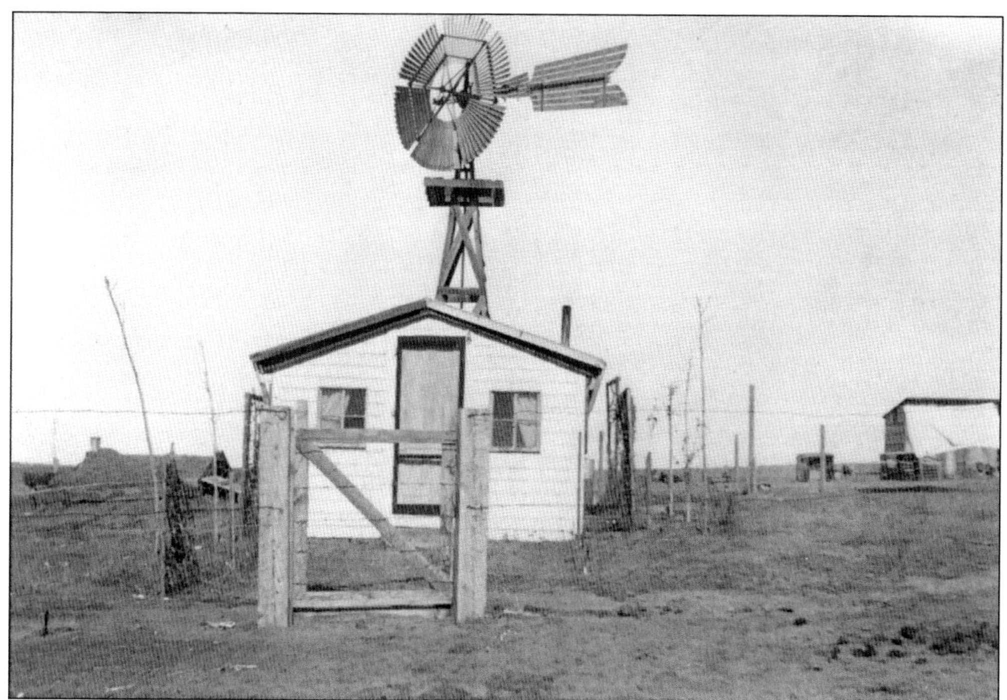

William W. Rickel's homestead, pictured here around 1888, depicts the typical Western shotgun house sometimes called a shanty. Beginning in 1871, hundreds of homesteads were granted in the Fort Morgan area. The 1862 Homestead Act allowed up to 160 acres with the promise to live, work, and prove up the land.

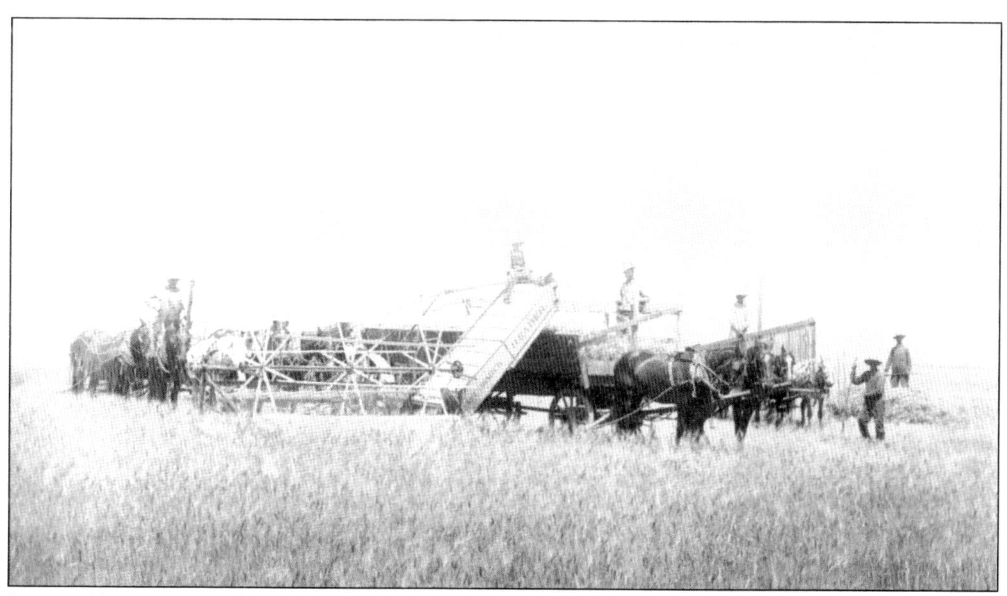

Pictured here is an early McCormick-Deering horse-driven harvester, made by the International Harvester Co. IHC was formed in 1902 and marked a merger between longtime competitors McCormick and Deering, as well as several smaller companies.

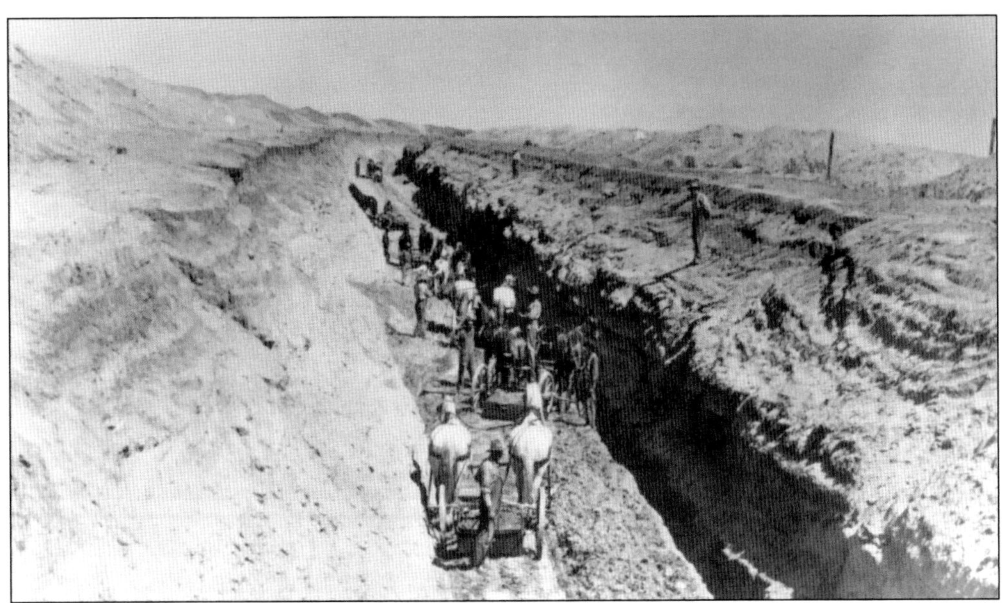

Several irrigation ditches were built during the late 1800s and early 1900s. This photograph displays the Robert "Bob" Wellington Atchison construction team digging the cut for the Bijou Ditch. All work was done without the aid of steam- or gas-powered machines to dig the seven-foot-deep, 50-foot-wide ditch.

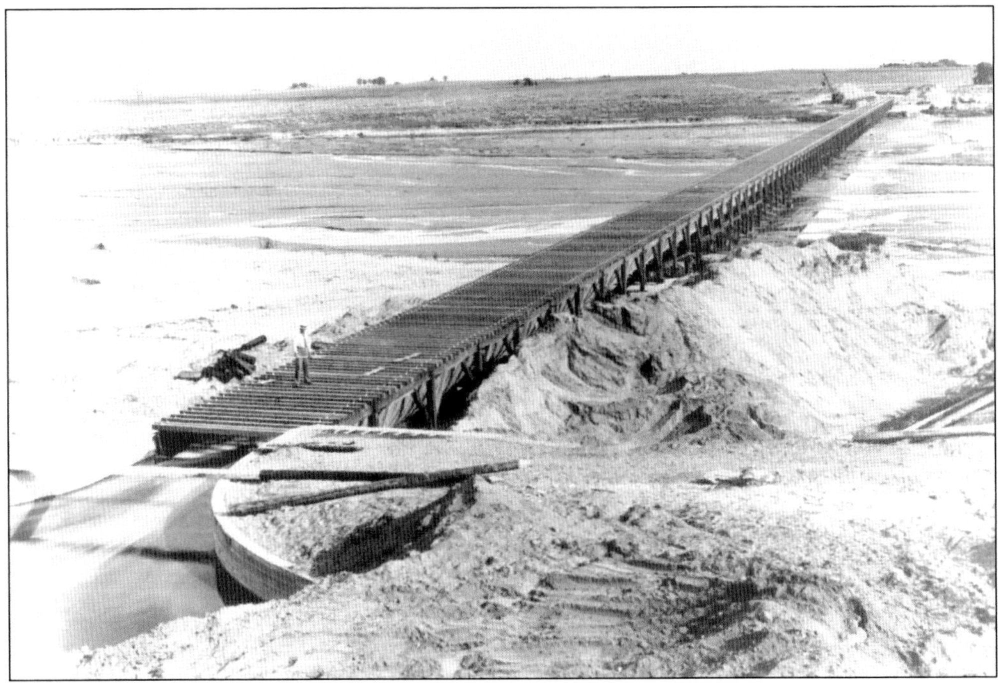

The first flume at this location over Bijou Creek, built in 1883, was rebuilt by shareholders in 1904–1905. The 1,578-foot-long steel flume pictured here replaced the old wooden flume, which was destroyed by a flood on May 31, 1935. The steel flume was constructed at a cost of $45,000.

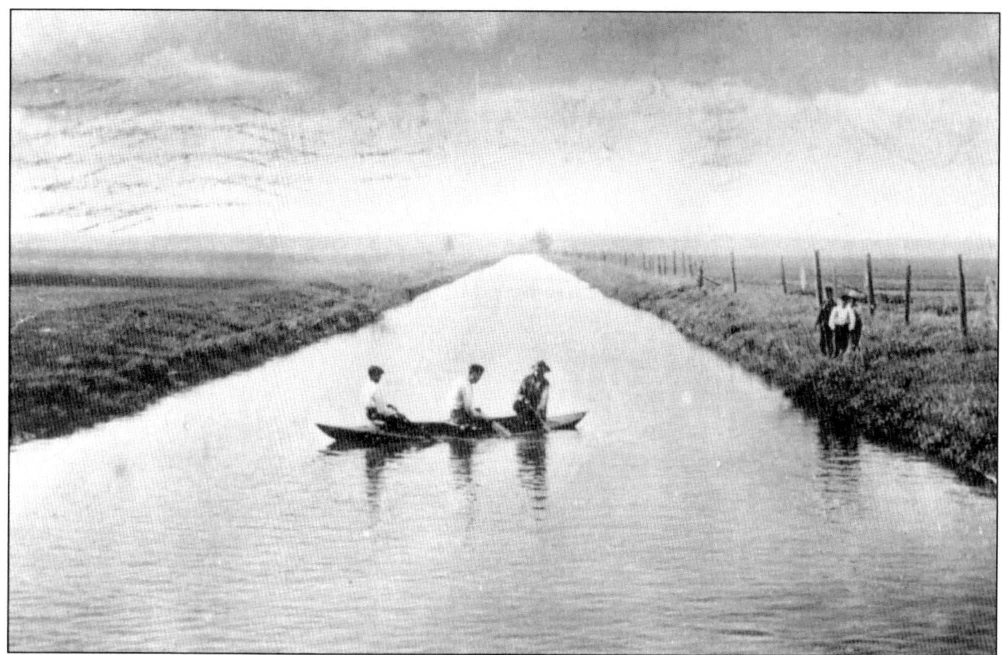

For those making a living on the semiarid plains, water is a precious commodity. Abner Baker conceived the idea of the Fort Morgan irrigation ditch and financed it with proceeds from the construction of other irrigation ditches. Three children stand on the right bank watching as three men canoe on the irrigation ditch.

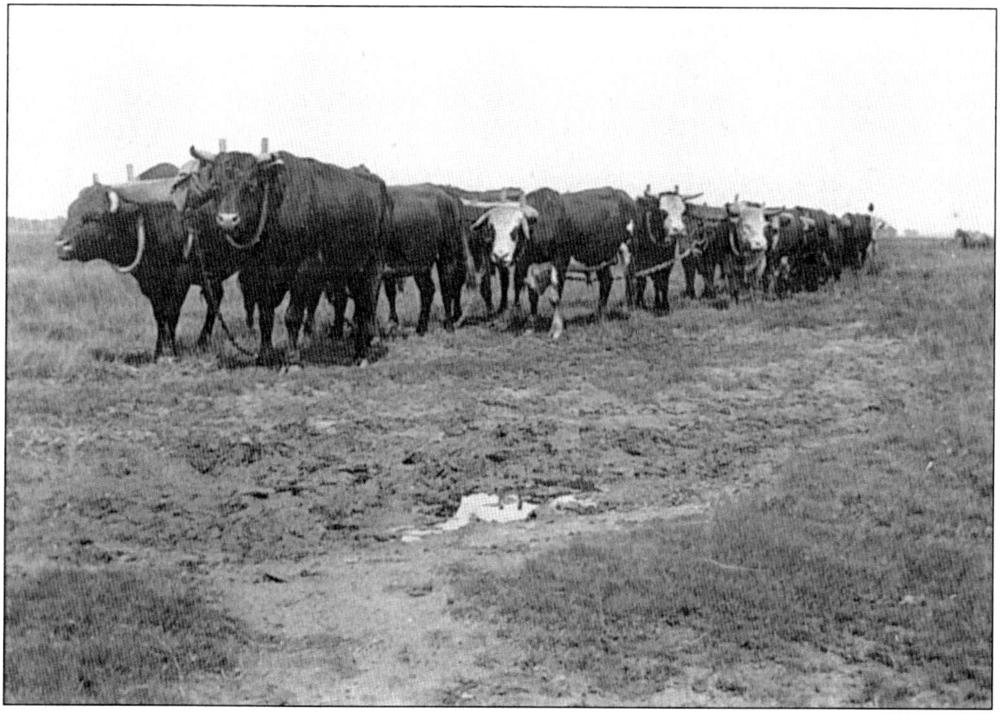

Some 30 to 40 oxen were used in early farming days to pull huge plows to dig out ditches to help drain seepage from land near the river. This photograph is from the Weldon Valley around 1905.

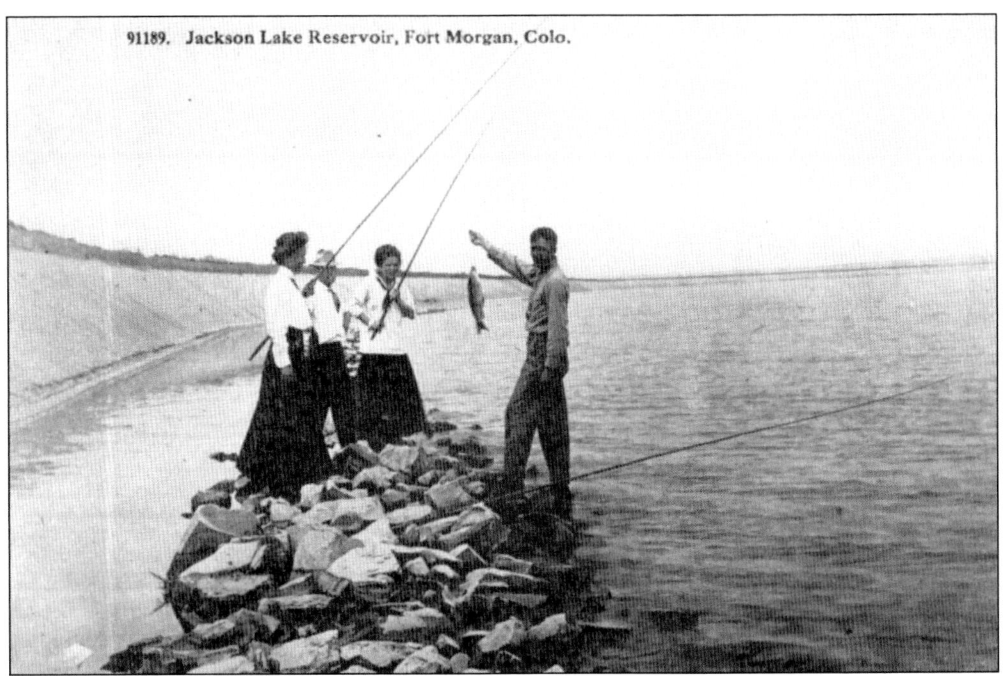

Jackson Lake was built in 1901 and is a water-storage reservoir with a capacity of 1,552,000,000 cubic feet. It was named for Leonard A. Jackson, a Weld County pioneer who came to the area in 1875 after freighting between Denver and Leadville (1865–1875). Jackson helped construct many irrigation canals in the Orchard district. The lake quickly became a place of recreation for both fishing and boating.

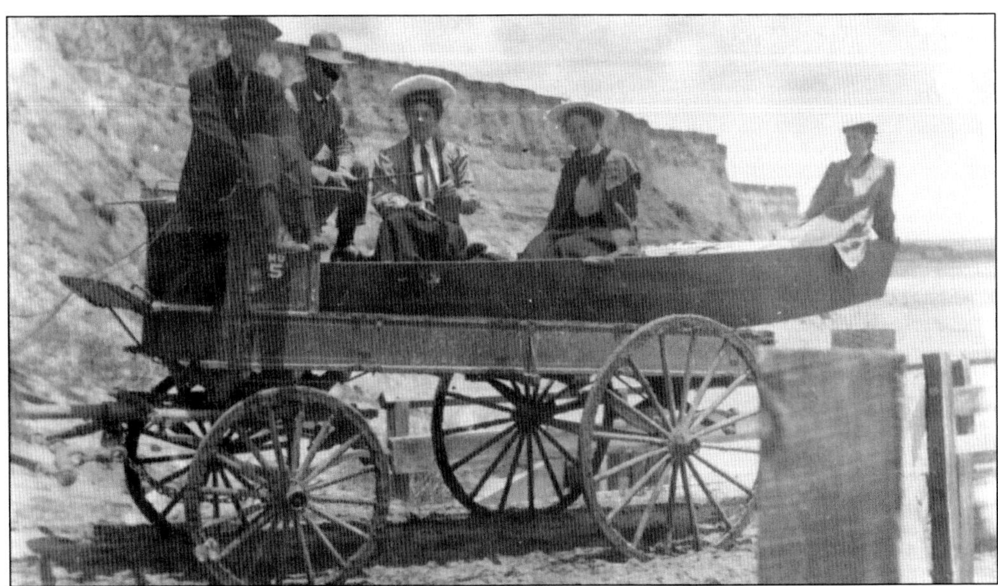

A few of the people in this recreational photograph are identified as Harold, Brose, Harriet, Florence, and Fred Stanley.

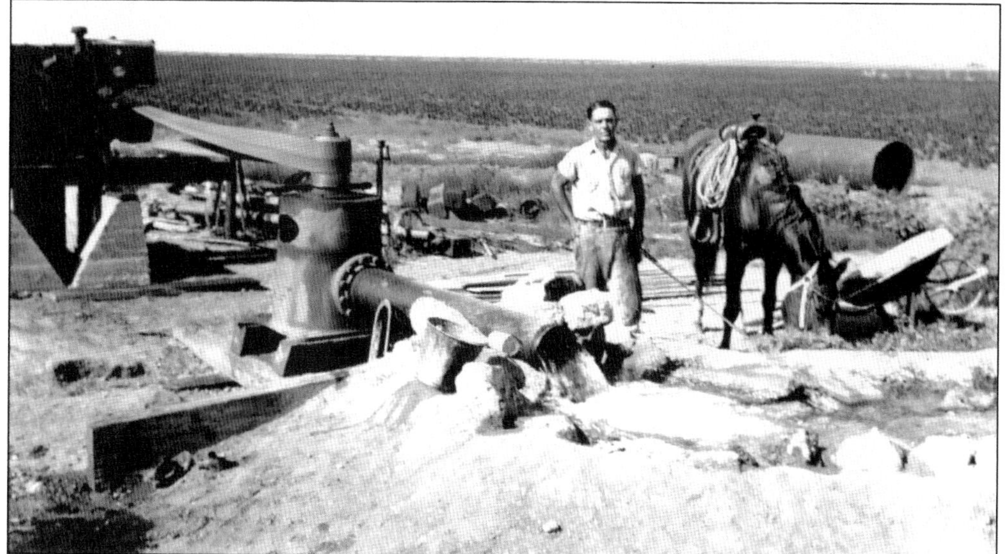

Chuck Harshman is pictured here at his irrigation well, which pumped 2,000 gallons per minute, near Wiggins in 1934.

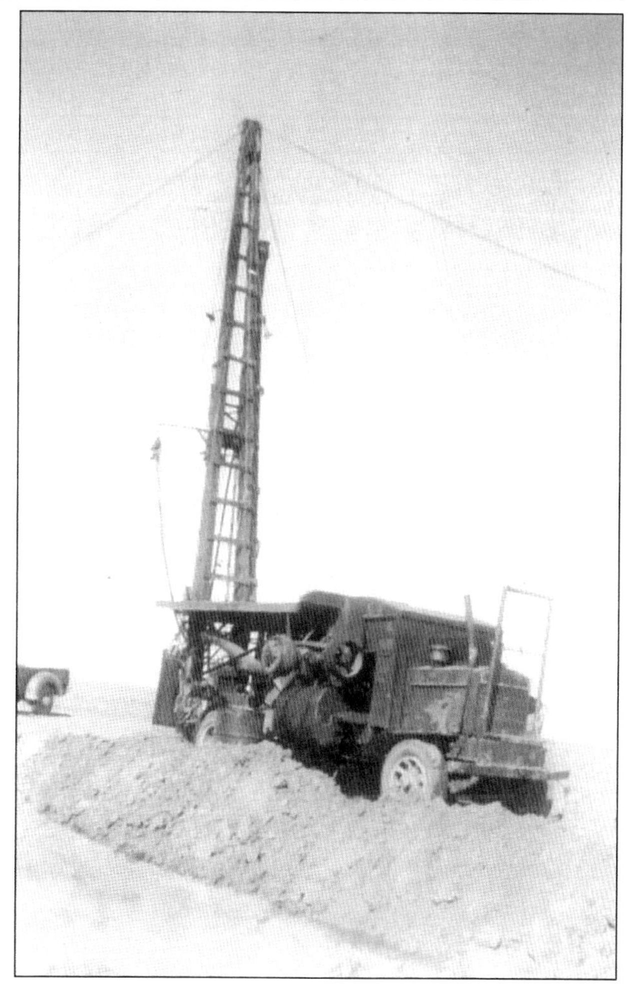

Successful deep-well irrigation started in Fort Morgan in the early 1930s with Fort Morgan's own Les Canfield leading the way. He discovered a system that used a pump and reverse circulation, allowing the drill bits to go deeper. He had Jack Dove, an early Fort Morgan machinist, fabricate a rig that would allow drilling through five-inch layers of rock, thus reaching the deeper sources of water. In later years, Canfield's drilling activities stretched from southern Colorado to the Canadian border.

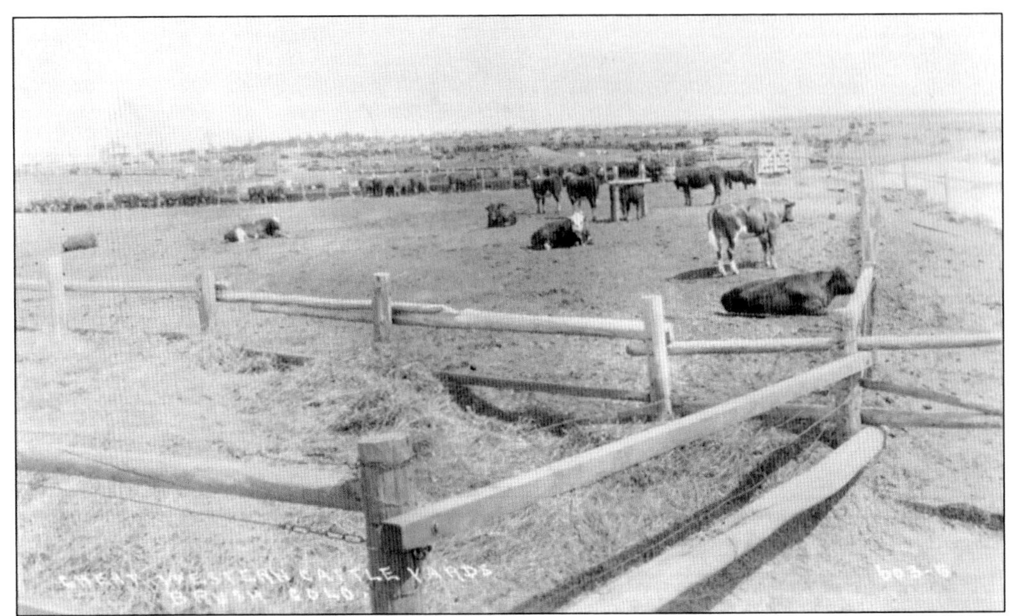

A valuable by-product of the sugar beet industry was pulp. Numerous cattle and sheep yards began with the introduction of two sugar factories in the county during 1906.

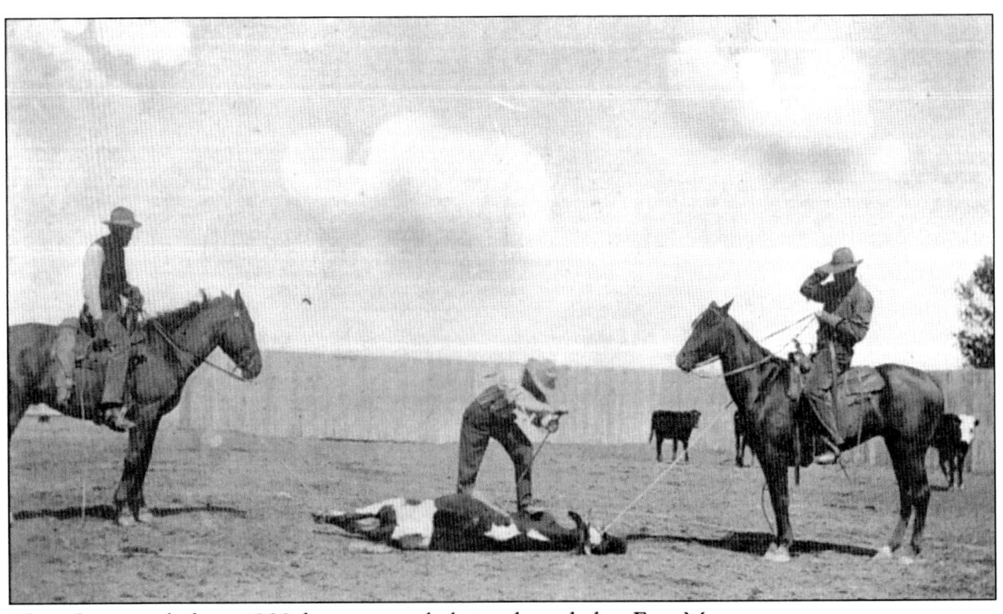

This photograph from 1908 features cattle being branded at Fort Morgan.

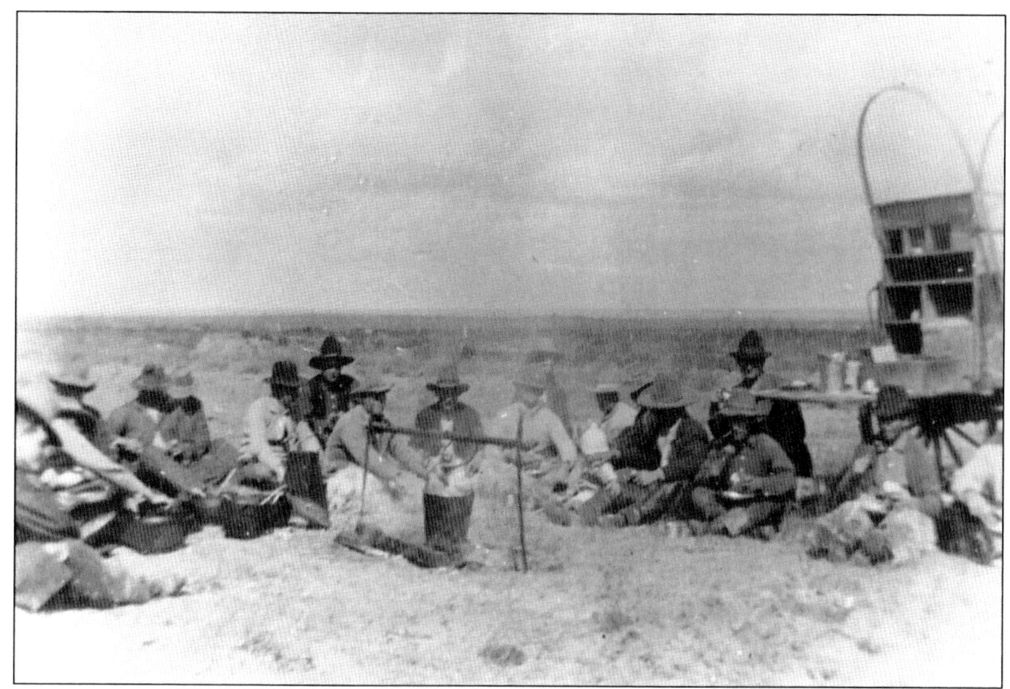

Cowboys sit around a campfire with the chuck wagon at right in October 1914, reportedly the last roundup meal eaten in Morgan County. This photograph was taken on a homestead 12 miles west of Fort Morgan. From left to right are Billy Baird, Emile Youngblut, Tom Price, Walt Ripply, S. Sanford, Jim Prescott, Charley Wait, Gordon Sanford, Tommy Igo, George Glenn, Walter Dodge, Sam Clem, Will Clem, Little Marvin Milheim, Fred Milheim, Bill Kelly, Bud Campbell, and Arl McCasky. A note on the photograph reads, "There were eight men out with cattle—will eat later."

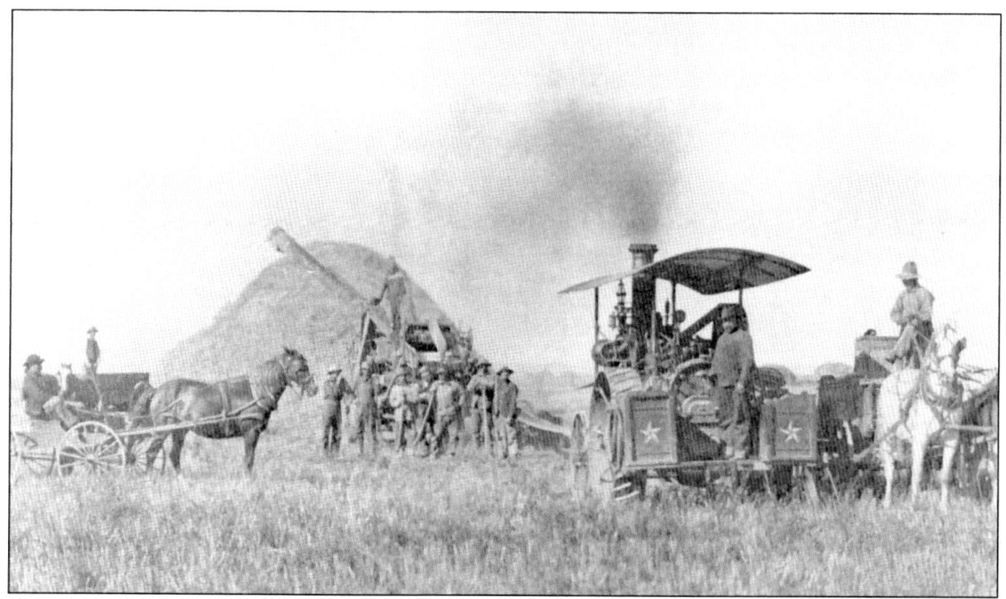

Pictured here is a group threshing wheat in Morgan County using Clarence Work's traction engine. This irrigated land produced 50 bushels per acre—irrigation brings results.

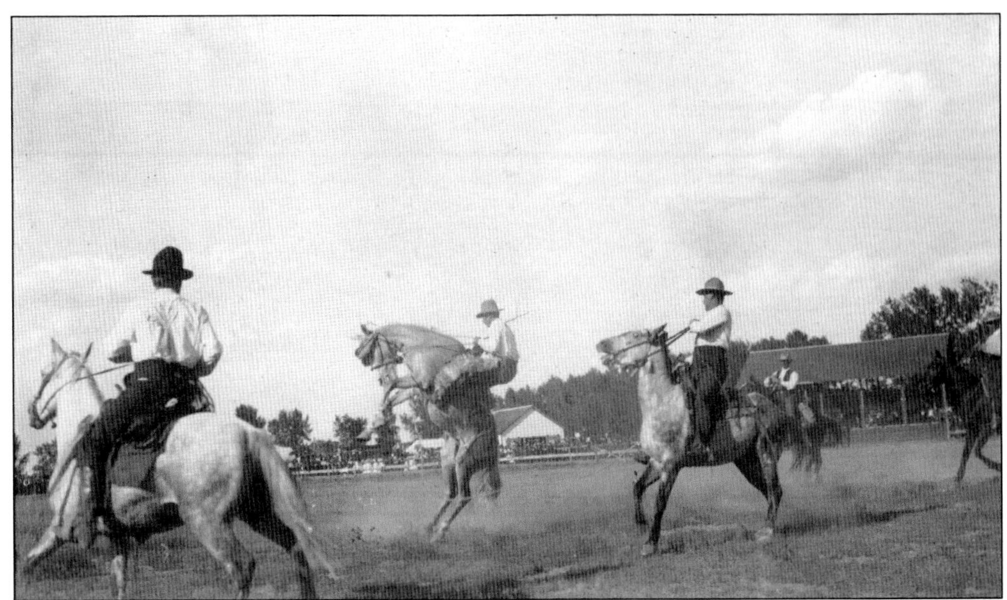

A bronc rider performs at the Morgan County Frontier Days around 1915. The fairgrounds were located in Fort Morgan south of the Chicago, Burlington & Quincy Railroad tracks east of West Street.

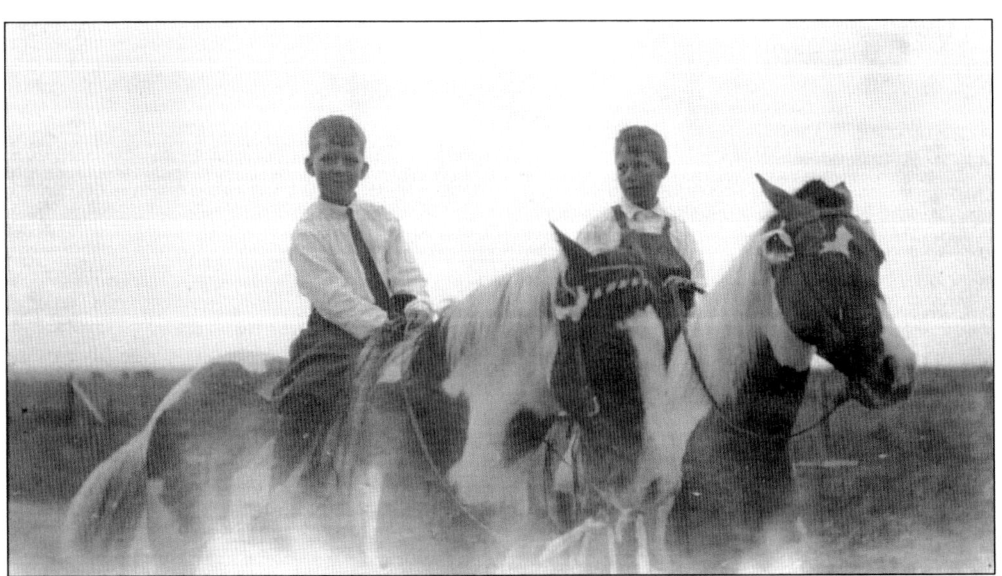

Robert Hogsett (left) and Mel Rosencrans sit atop paint horses in 1913.

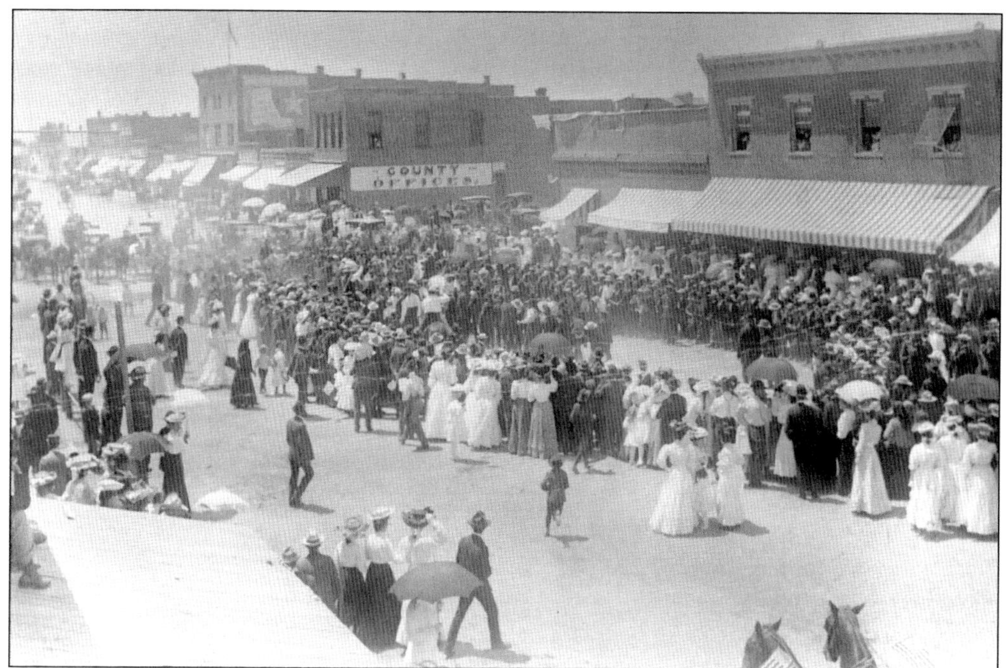

Pictured here is a Fourth of July celebration in downtown Fort Morgan in 1904 or 1905.

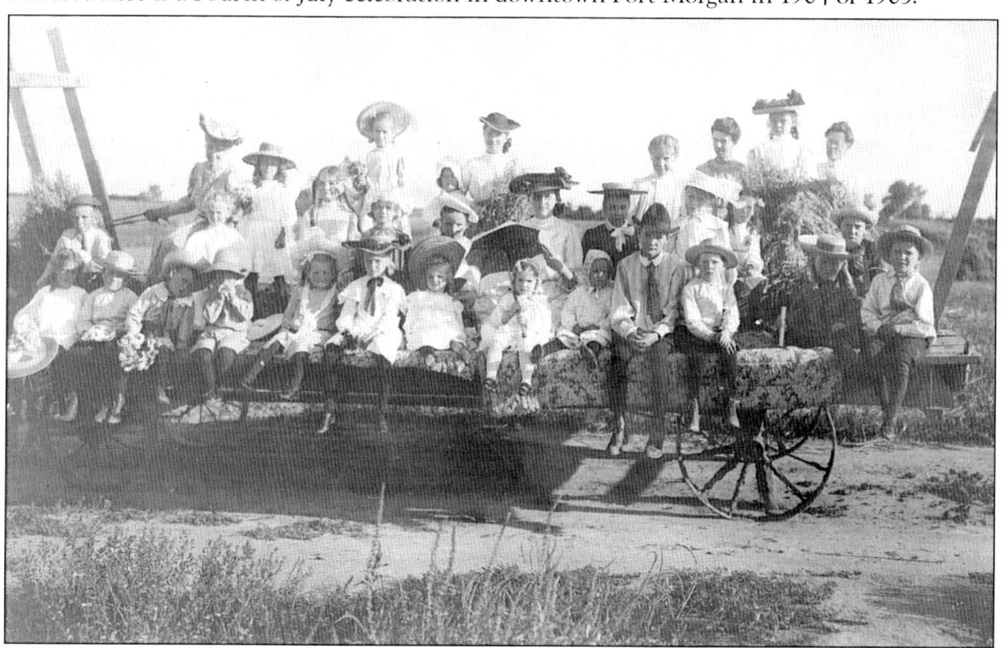

Pictured here are children enjoying a hayride party given by the Tuttle family in 1907. From left to right are (first row) Adrienne E. Jones, unidentified, George Beggs, unidentified, Louise Kinkel, Margaret Simpson, unidentified, Louise Warner (with umbrella), two unidentified children, Bundette, unidentified, and Carl Kinkel; (second row) two unidentified children, Edwynne Cutler (standing), Elizabeth Brown, Ethel Grahm, Helen Lytle, Esther Warner, Mildren Gordon, Nellie Samples, and Helen Simpson; (third row) Miss Tuttle (driving), Beulah Grahm, Leona Warner, unidentified, Marjorie Crouch, and four unidentified girls.

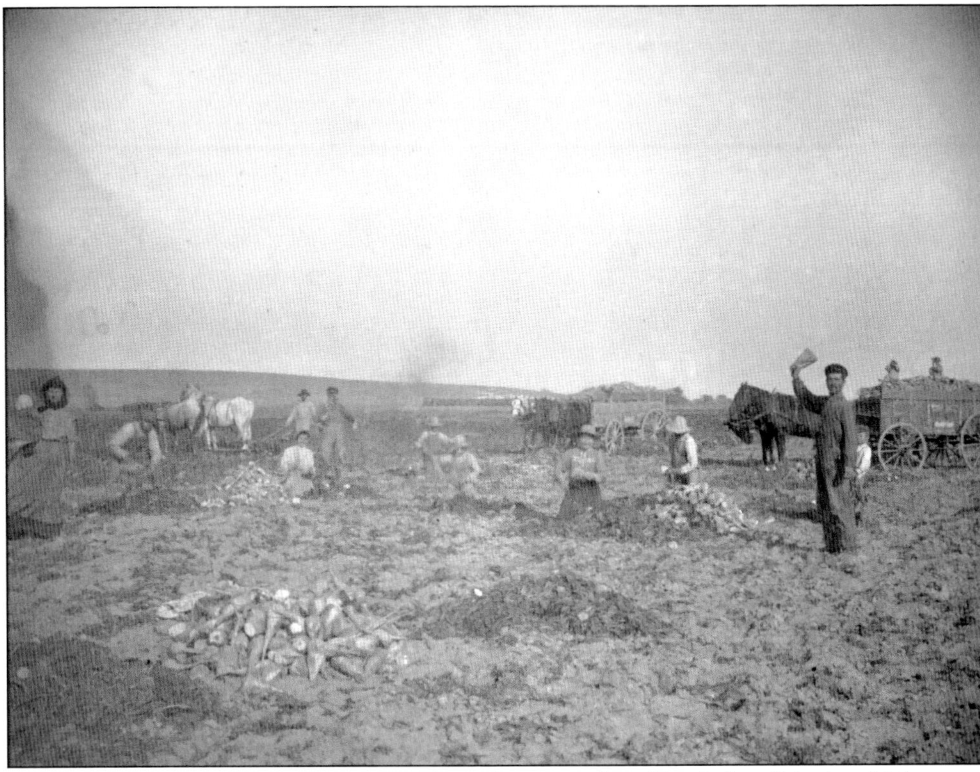

Sugar beets that have been pulled from the soil, trimmed, and loaded—all by hand labor—are shown here ready to be taken by teams of horses to a beet dump near the railroad.

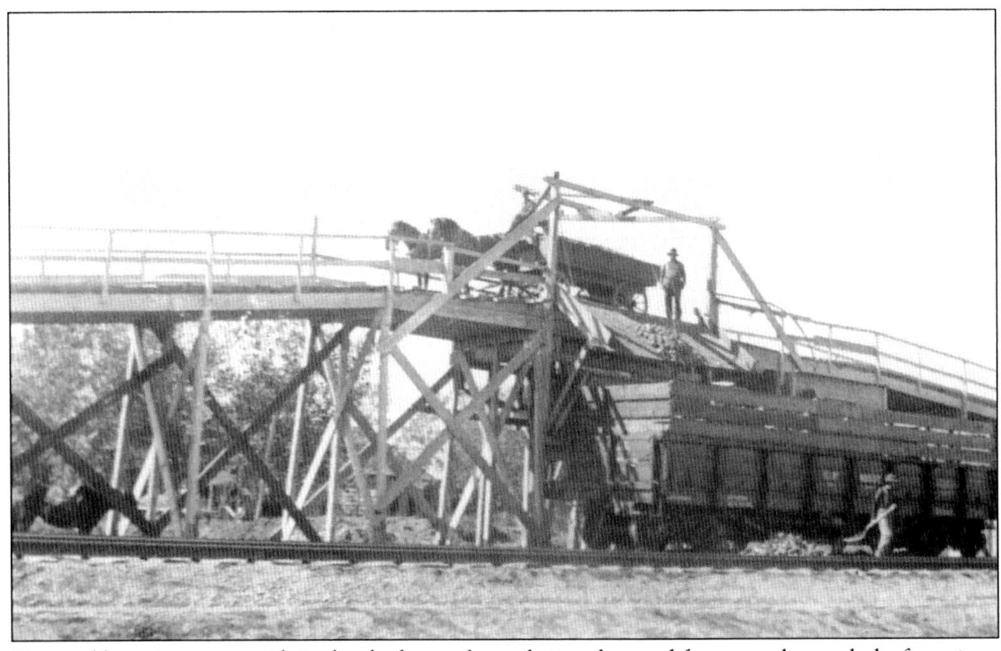

Pictured here is wagon with its load of sugar beets being dumped from an elevated platform into the railroad gondola below. This photograph is believed to be from the Fort Morgan plant.

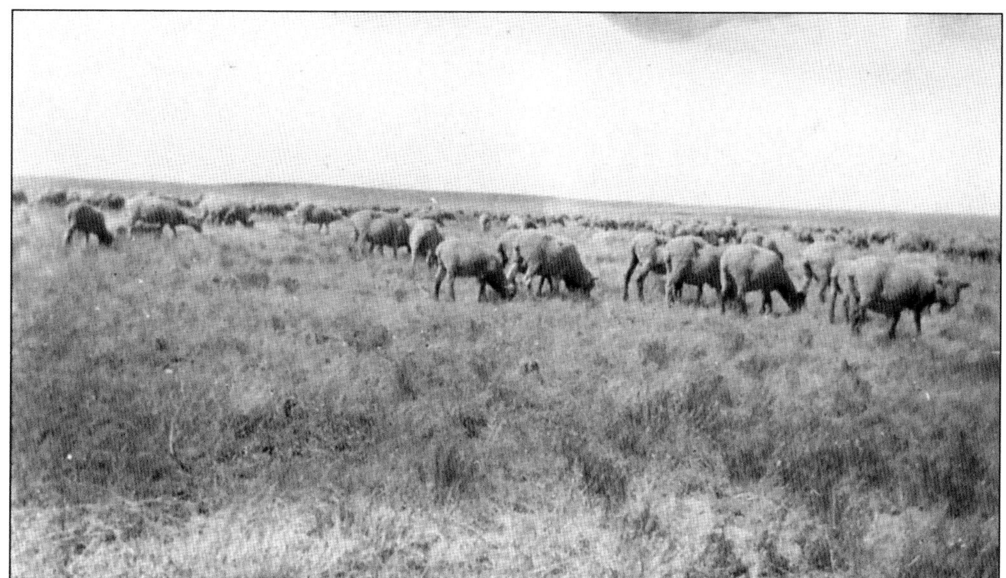

The prairie also proved suitable for sheep grazing, as seen here in the Adena area in 1913. As fences began to be constructed around the best forage sources, the open range came to an end.

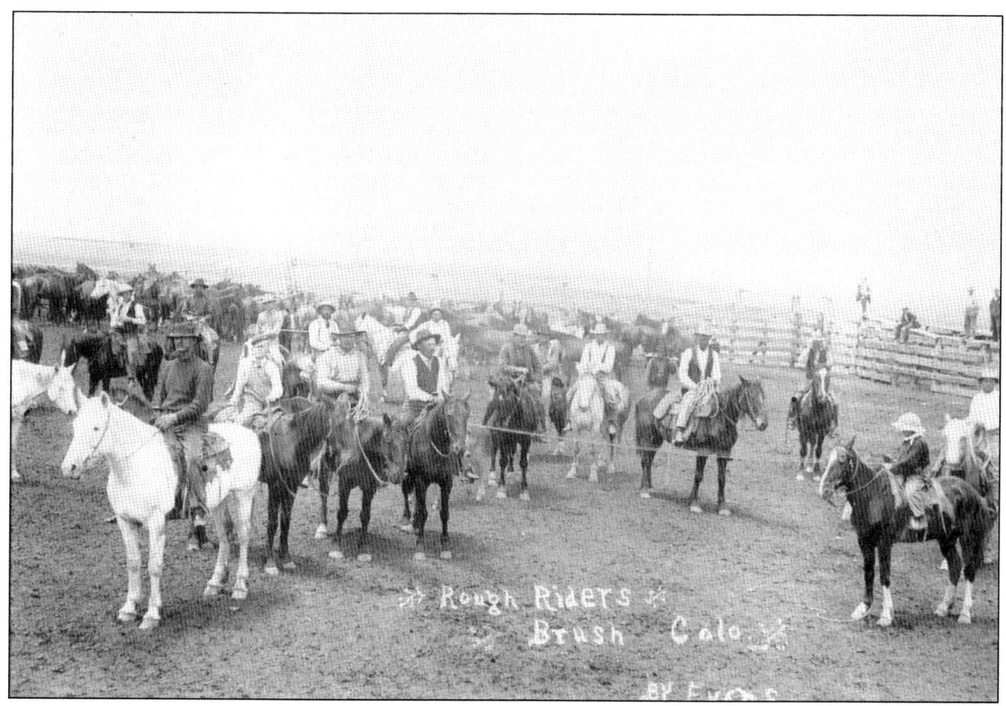

Three years before Teddy Roosevelt became famous with his Rough Riders in the Spanish-American War, Brush boasted its own "Rough Rider" group. These were not trained military men but ranchers who honed their craft with rodeos. To the left, seated on a white horse, is Hurd W. Twombly. His six-year-old son, George C. Twombly, is on the far right after having roped a calf.

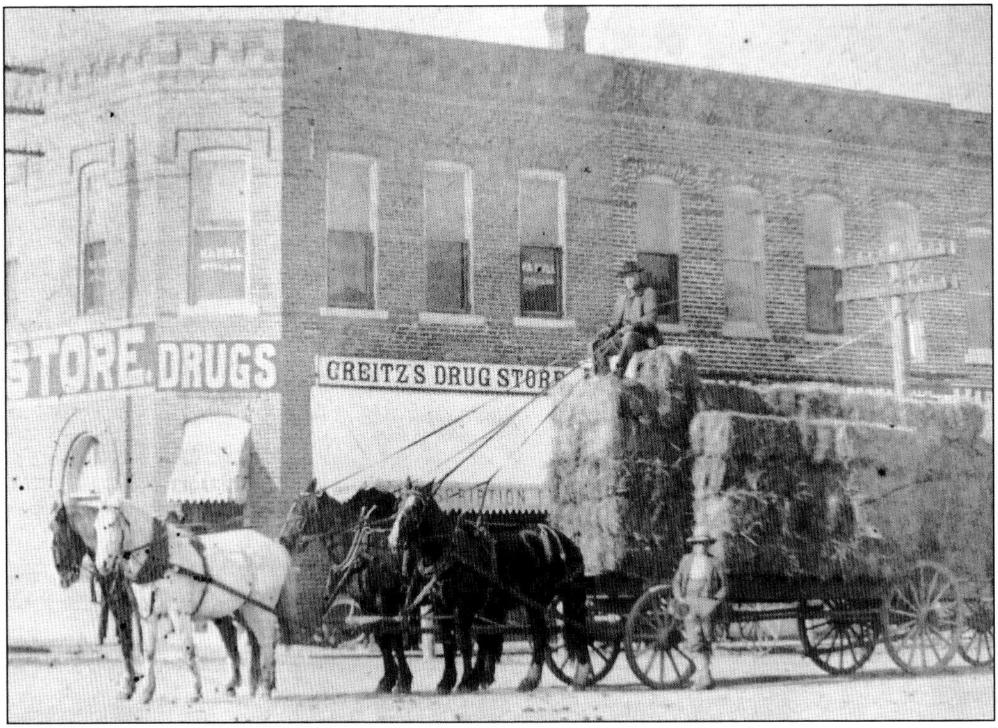

Pictured here is baled alfalfa on its way to market in Fort Morgan. This crop was a result of irrigated land.

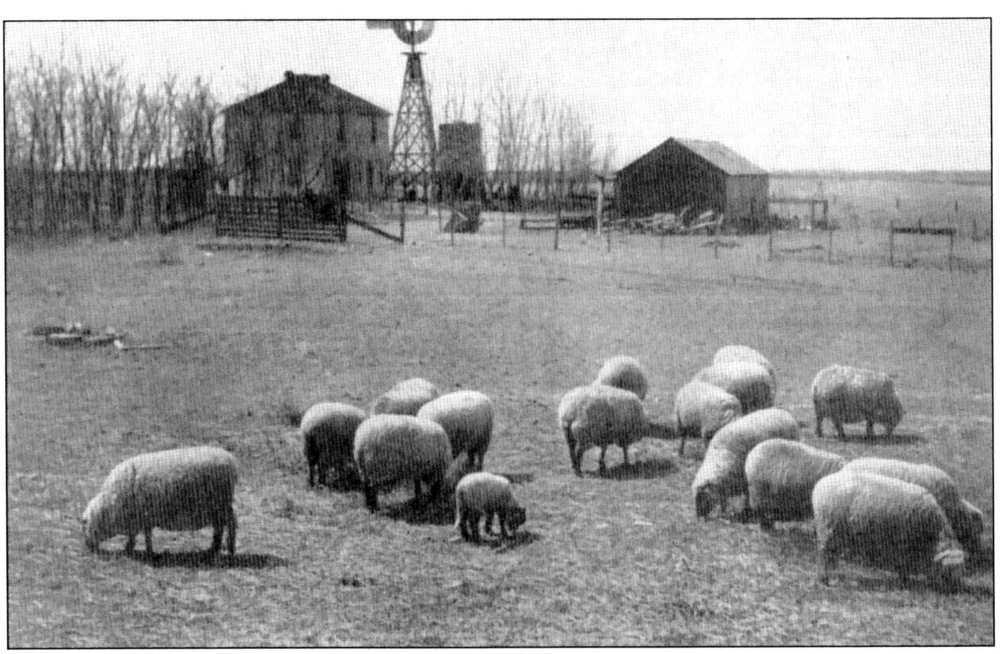

These grazing sheep are the wealth producers of Morgan County.

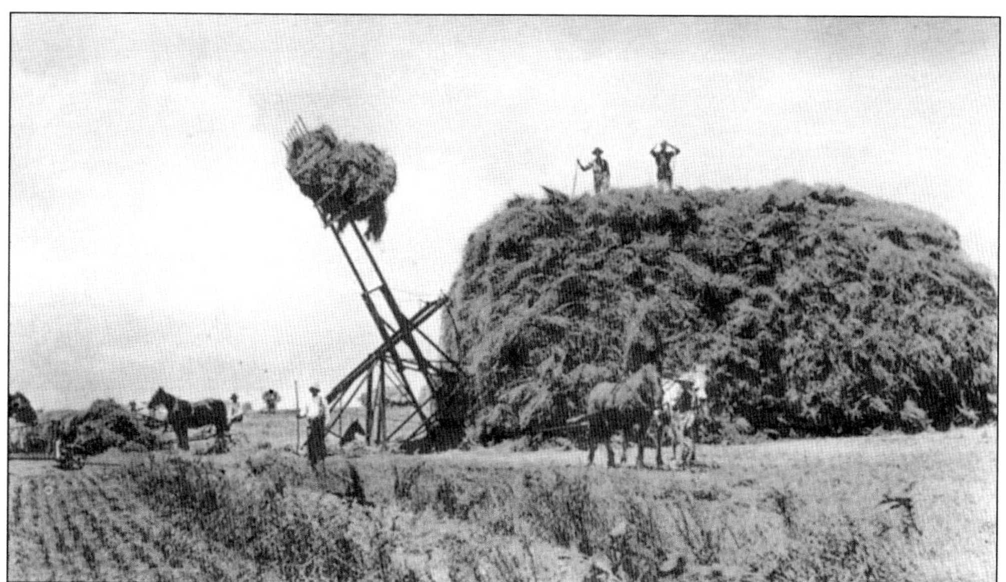

Harvest was a team effort, with many workers required to get the job done in the days before mechanized machinery. This overshot haystacker hoists up another load of alfalfa.

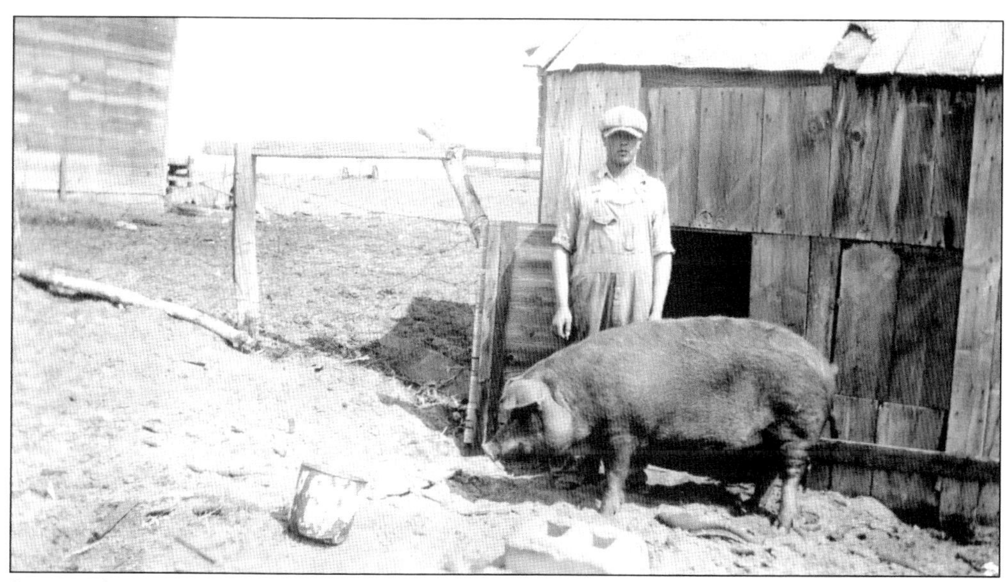

Bert Anderson, wearing bib overalls, stands behind a Duroc gilt pig. This photograph was taken in 1932 south of Fort Morgan on a dry land farm.

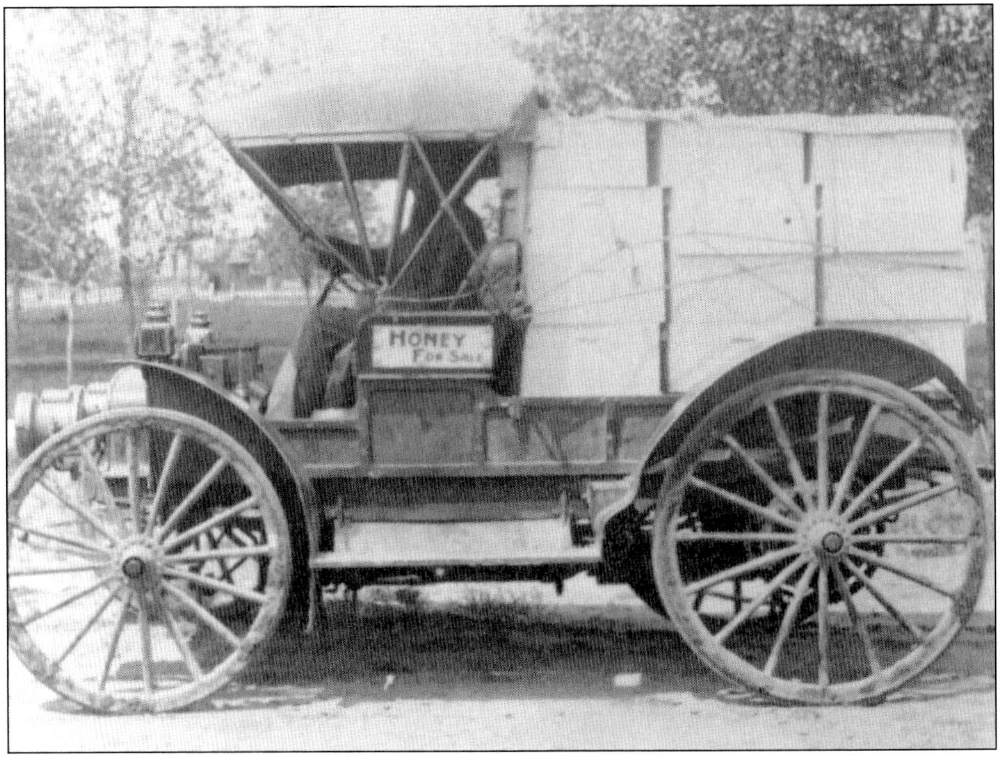

Daniel Danielsen is shown here hauling beehives. Danielsen started his apiary in 1900. Honey production was common in Morgan County, with the Danielsen Apiary, the Wankelman and Tomasini Apiary, and "Chick" White's operation.

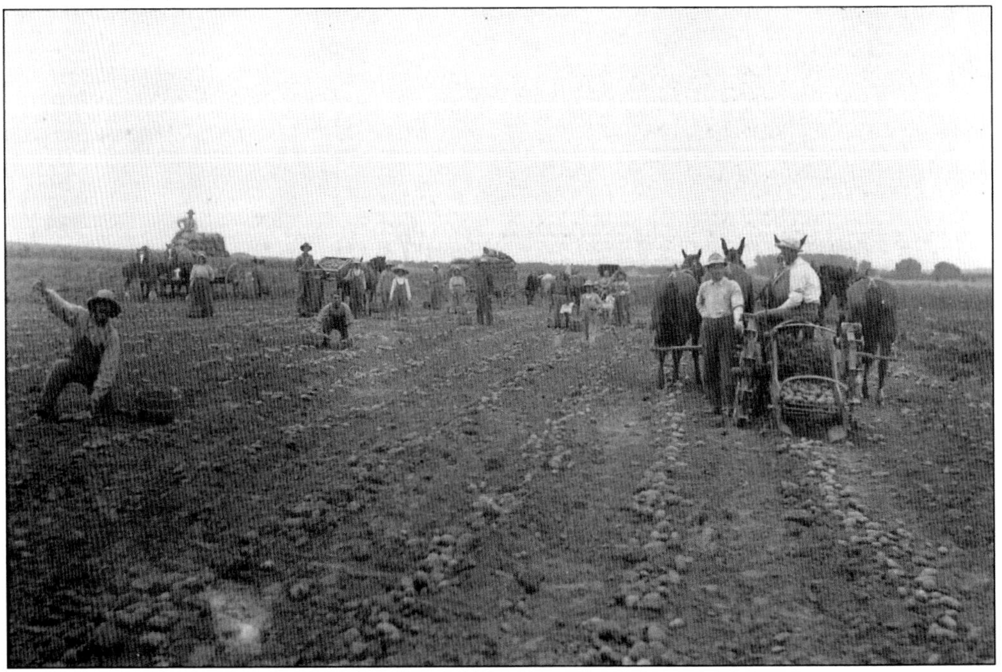

Potatoes were a staple crop of Morgan County beginning in the 1930s.

Three

Transportation

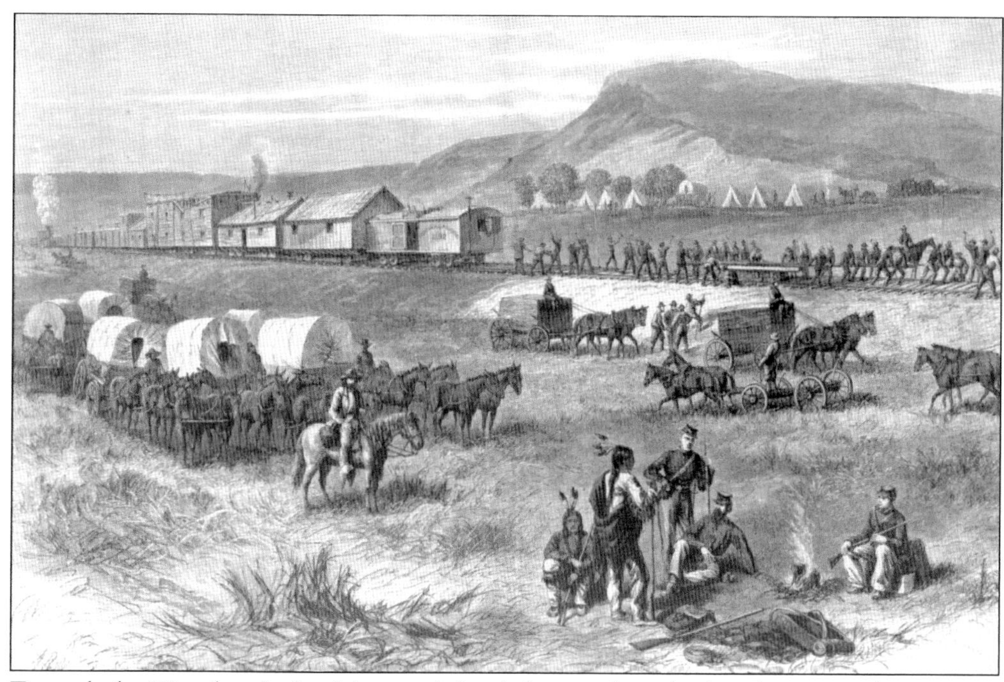

To reach the West, hundreds of thousands headed out on horseback and in covered wagons. By 1869, the railroad reached from coast to coast, creating a new link between people and places. What was once a grueling trip of up to eight months by wagon or 110 days by ship around Cape Horn was cut down to 10 days from coast to coast, as trains averaged speeds of about 30 miles per hour. The development of trains allowed the transport of people and goods from the largest cities to the most isolated areas of the country.

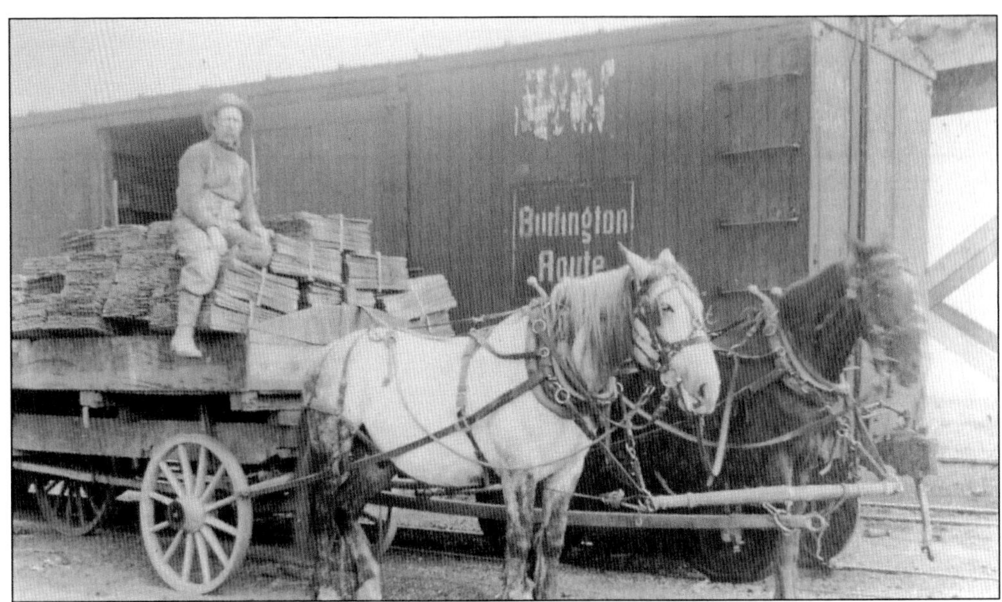

The Chicago, Burlington & Quincy Railroad (CB&Q) reached Fort Morgan on April 17, 1882. The original railroad station on the Burlington line was at Ensign, a couple of miles west of the town of Fort Morgan. Baker knew that for his town to survive it had to have a railroad station. He persuaded the Lincoln Land Company to move the station to Fort Morgan by deeding alternate plots of the newly platted town to the company. In 1884, the section house at Ensign Street was moved two miles and placed in Fort Morgan at the head of the thoroughfare.

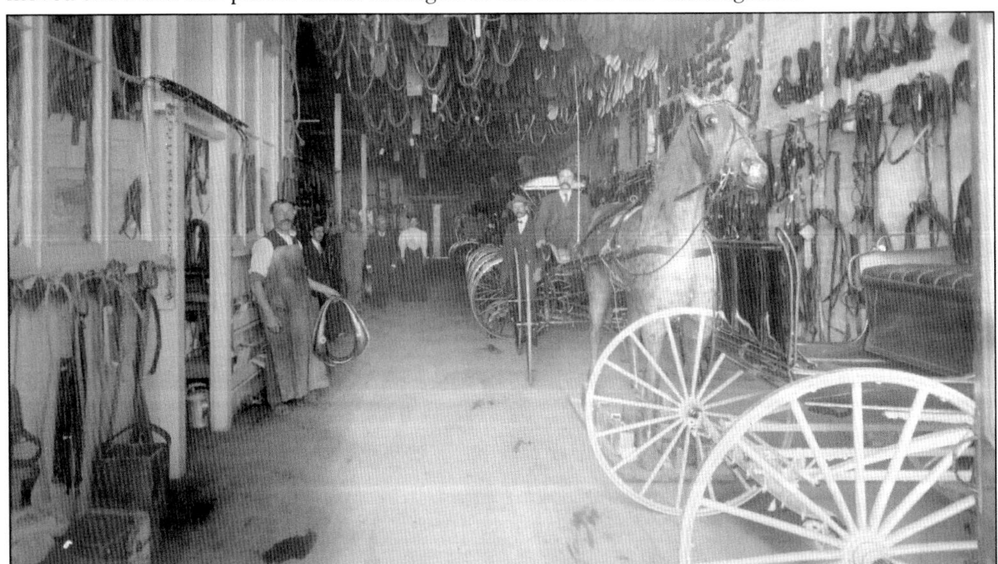
In 1890, M.N. Wagner and Marion Simpson formed a partnership under the name Wagner-Simpson Implement Co. Wagner is standing next to the buggy in the middle of this photograph. Although the automobile was able to travel faster and farther, the farmer's wagon was more efficient in hauling raw goods to market or the train and transporting products back to the farm as well as traversing the county roads in all weather conditions. The change from horse-drawn vehicles to automobiles did not happen suddenly. From the late 1890s to the 1920s, they shared the road, but by 1925 there were fewer than 90 carriage companies operating in the United States.

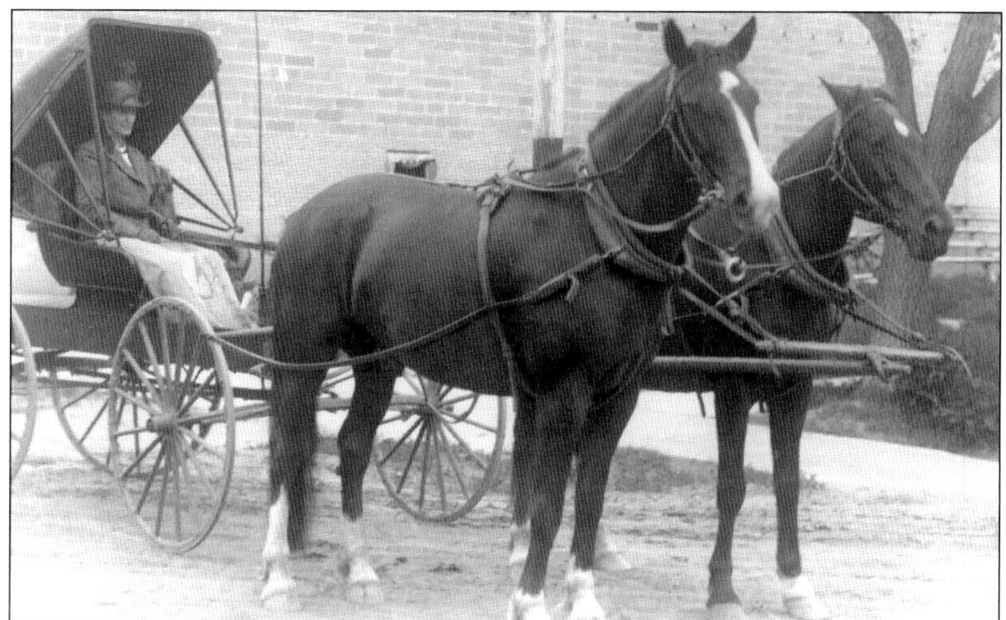

The buggy, a light, four-wheeled carriage for one or two people, was the most popular vehicle in the late 19th century. Although buggies were listed for as little as $20 in mail-order catalogs, most people could not afford or did not have the facilities to feed and care for more than one horse, so livery stables had horses and carriages available for rent. Gertrude Rickel is pictured here sometime between 1907 and 1915 with her favorite riding horse, Lundy, on her left. Blaze is on her right.

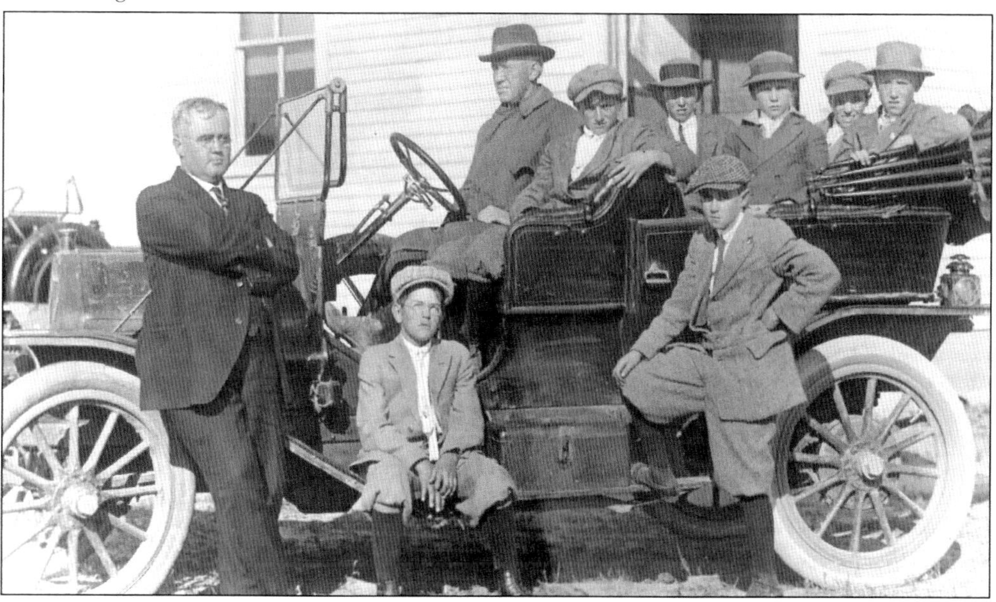

F.W. Carruth is pictured here at the wheel of his 1901 EMF Studebaker, parked in front of the Wiggins Methodist Church. The year is 1913, and the boys of Arlington Taylor's Sunday school class are decked out in their knickerbockers and hats. Members of the class are, from left to right (first row) Arlington Taylor, Ernest Dandridge, and Russell Taylor; (second row) F.W. Carruth, Charles Samples, Ward Roby, Elmer Petersen, Warren Leonard, and unidentified.

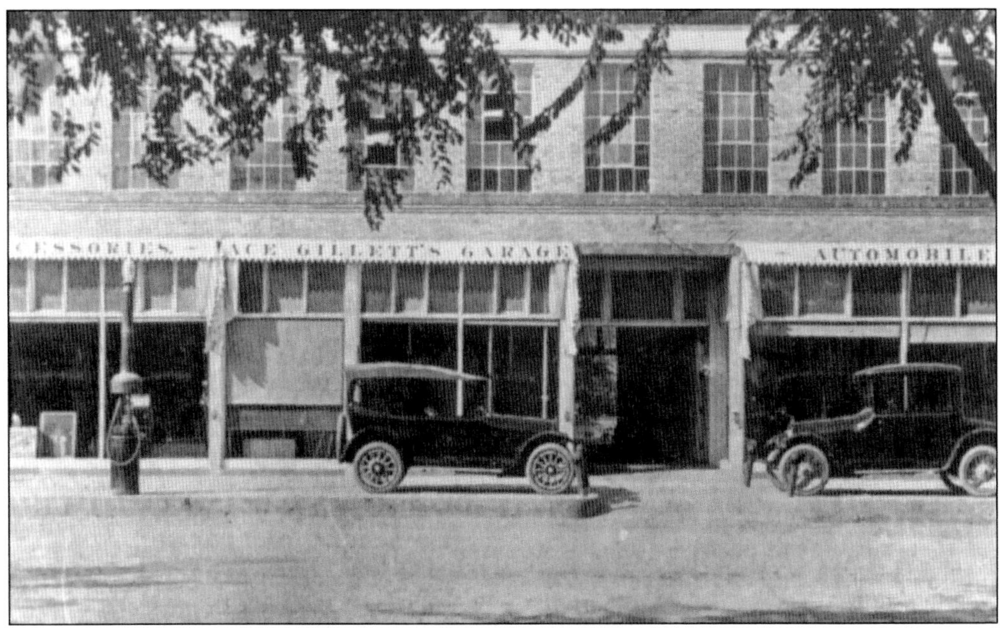

In 1916, A.C. Gillete razed the temporary tabernacle used to house Chautauqua meetings. In its place, he built a structure considered to be the most architecturally refined of the automobile dealerships that had emerged on the north end of Fort Morgan's commercial district. Ace sold and serviced Willys automobiles from the garage and sometime before 1927 sold the building to Headrick-Rothrock, who sold Plymouth and Dodge Brothers Motor Cars. Later, by 1934, the partnership had changed to Dixon-Rothrock Inc., and an auto parts store was added. The building was later occupied by Morgan Auto Parts, and after a period in which it lay vacant, it became M&H Auto Parts. A popular bar and grill currently operates at this location.

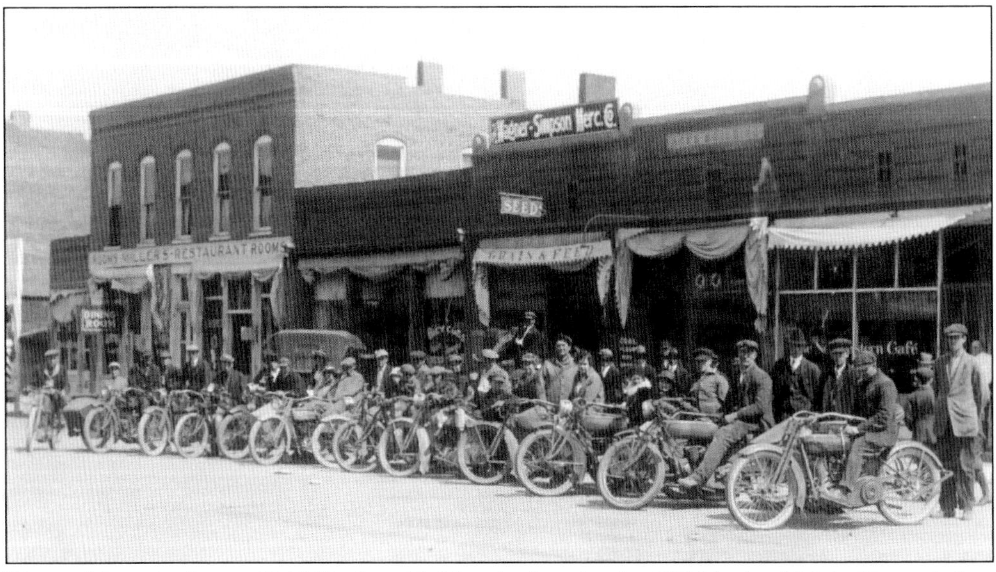

Pictured here in front of L.V. Rothrock's bicycle shop in the 200 block of Main Street is Lee Stickney, who started Stickney's, Inc., at Sterling. He organized the Sterling Motorcycle Club. Members rode to Fort Morgan to attend dedication ceremonies of the Rainbow Bridge in 1923.

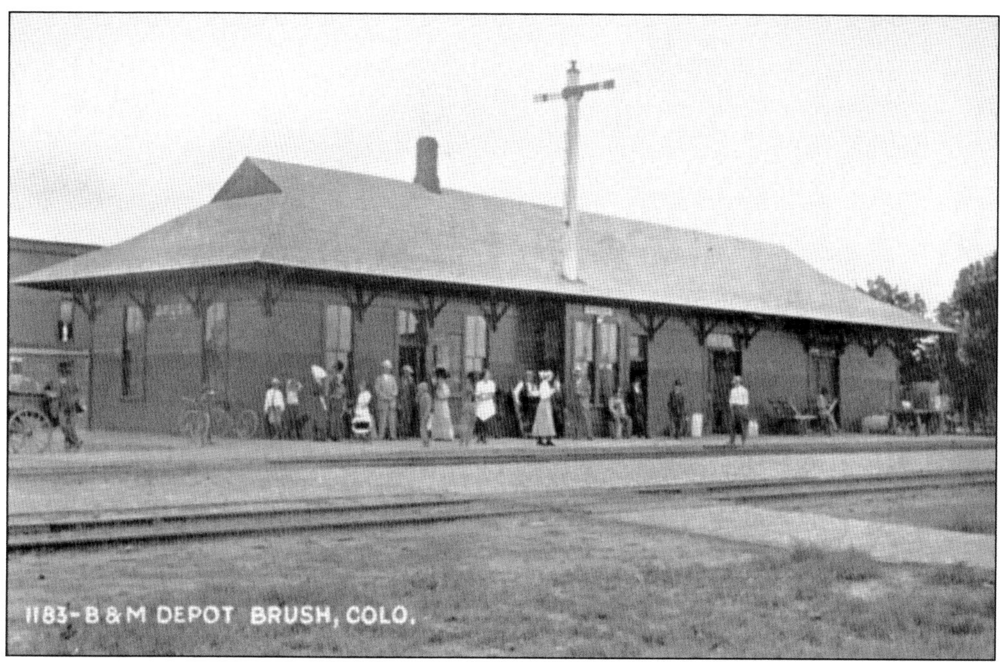

The third depot in town, the wooden Burlington and Missouri Depot in Brush, Colorado, was built in 1902. It was torn down in the late 1920s and replaced with a brick structure.

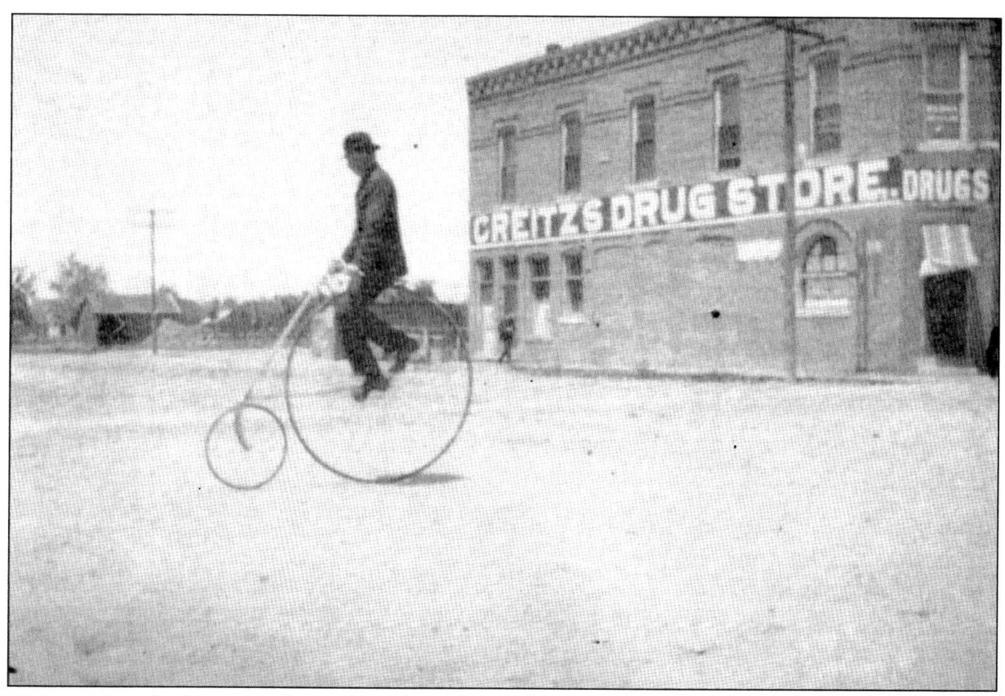

This unidentified man is riding a bicycle in front of Creitz Drug Store, located at 201 Main Street in Fort Morgan. The bicycle is similar to the American Star Safety Bicycle, patented in 1881; it has a large wheel in back to give the rider more stability. There was less chance of the rider going headfirst over the front wheel.

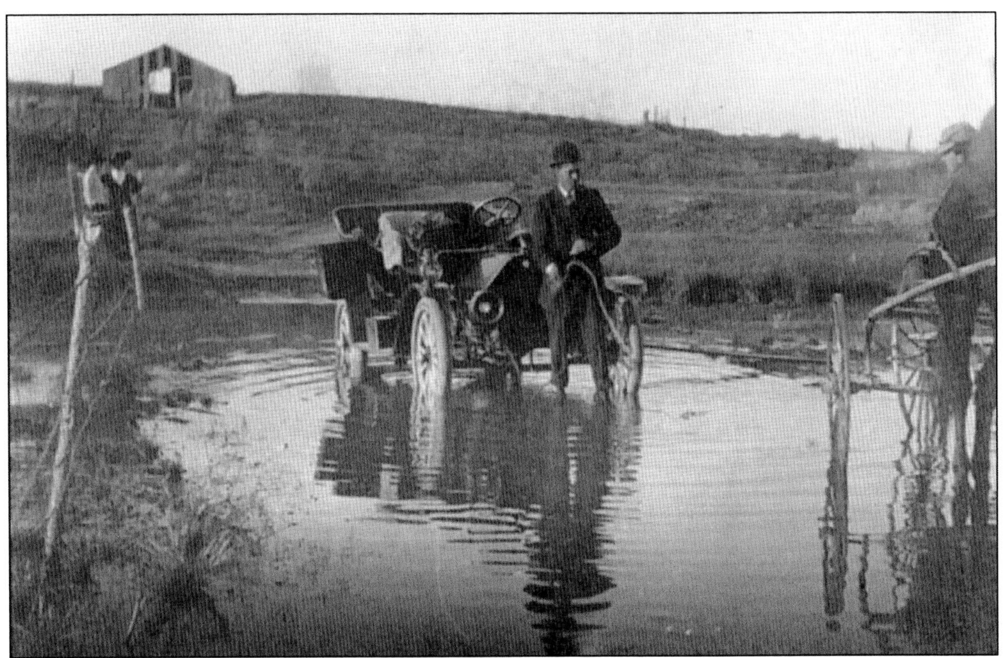

Dr. George M. Anderson ran into some of Mother Nature's problems, as evidenced by this photograph taken about 1910, when he attempted to cross the normally dry Bijou Creek in his automobile. The flooded creek presented no problem for the horse and buggy shown assisting him on the right.

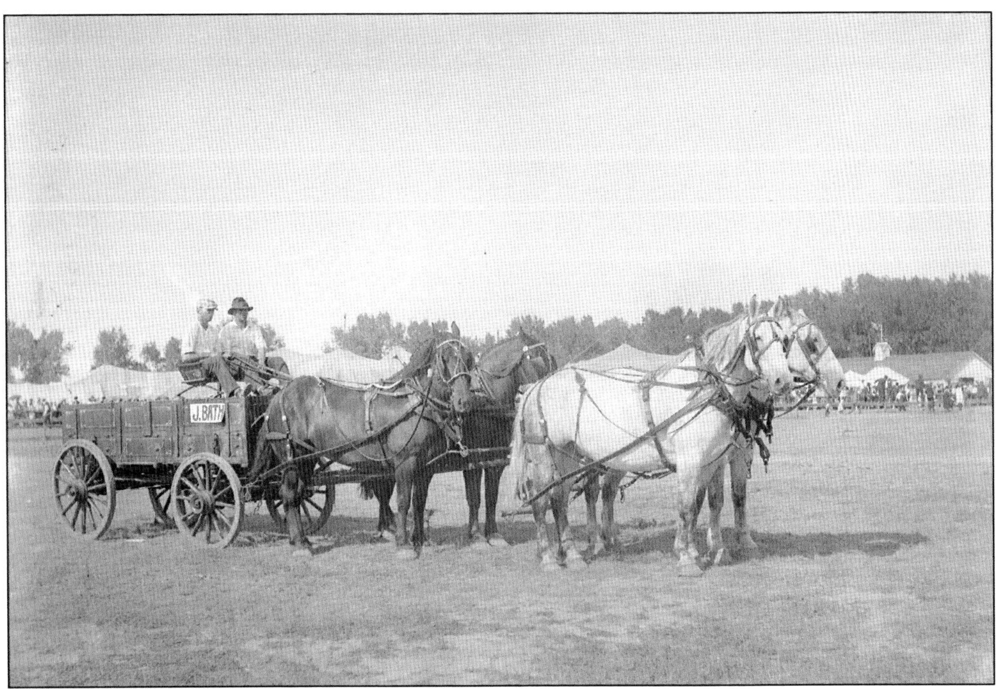

In this photograph dated about 1910, "J. Bath" is written on a small sign on the side of a wagon drawn by four horses.

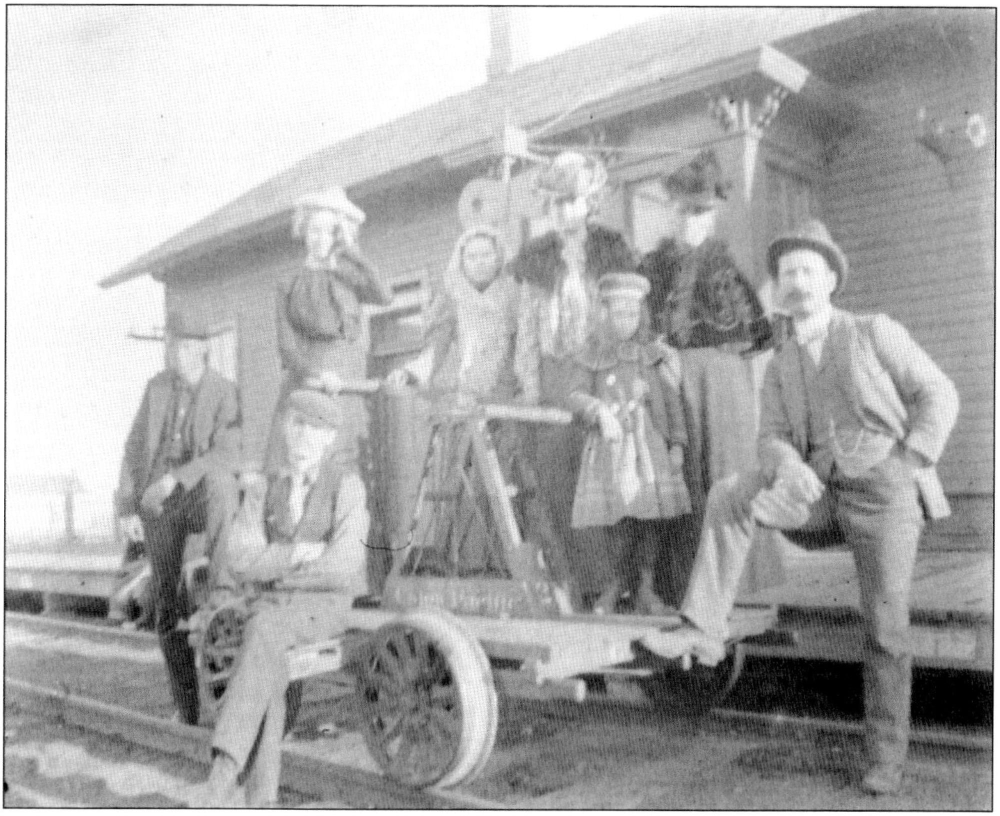

A group from Orchard travels to a dance on a handcart around the year 1890.

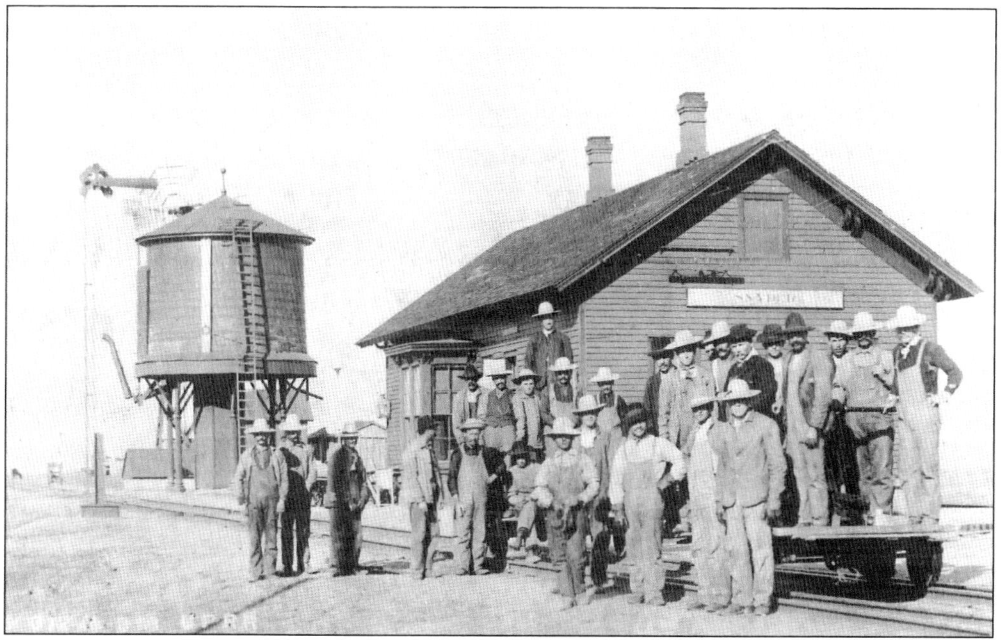

The Union Pacific Railroad ran along the north side of the South Platte River. Pictured here about 1880 are the Snyder Depot and water tower needed by the steam engines of that era.

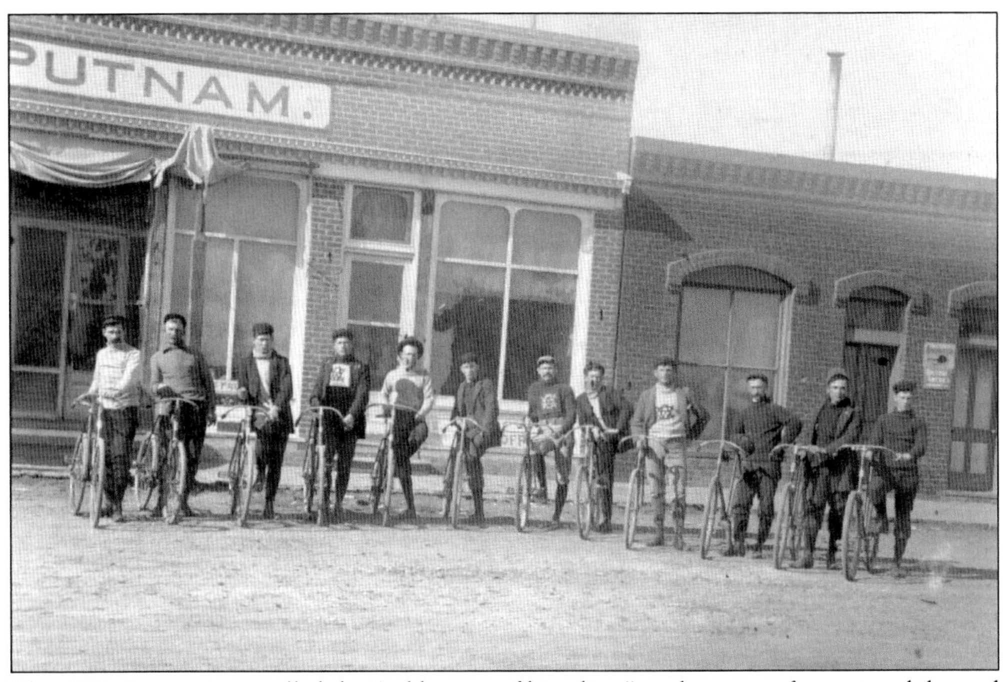

The 1890s is sometimes called the "golden age of bicycling," as there were few automobiles and bicycles provided an alternative to walking, but they were expensive. By 1900, they became more affordable, but in the rural community, mud, snow, and sand on the predominantly dirt roads left the rider dusty and disheveled when he or she arrived at a destination. Appropriate dress for women made it difficult for them to ride, and the size of the town lent itself to walking to shops. Here, Fort Morgan Bicycle Club members gather for a portrait in front of Putnam's Notions Store, located at 213 Main Street in Fort Morgan. The building was constructed by George Gordon, a brickmaker and builder.

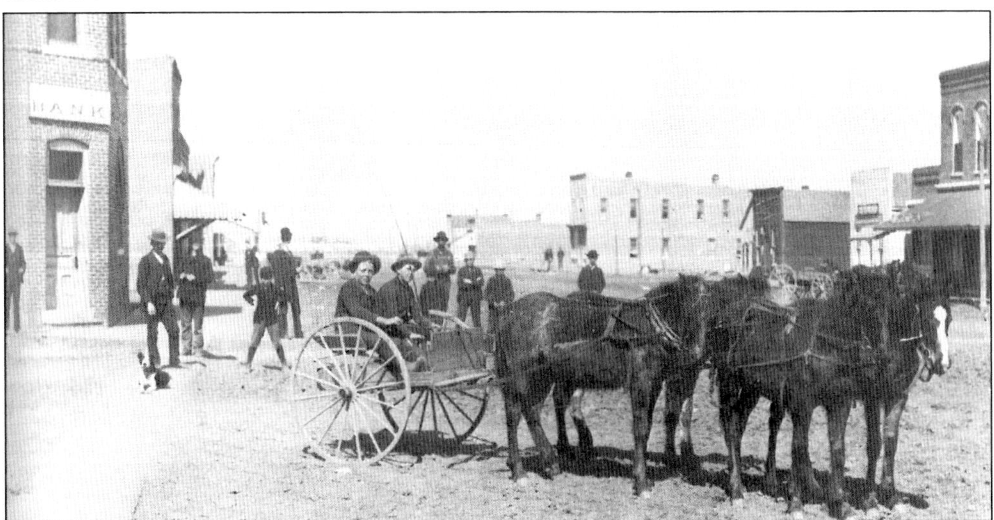

Two youngsters, George G. Baker (left) and Fred Killebrew, sit in their buggy pulled by a four-horse team. The photograph with a view looking north was taken at the corner of Main Street and Railroad Avenue. Baker was the eldest son of Abner S. and Sarah Baker and was about 12 or 13 years old when this photograph was taken in around 1891.

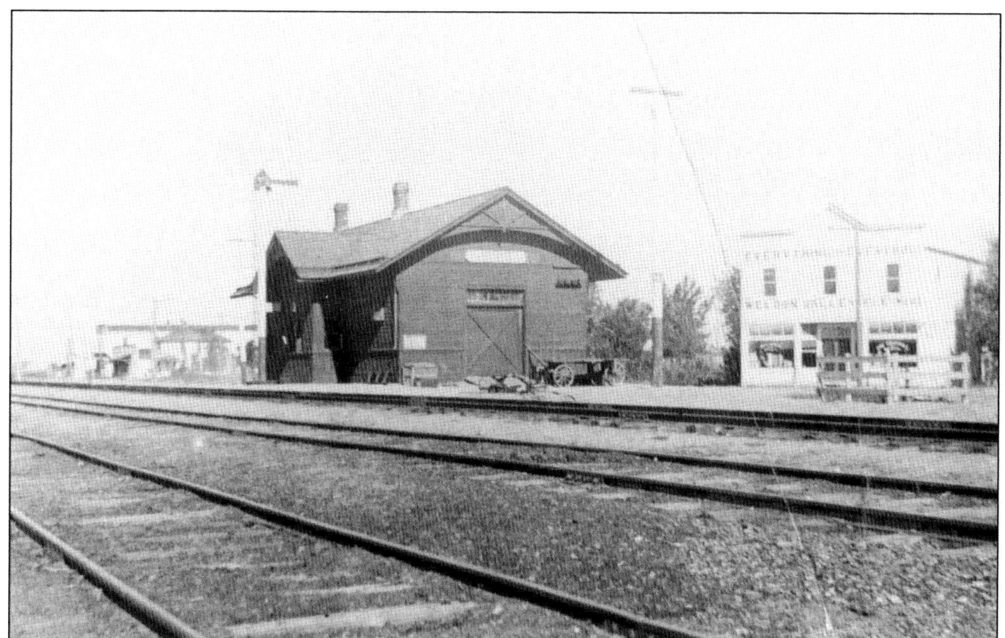

The Weldona Depot was once located on the north side of the South Platte River and functioned as the Deuel station of the Union Pacific Railroad.

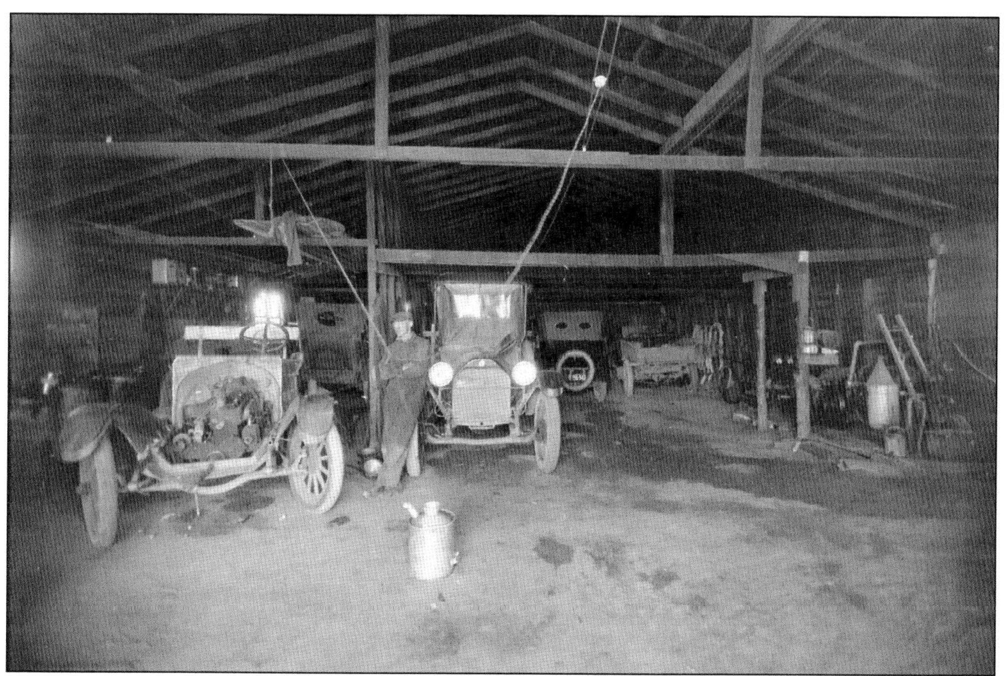

This 1920 photograph of a service station in Wiggins features Model T cars under repair in the dirt-floor building. The DLD connected the cities of Denver, Colorado; Lincoln, Nebraska; and Detroit, Michigan, and was a major thoroughfare for commerce. Later, the Eisenhower Interstate Act established the interstate system and eliminated the importance of the DLD.

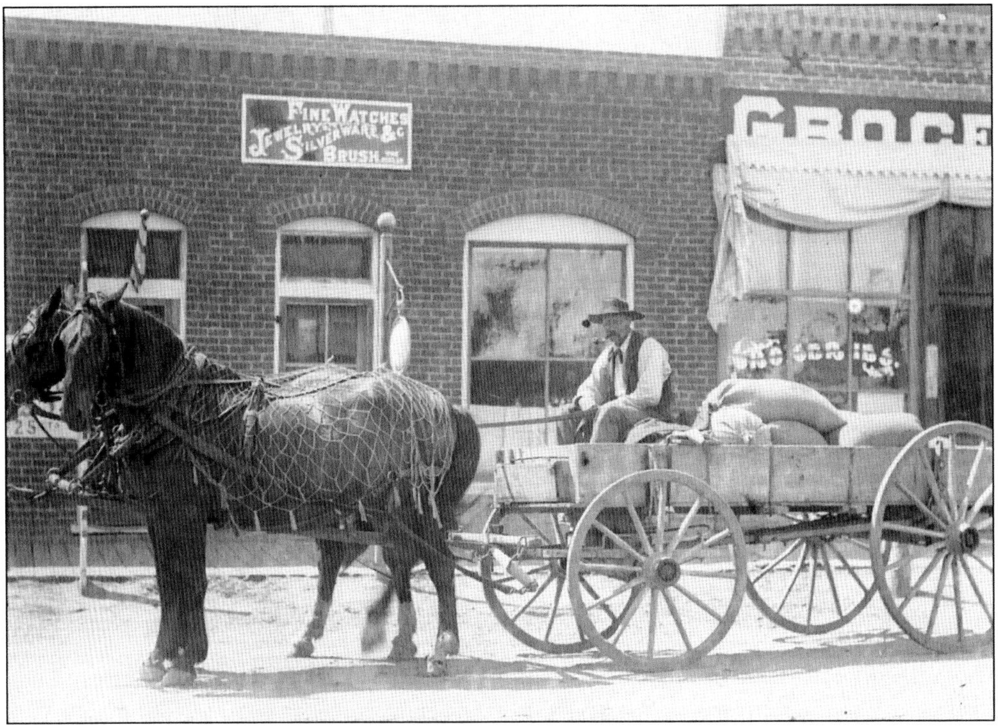

This photograph features Brush's jewelry store and a grocery store, both built of brick. An unidentified resident driving a large wagon and a fine team of horses has gone to the feed store and purchased burlap bags filled with feed for his animals. The netting on the horses may have been used as a sort of fly protection during the hot summer months.

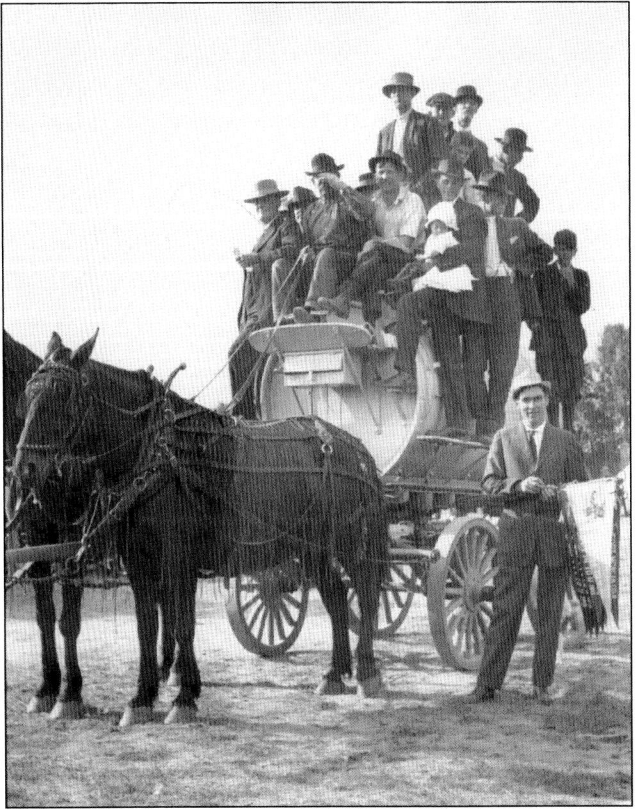

Pictured here is a Fort Morgan city water wagon in 1915. One man stands beside the wagon holding several felt pennants reading "Frontier Days – Fort Morgan, Colo – Sept 14 to 17 1915." The man holding the child is Erne Morse, and his daughter is Edith. R.L. Patterson is to the right of them. The driver is named Hawthorne.

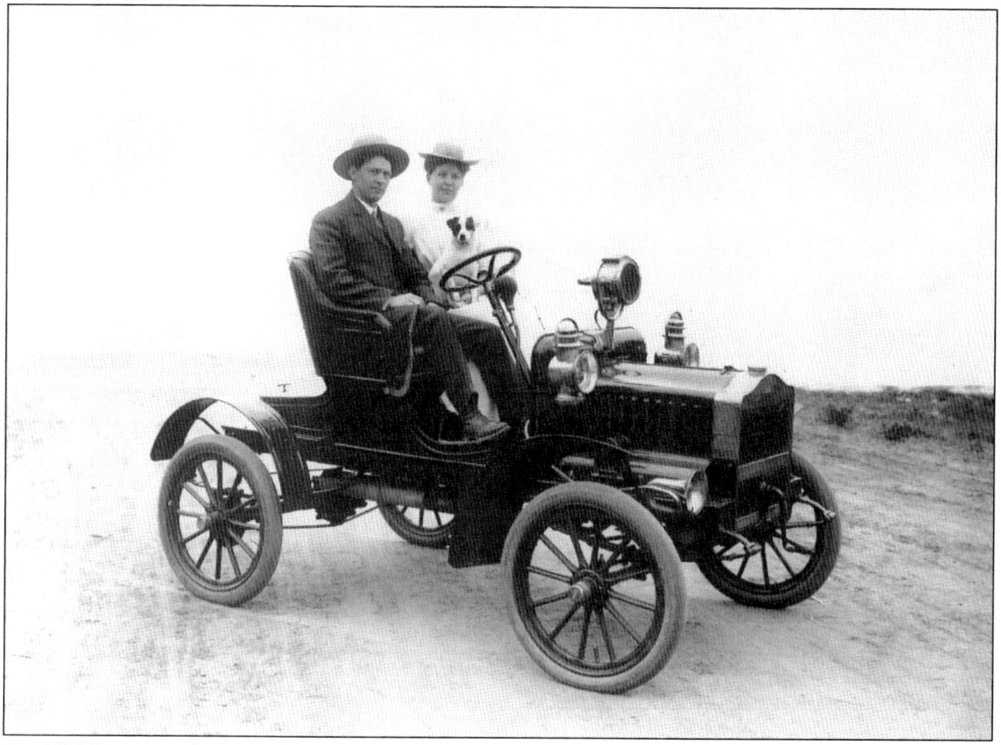

Dr. ? Williams and an unidentified woman are pictured here in a Maxwell car in May 1907.

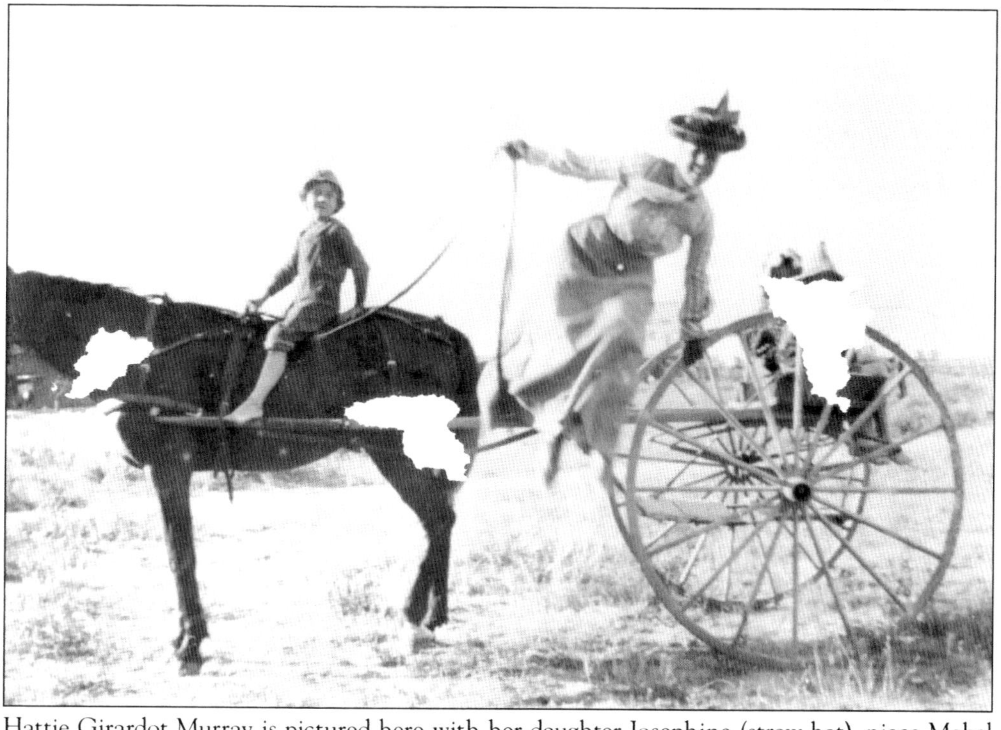

Hattie Girardot Murray is pictured here with her daughter Josephine (straw hat), niece Mabel Prichard, and nephew Bert Towne (on horse) at the Orchard Ranch.

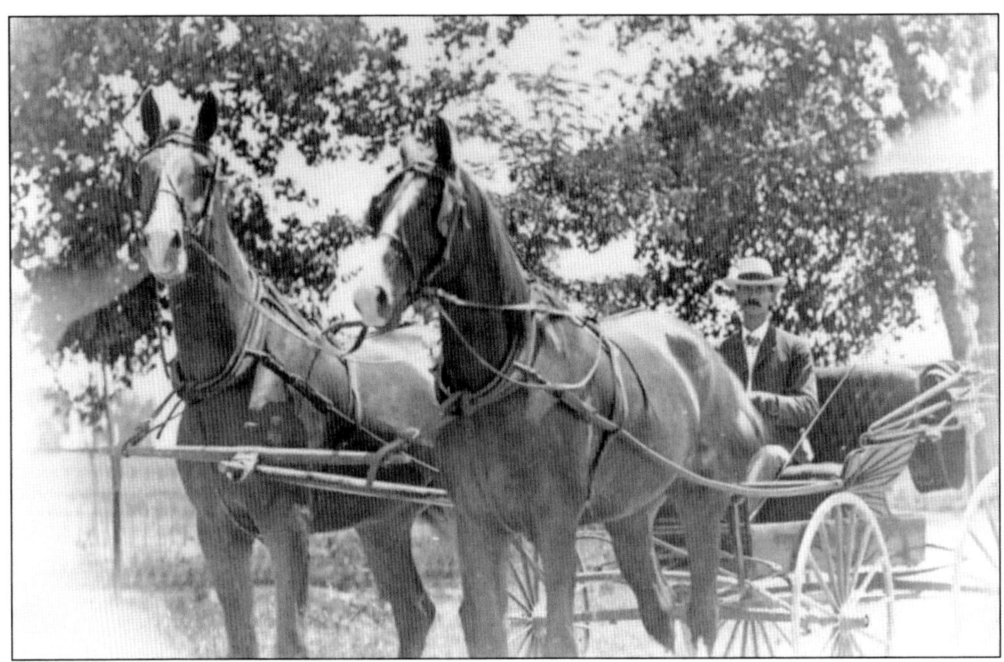

J.P. Curry, shown here in his carriage, was active in the promotion, founding, and administration of various financial institutions, including the State Bank in Fort Morgan, which became the First National Bank of Fort Morgan. He was president of the Fort Morgan Irrigation District for 20 years, until the last bond was redeemed, with never a default in payment of principal or interest.

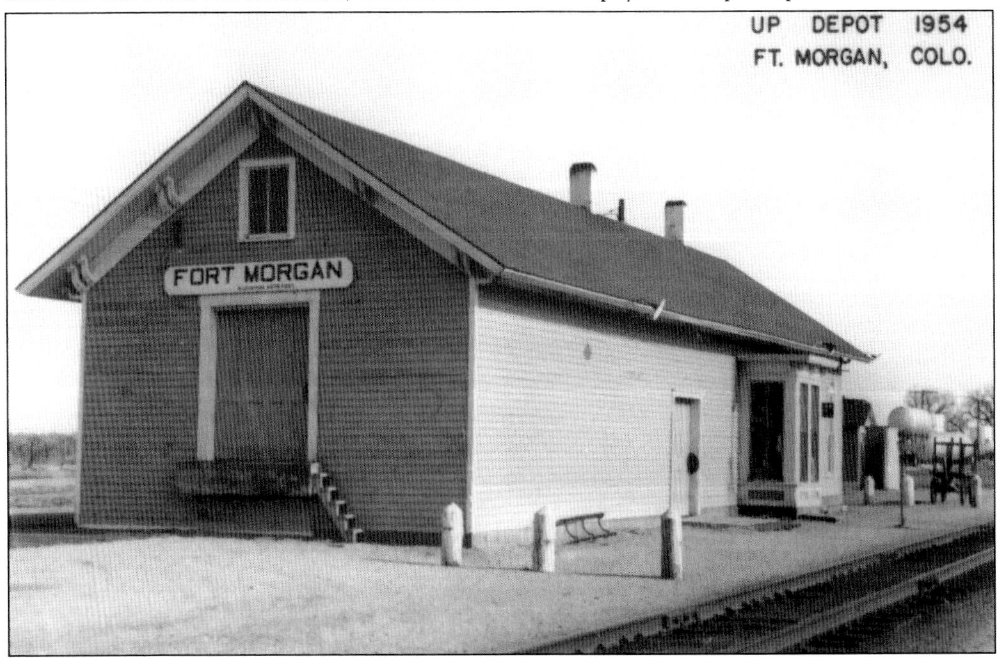

On the north side of the South Platte River was a station of the Union Pacific Railroad named Deuel. The Julesburg Branch of the UP from Julesburg to La Salle was completed in 1881. The town was surveyed in 1885 and became a true rival of Fort Morgan. Deuel was later moved west and in 1907 became Weldona.

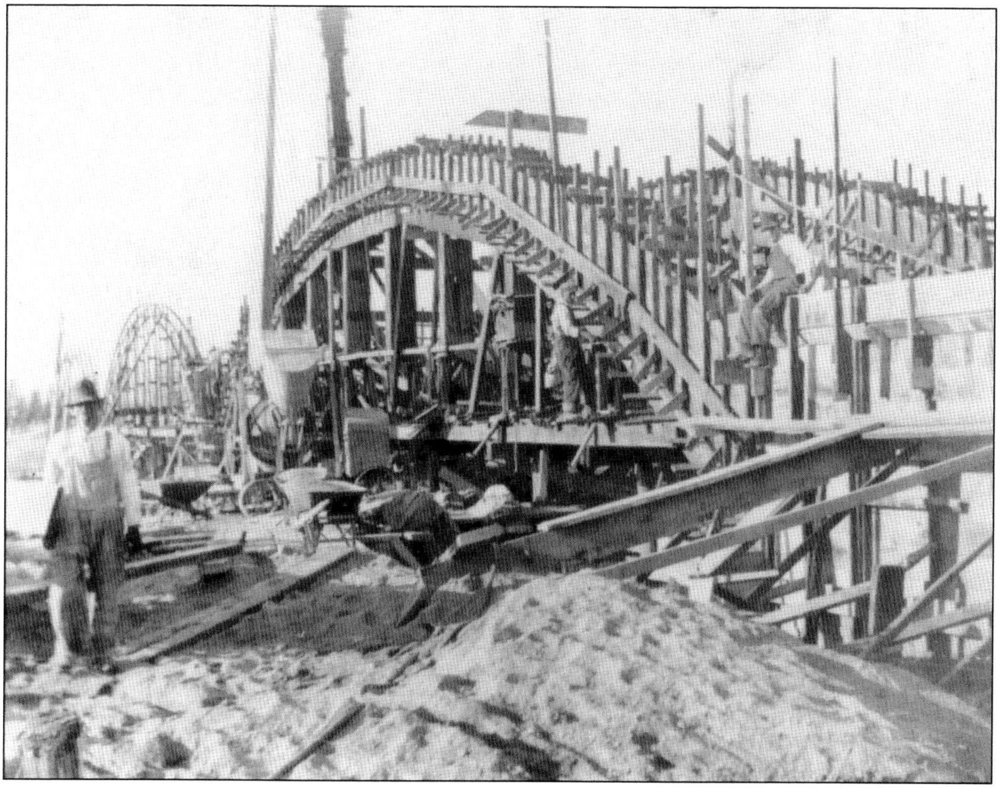

Pictured here in 1923 is the construction of the Rainbow Arch Bridge across the South Platte River, located north of Fort Morgan.

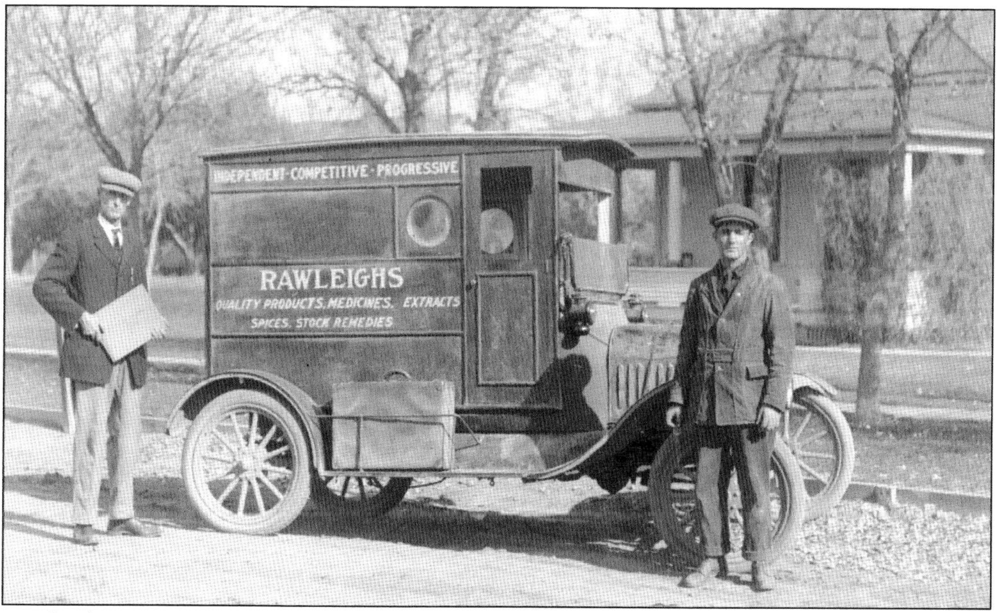

Rawleighs was a delivery service that brought goods such as medicines for both people and livestock, extracts, and spices to rural homes. The company was purely delivery and did not own any stores in the area.

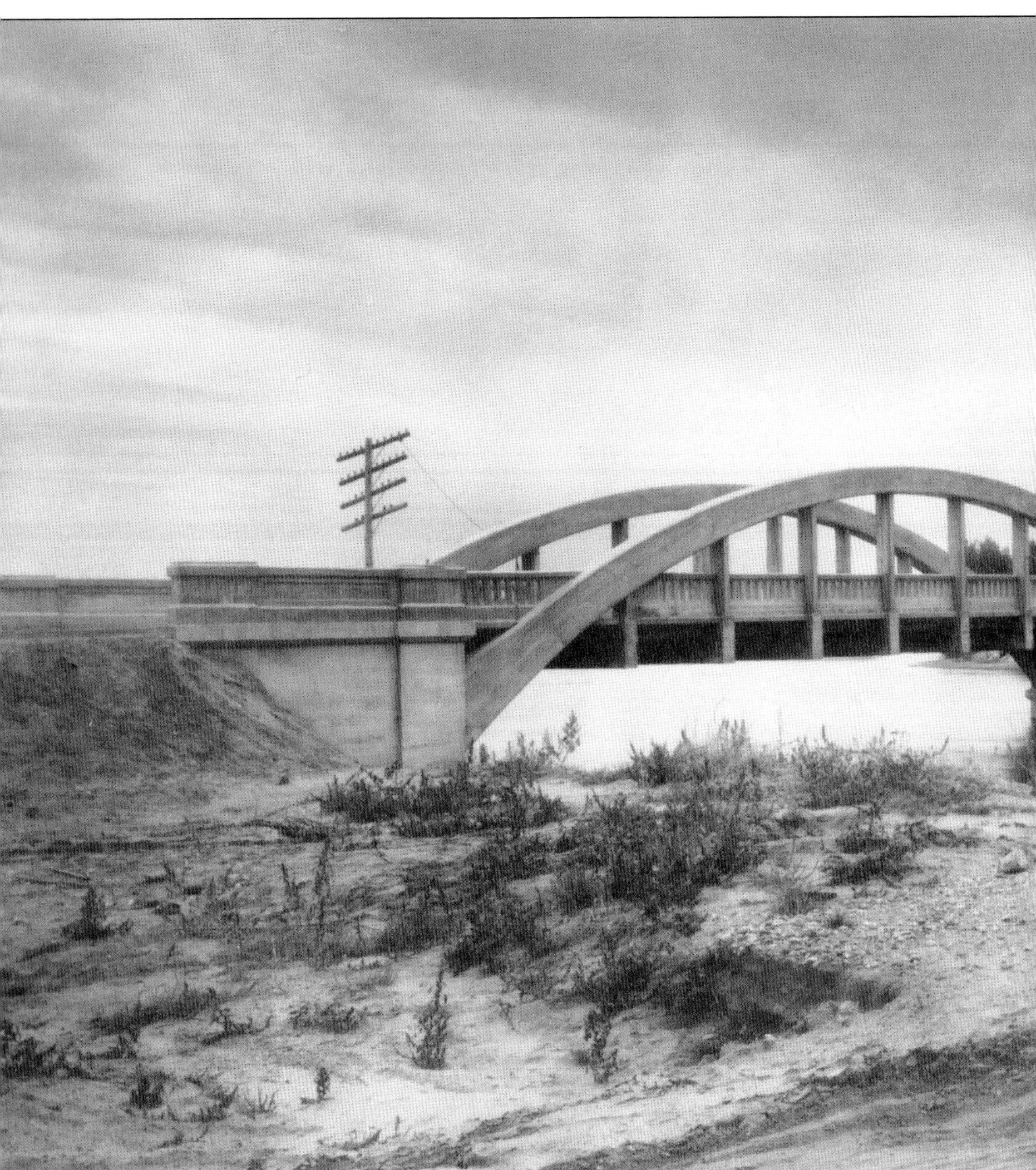

The Rainbow Arch Bridge, spanning across the South Platte was built between 1922 and 1923. The design was patented by James Marsh, an engineer from Iowa, and built by Denver contractor Charles Sheeley for $89,000. Built one mile north of Fort Morgan, 75 percent of the construction workers were from the area. Nort Carlson recalls, "I was a member of the construction crew during the summer of 1923. I remember 40 to 50 men that worked on the bridge at one time or another."

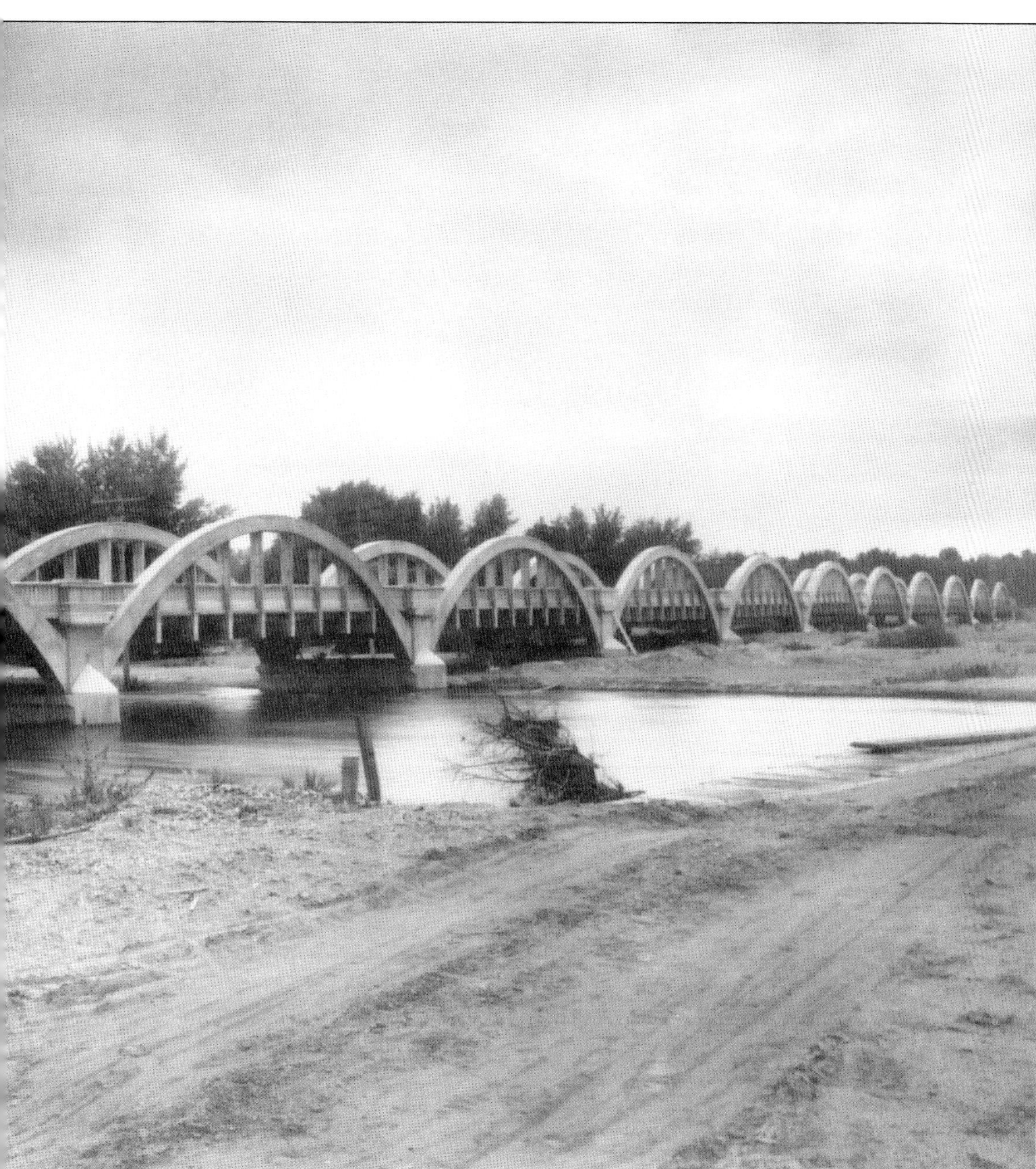

He continued, "I was paid 35¢ an hour." The 1,080-foot concrete arched bridge has a frame made of steel. The roadway is 24 feet wide. In the flood of 1965, the new wider bridge built upstream was washed into the Rainbow Bridge, which then acted as a dam. The Rainbow withstood the pressure and remained intact. The new bridge was rebuilt. The Rainbow Bridge is listed in the National Register of Historic Places and is a Colorado Civil Engineering Landmark.

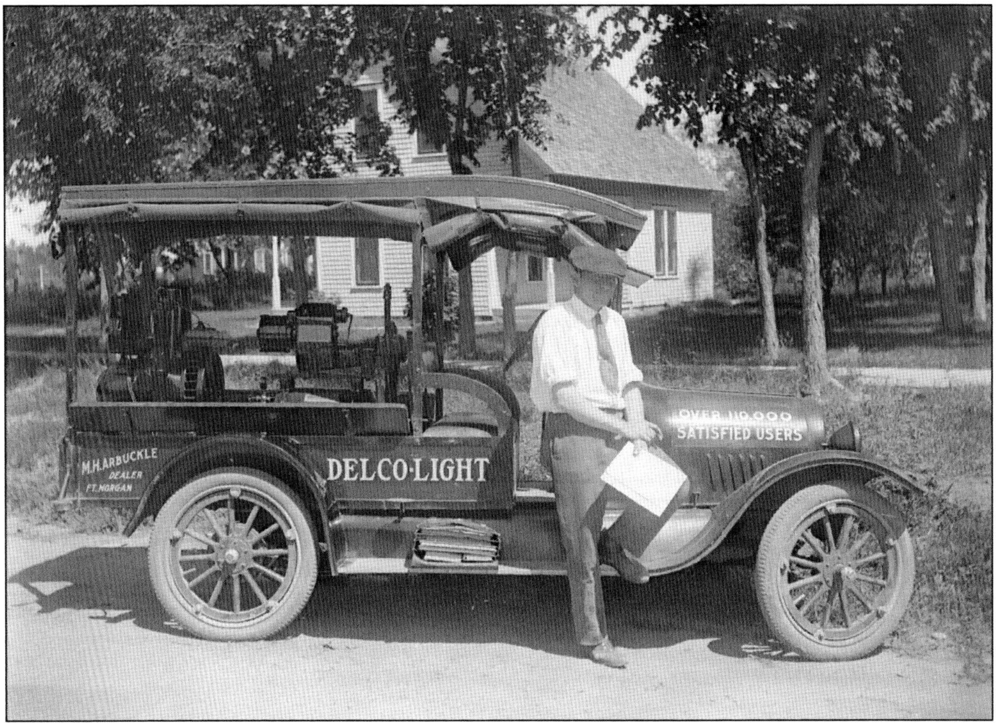

On the side of the car reads "Delco Light, over 110,000 satisfied users, M.H Arbuckle, Dealer, Fort Morgan." A note on the back says this man is Mark Arbuckle, an uncle of Mrs. Lionel Fisher, who married Gus Kammerer's youngest sister. This photograph was taken at the present site of Shamrock filling station on the corner of Ensign and Platte Streets around 1920.

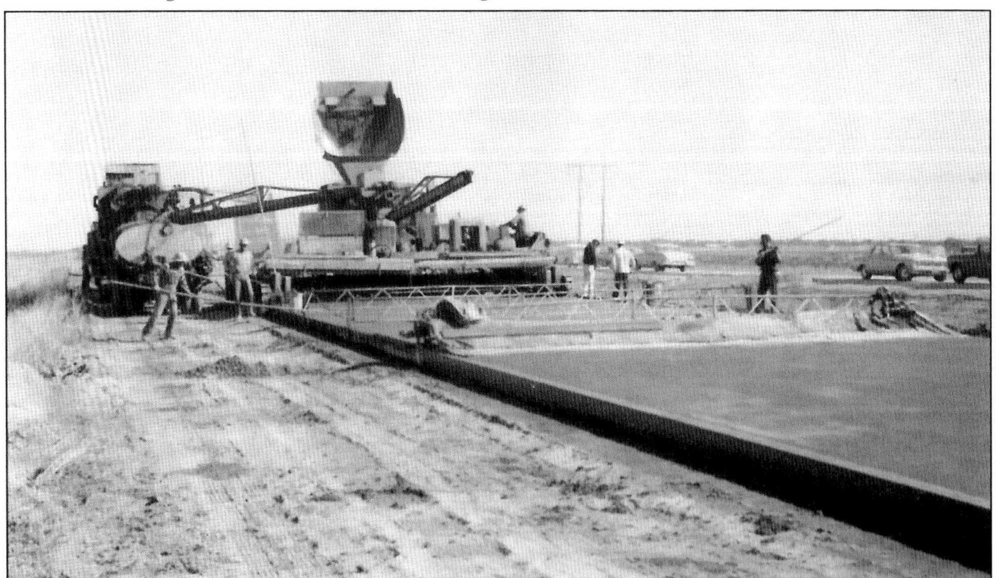

Pictured here is construction on Interstate 80S (renamed I-76 in 1976—Colorado's centennial year). The highway began emerging through Morgan County in 1962. The crew completed between 2,900 and 3,300 feet per day, and the road was opened in 1963. Dave Luna is pictured on the left edging concrete.

Four

Schools and Churches

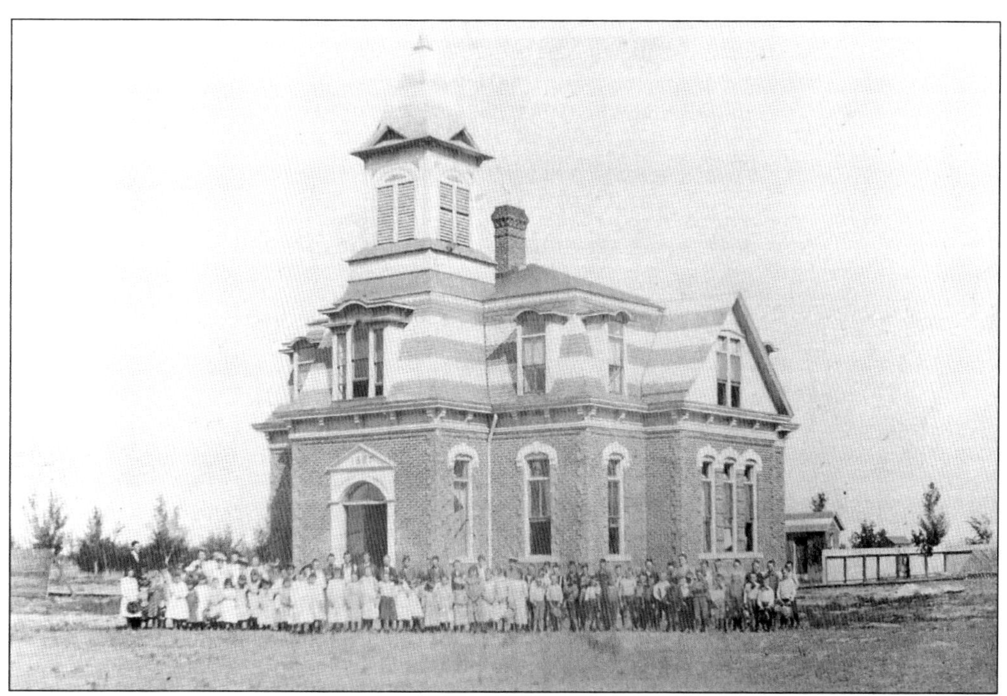

Pictured here is the first school building in Fort Morgan, constructed in 1887; this was also the first school on the Baker School Lake Street site.

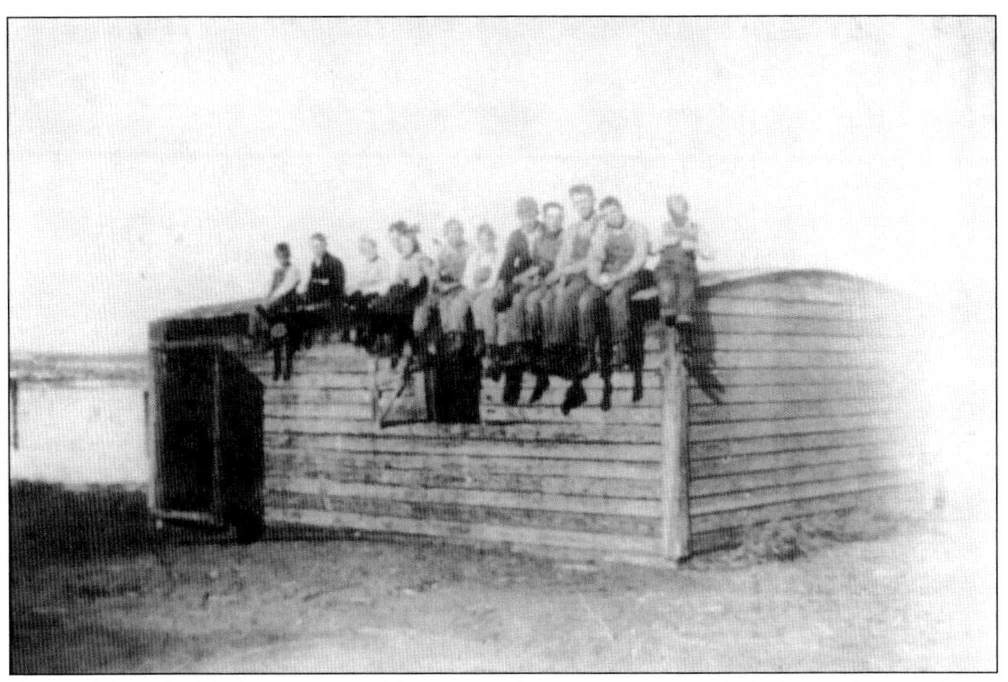

Pictured here in 1918 are some of Anna Busch's pupils on top of the horse barn at Long Meadow School.

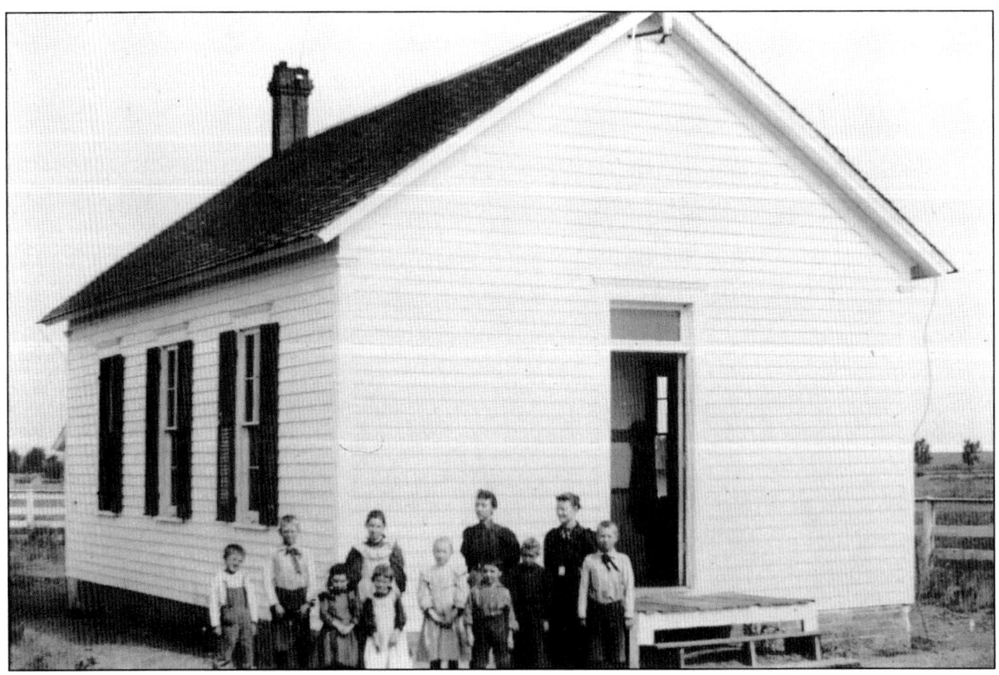

In 1890, four wooden buildings were constructed and placed around the district to be used as schools. This is an example of one of the four, believed to be the Orchard School.

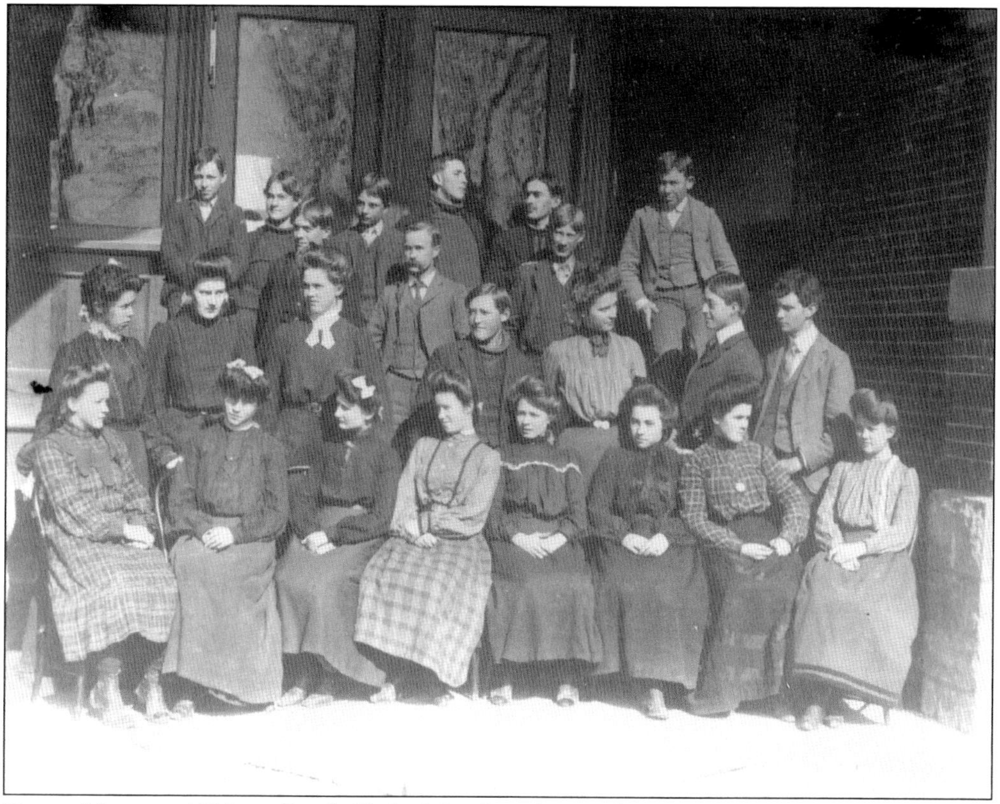

Pictured here in 1904 are Brush High School students. Identified are, in no particular order, Dagmar Peterson, Josie Wier, Gertrude Mortensen, Ivy House, Marie Rasmussen, Hattie O'Dell, Ethel Roberts, Clara Nelson, Kate Burchsted, George Peterson, Hattie Siever, Merton Smith, and Roy Bolton.

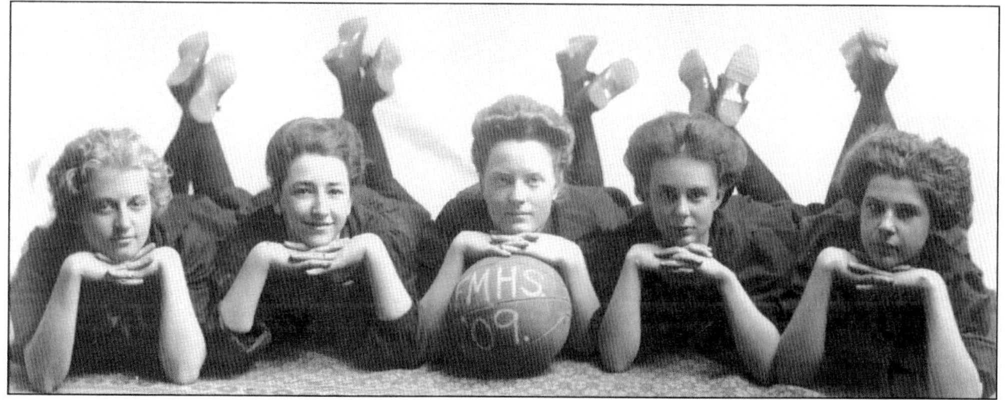

Members of the 1909 Fort Morgan High School Basketball team pictured here are, from left to right, A.J. Masher, Josephine Ballard, Alma Heiskell, Alma Eyser, and unidentified. Both Alma E. and Alma H. were named after Alma Curry, who taught school in Fort Morgan.

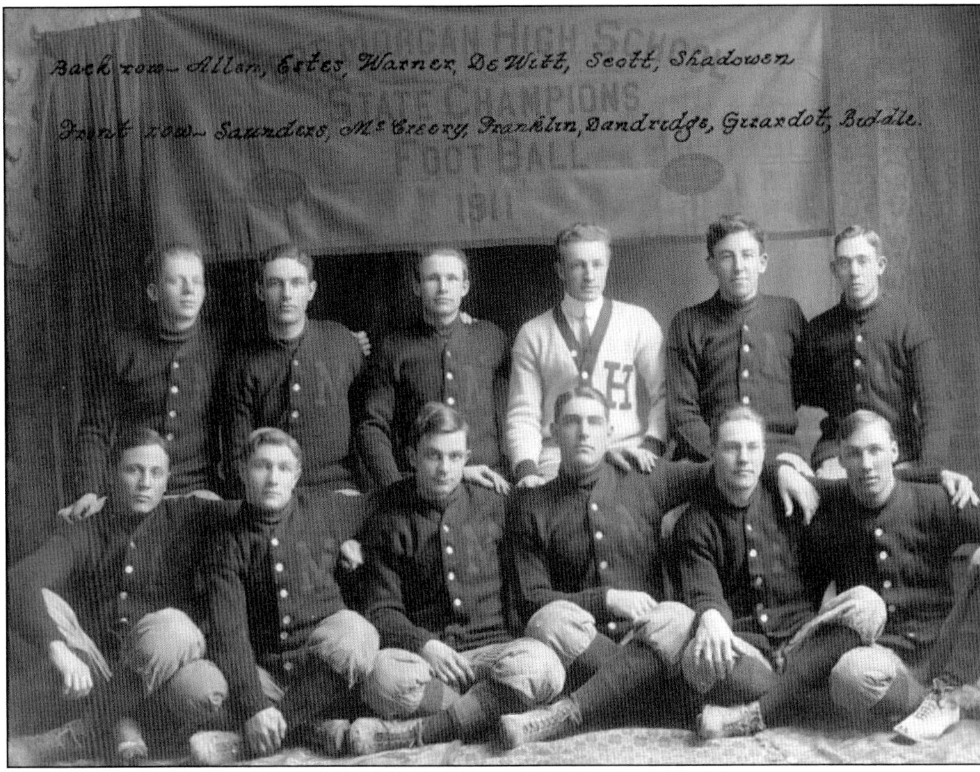

The 1911 Fort Morgan High School football champions are pictured here.

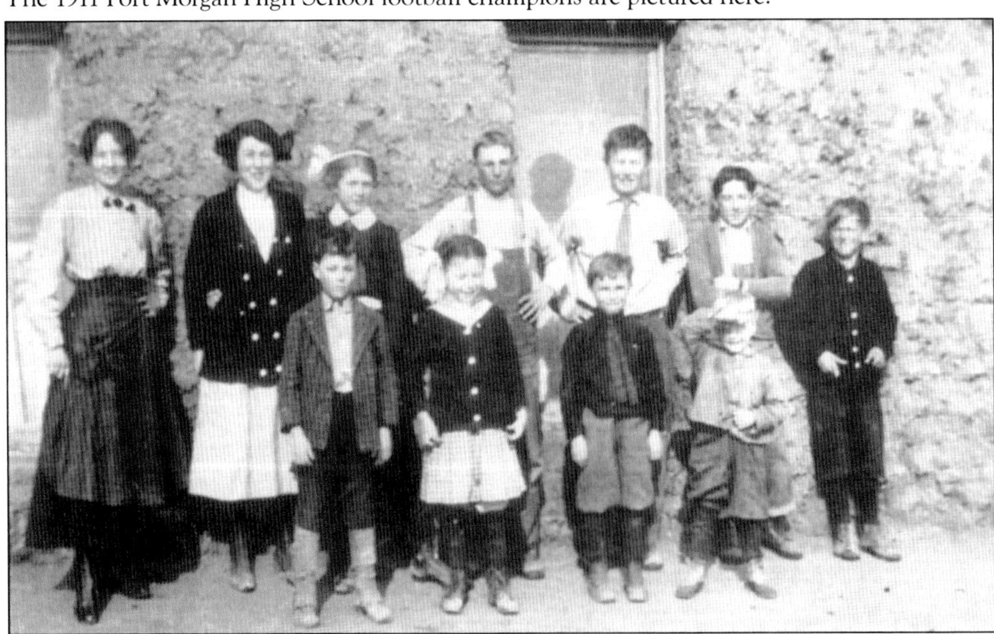

Adena School students pictured here in 1912–1913 are, from left to right (first row) Clarence Nevell, Alice Nevell, Bennie Spencer, and Paul Fryar; (second row) Lillian McVey, Irma Hawley, Gertrude Hauermann, George Chittick, Arthur Smith, and Ralph Rogalls. The schoolteacher (far left) is unidentified.

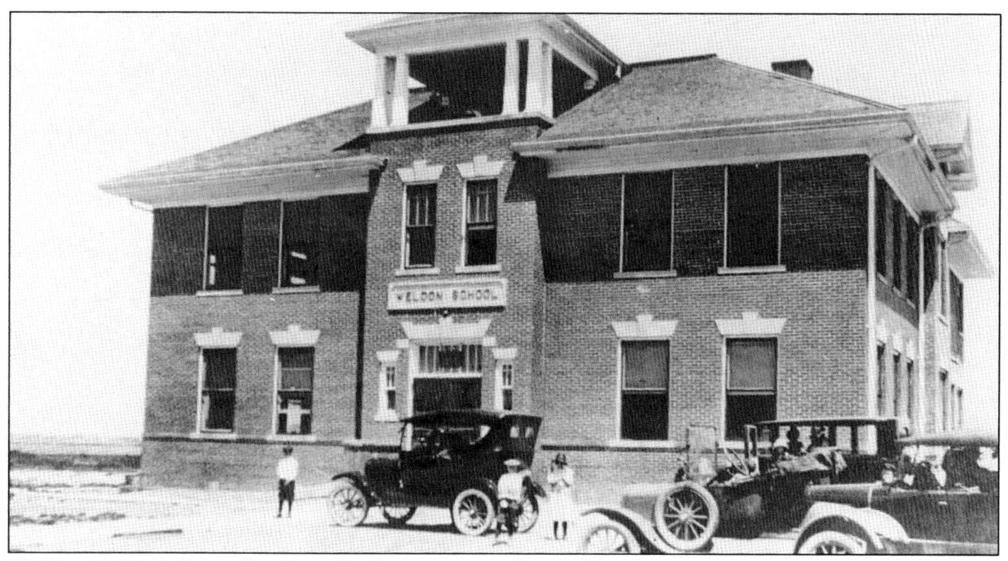

Weldon Valley's first school was built in 1906, and an addition of two rooms on the ground level and a second floor was completed in 1917.

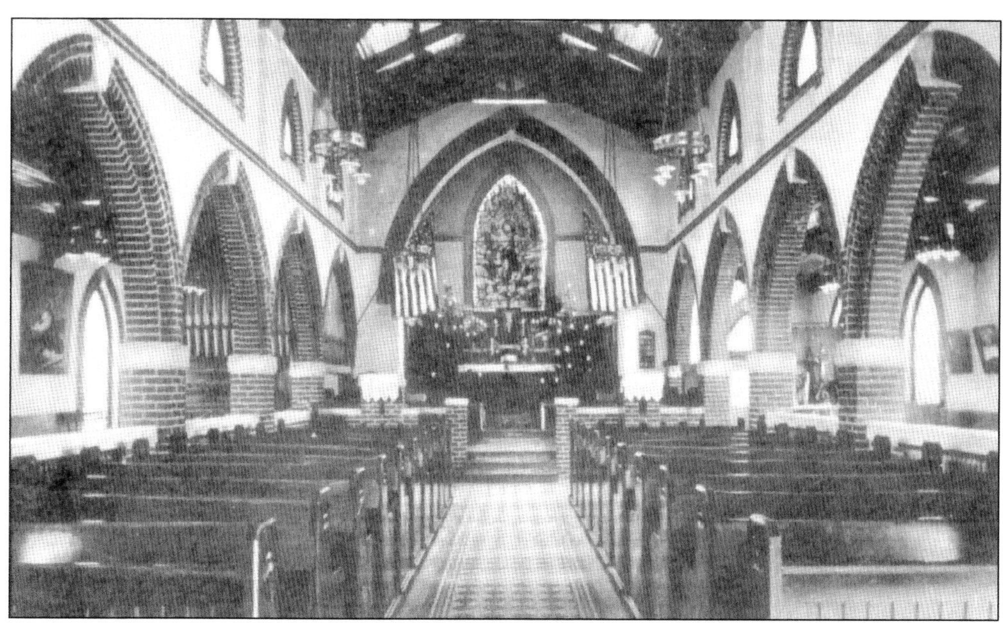
All Saints Lutheran Church was built in the Danish Gothic style in 1918. It is part of the Eben-Ezer complex, which was opened by Pastor Jens Madsen in Brush in 1903 as a tuberculosis sanitarium.

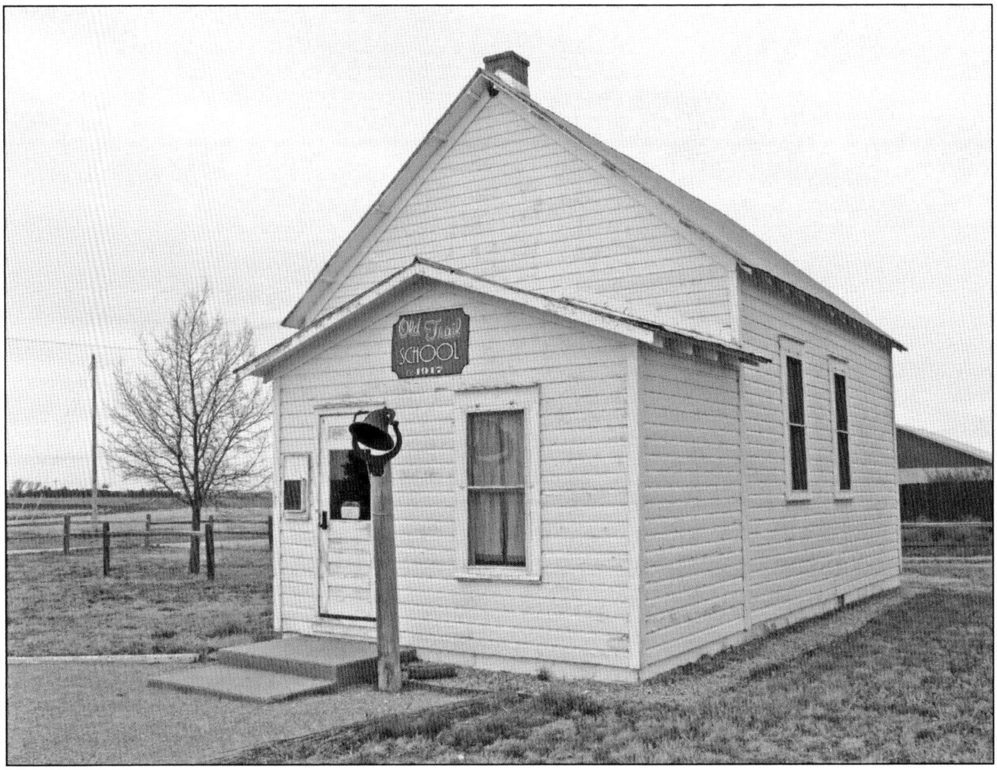

This school was originally the Reed School, built in 1909 on the George Reed Homestead. It was moved from this site in 1919 to a site south of Wiggins and renamed Old Trail School because it was relocated there on a branch of the Overland Trail. It was again moved to Wiggins on school property and used as a music room. In 1964, it was purchased by the Wiggins Historical Group and moved to its present location at 421 High Street in Wiggins. The building has been registered in the Colorado and National Registers of Historic Places, which points to the fact that the 1912 Old Trail School exhibits the distinguishing characteristics of a rural one-room schoolhouse.

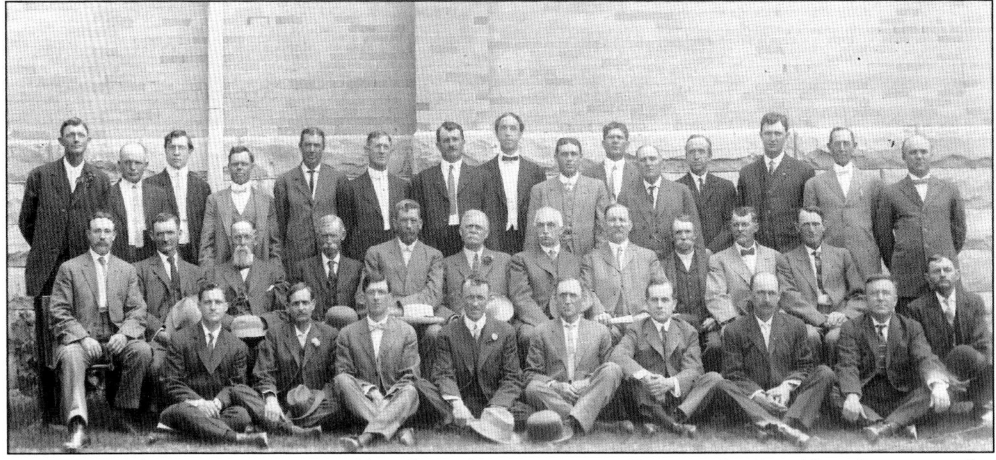

Members of the Business Men's Bible Class of Fort Morgan's First Methodist Church pose in the proper businessman's apparel of the early 1900s.

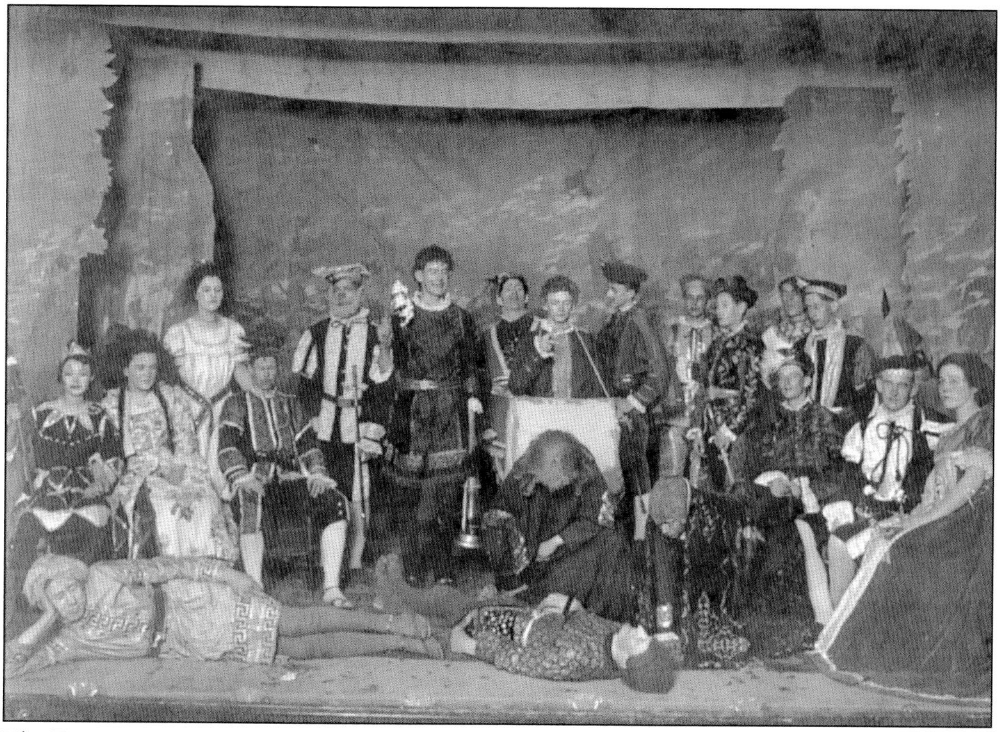

The Fort Morgan High School drama students of 1910 are posing onstage in their Elizabethan costumes for a production of Shakespeare's *As You Like It*.

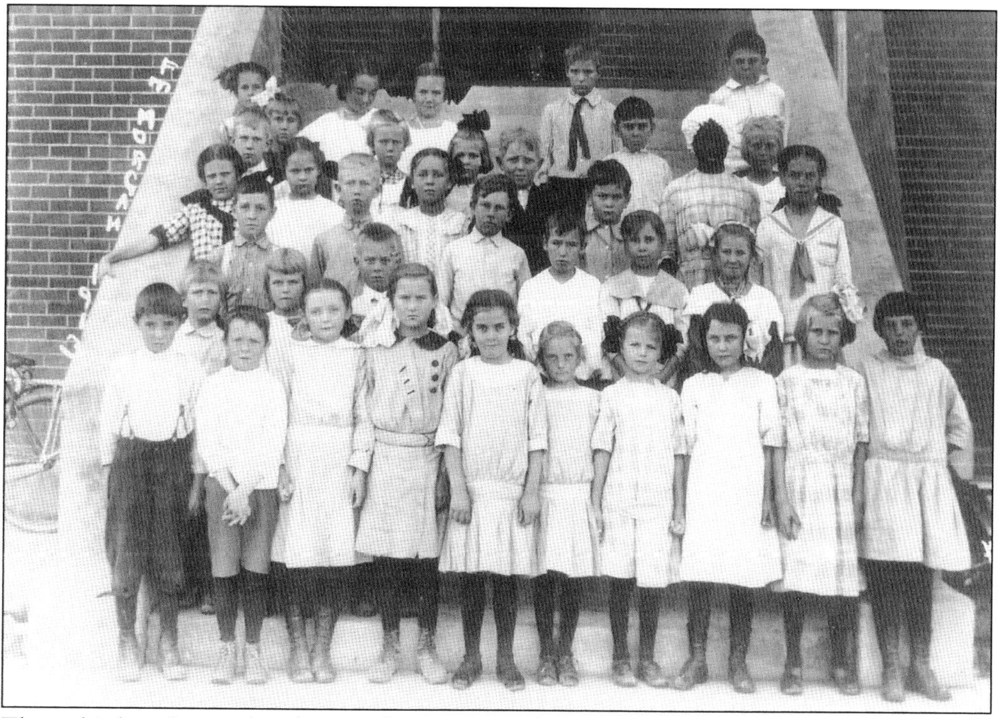

These third graders are lined up on the stairs outside Fort Morgan Central School in 1913.

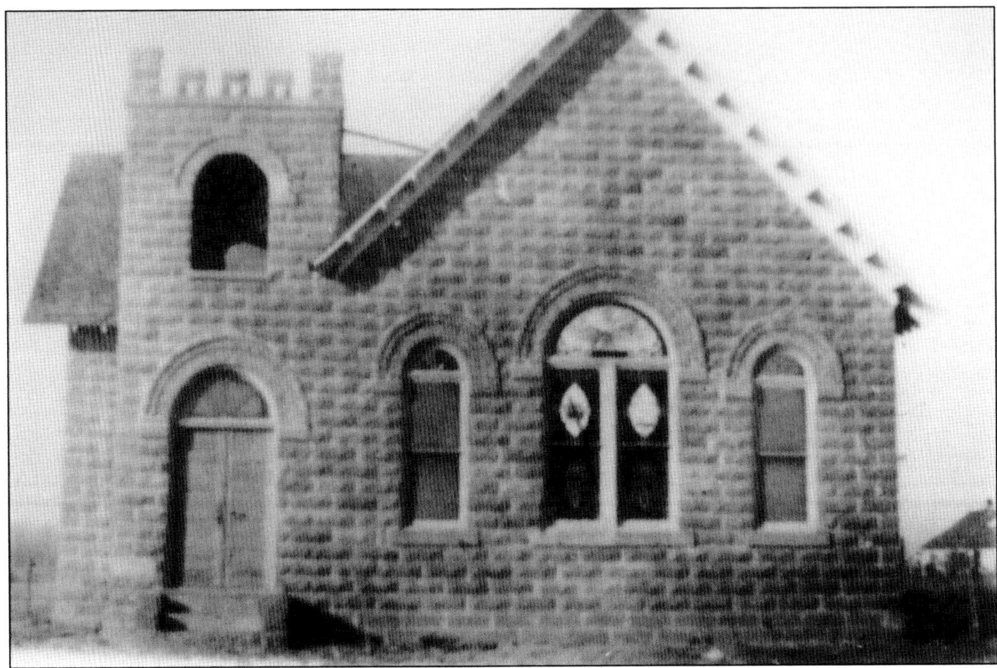

The Weldona Presbyterian Church was built in 1915 and was dedicated to Conrad Schaffer, an early resident of Morgan County. Reverend Hanes served as the pastor at that time and Marie Schaffer was a charter member. Due to its small size, the church was no longer in use by 1952 and torn down in 1956. The church bell on display at the museum came from this church.

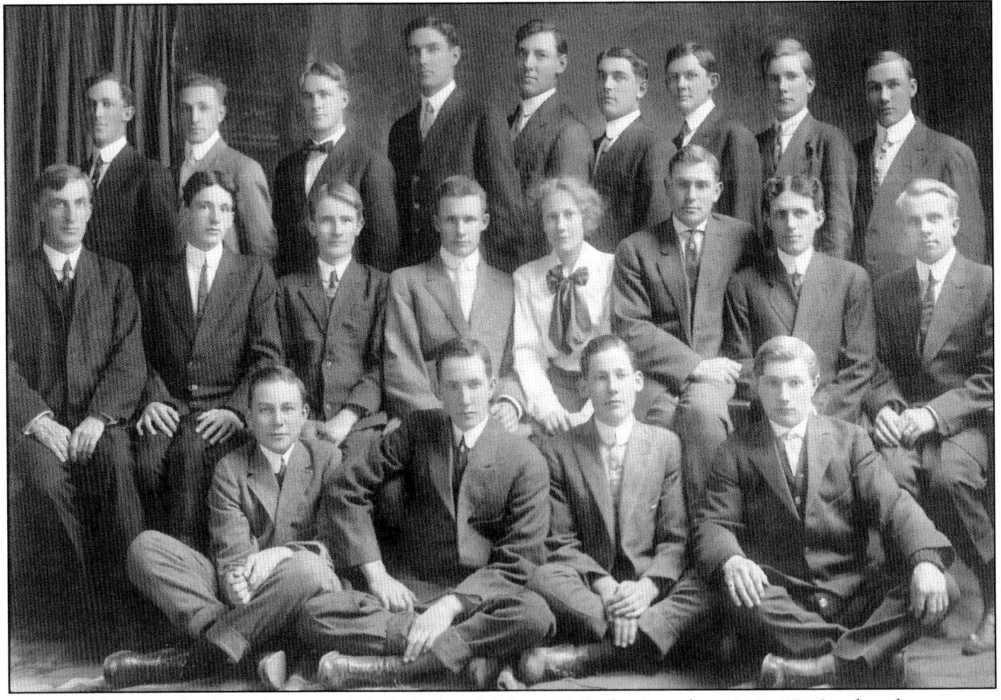

Pictured here is the Fort Morgan High School Glee Club during the 1912–1913 school year.

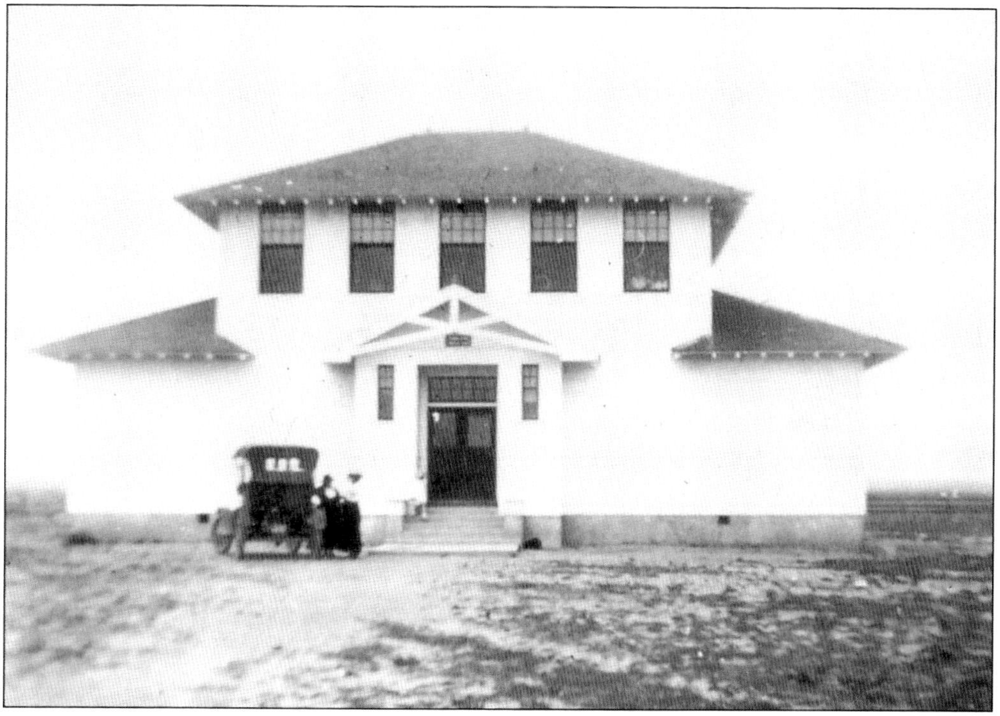

In 1871, the first Snyder School—a three-room structure—was painted pink. In 1881, a second school was built, named McGil School. The third school was built in 1901, and in 1916 the fourth school, White School (pictured) was erected.

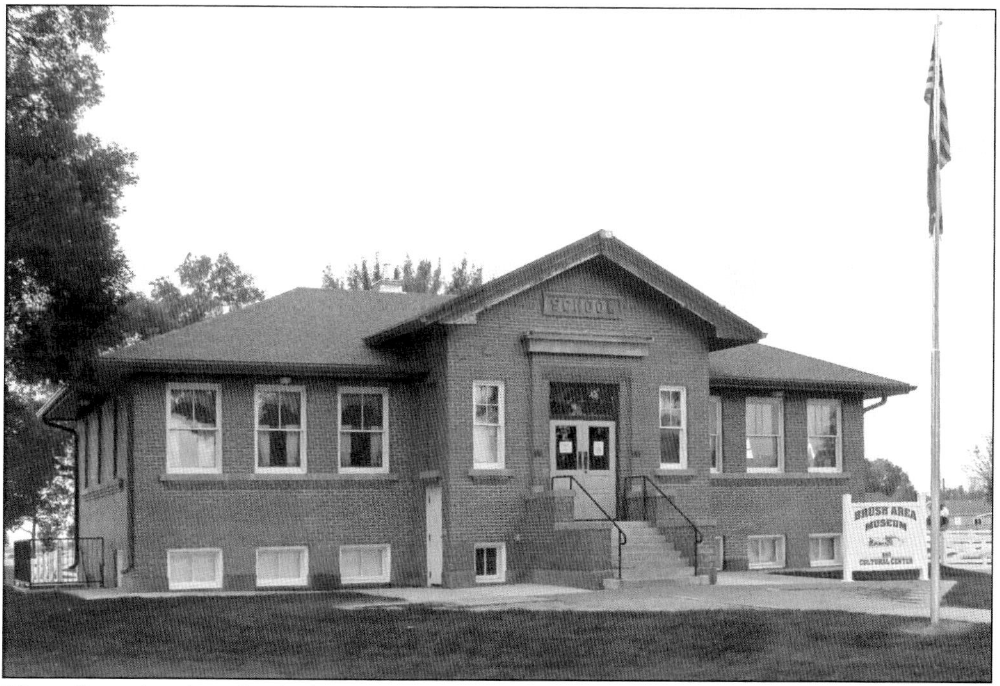

The influx of workers for the beet industry merited the building of Knearl School in 1910. The school opened in 1911 with around 100 students. It is the current home of the Brush Museum.

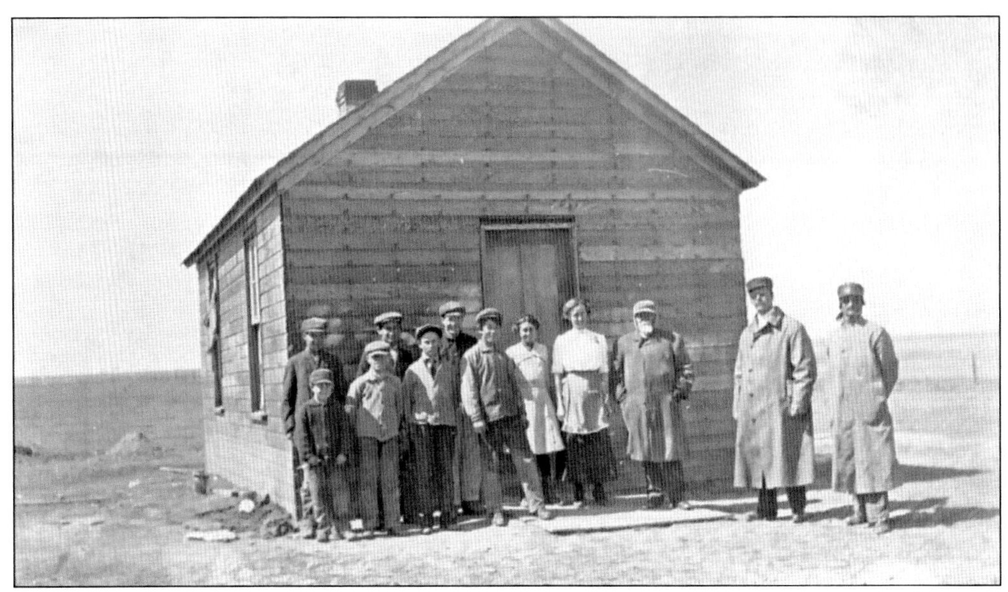

Centerville School, located 13 miles south of Fort Morgan, is pictured here in 1914.

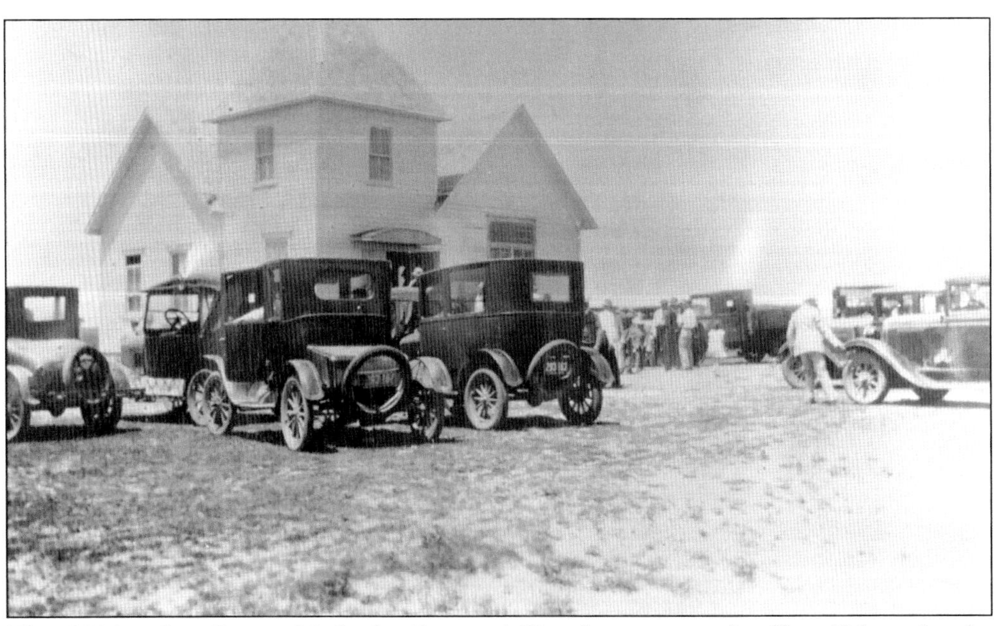

The 1915 Antelope Springs Methodist Episcopal Church is an example of late-19th- and early-20th-century buildings found in rural areas on the Colorado Plains.

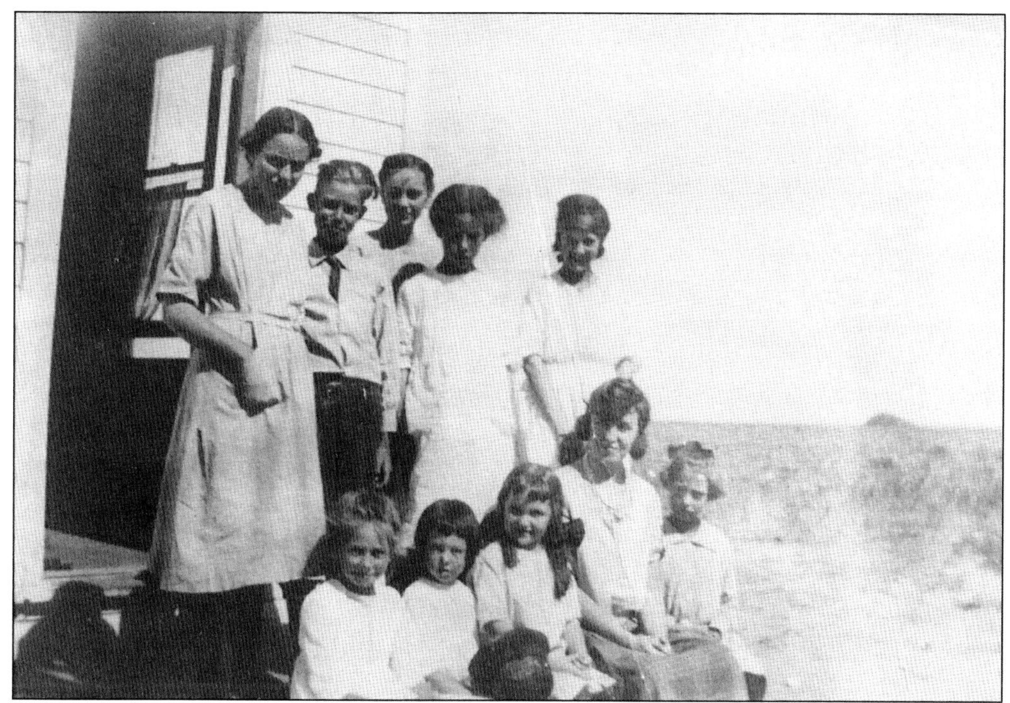

Pictured here in 1922 at Antelope Valley School are nine students and the teacher, Anna Busch (sitting on the front steps). A note on the back reads, "Quite a few of the boys were absent as they had to work in the field that day."

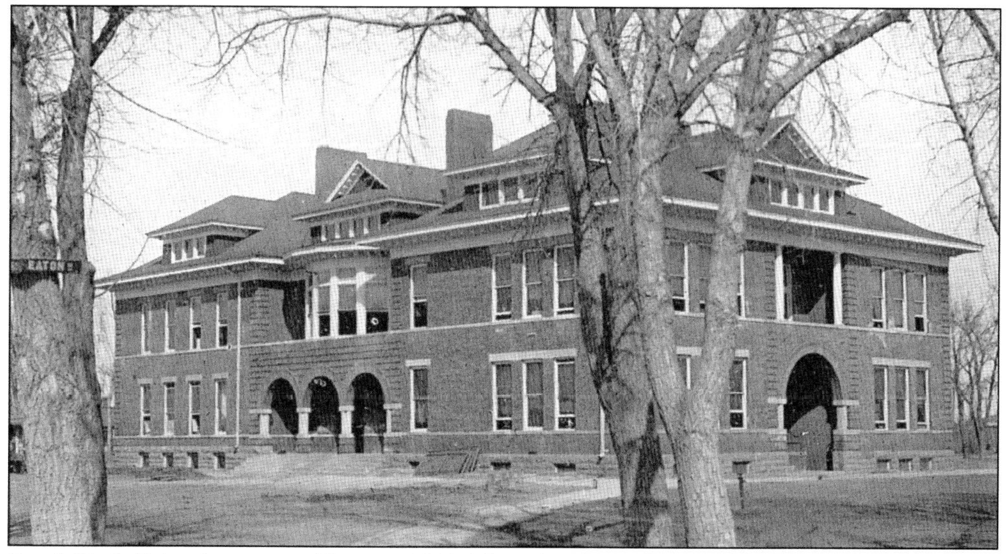

Brush High School is pictured here in 1910. The school was destroyed by fire in 1927.

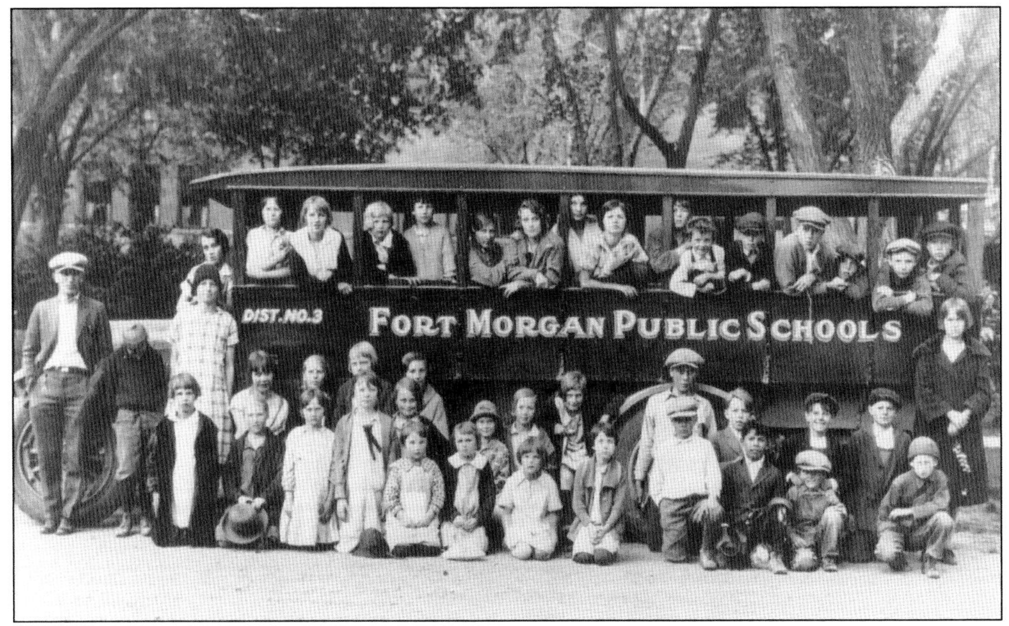

Pictured here in 1924 is a Fort Morgan Public School bus. There are 43 children in the photograph; some are on the bus, and others are kneeling in front. The schoolteacher, who was also the bus driver, is standing by the left front tire.

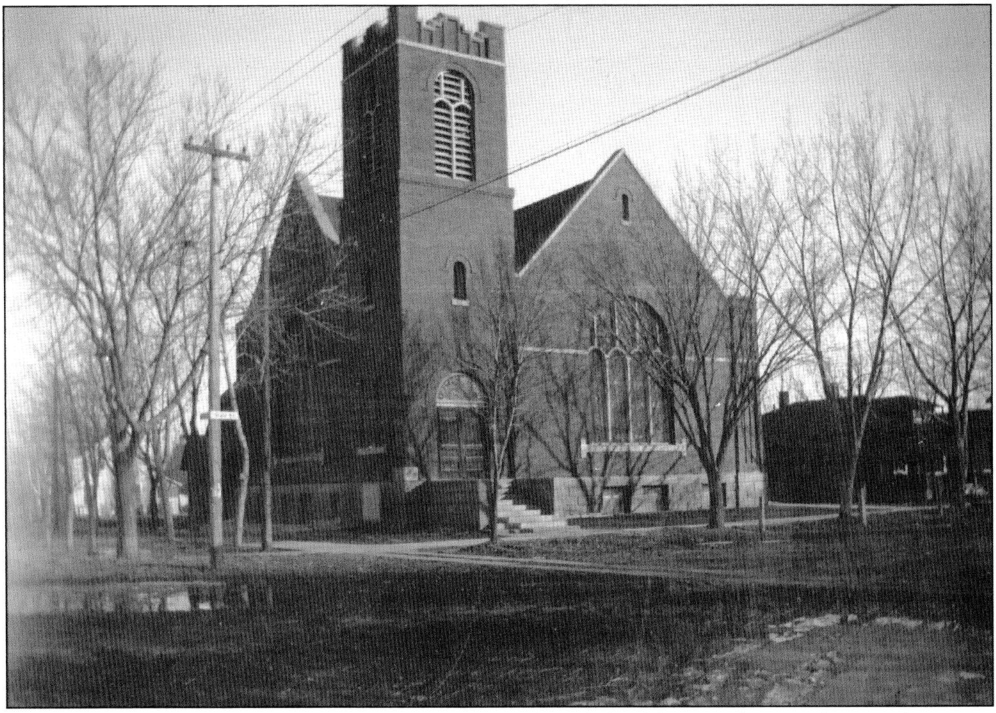

This photograph from 1928 features the third church building to house the Presbyterian congregation, on the original site at State Street and Beaver Avenue. The first structure, which was wood, blew down in a fierce wind; the second, which was brick, was razed to build this church. An educational wing was added in 1928.

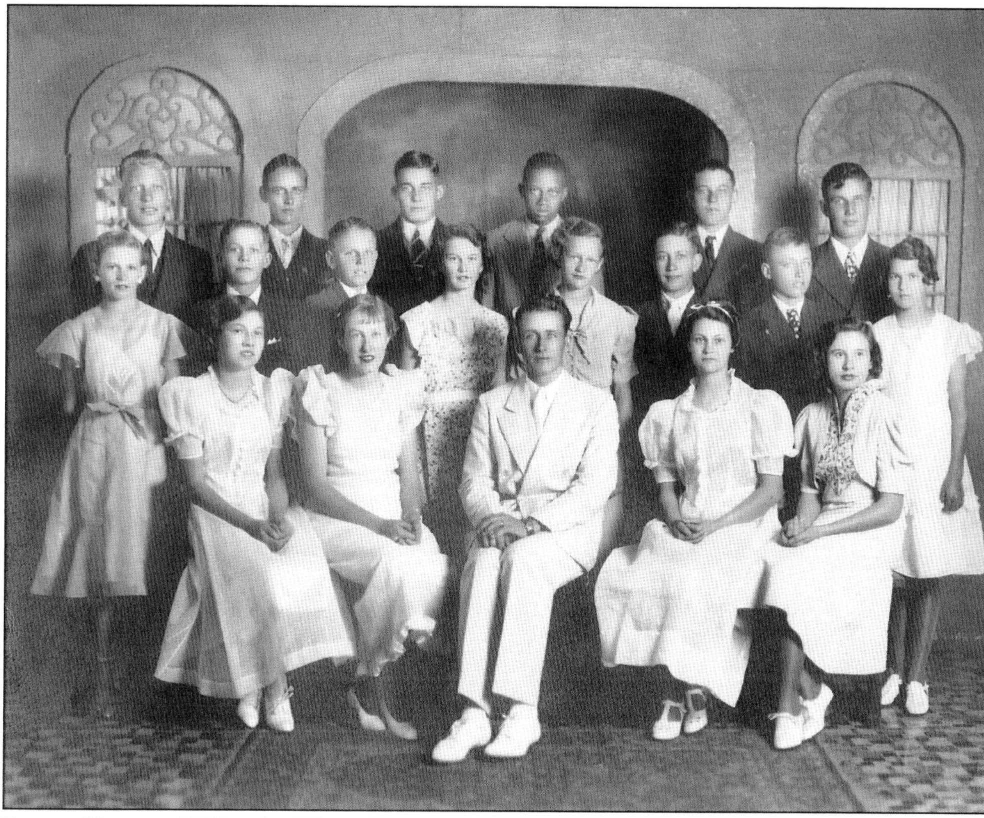

Pictured here in 1937 is the Wiggins eight-grade class; from left to right are (first row) Eileen Campbell, Pearl Johnson, Dean D. Stinson (teacher), Bobby Lee Jones, and Betty McAfee; (second row) Phyllis Vance, Alvert Loose, Edward Weimer, Ethel Horton, Mane Jane Cross, Billy Graff, Lee Marts, and Buela Wohlford; (third row) Bob Ledford, Melvin Barhite, Royal Palmer, Conelius Collier, Dale Richter, and Claud Kinnaman.

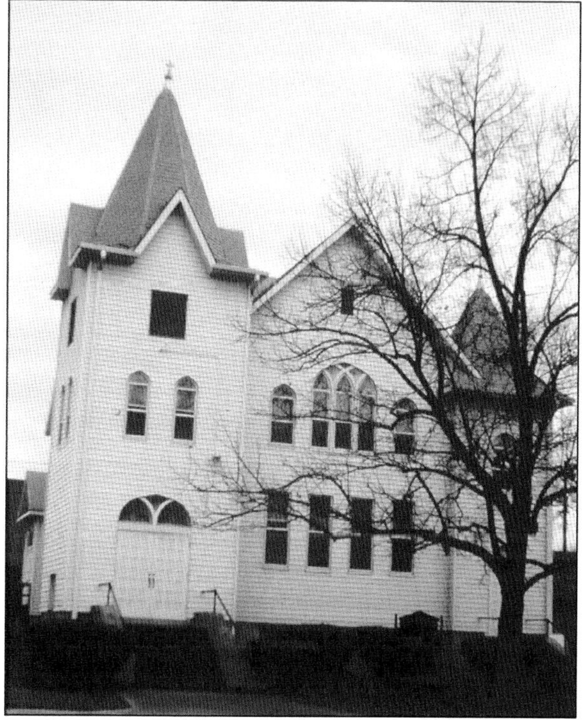

German beet workers from Russia built their first church in 1907 and named it Deutsche Evangelische Congregational Christus Gemeide. It was located at Seventh Avenue and Ensign Street. In 1917, the present church was built, incorporating the original church in its northeast corner. Services were conducted in German until 1940 and gradually merged into English by 1960.

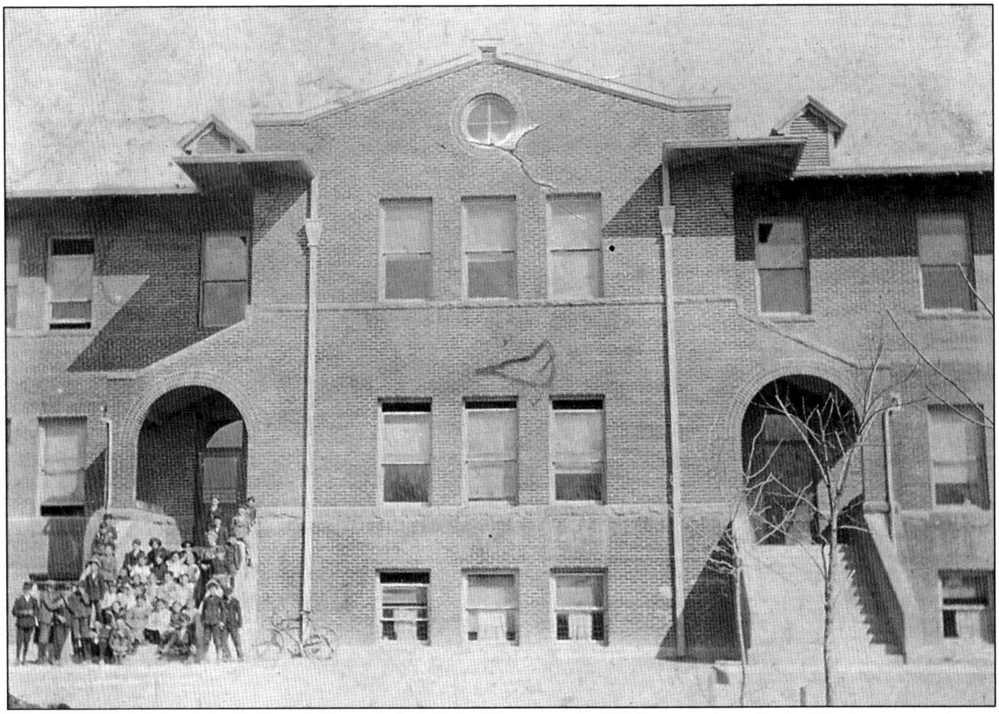

Central School was built in 1884 and enlarged in 1903. On December 9, 1927, the school was destroyed by fire. On February 27, 1928, a new school was built for $150,000 on the same site.

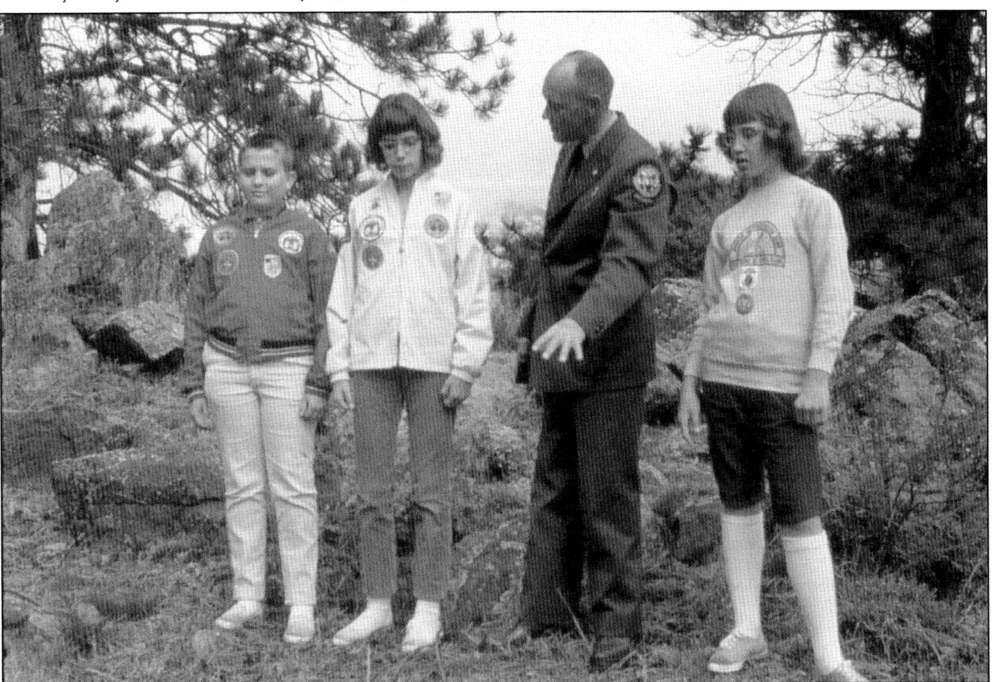

The Junior Conservation Club, the first of its kind in the nation, was founded for the preservation of local game. It began in 1946 and was founded by Herb Hockstrasser. No one in this image is identified.

Five

Industry and Business

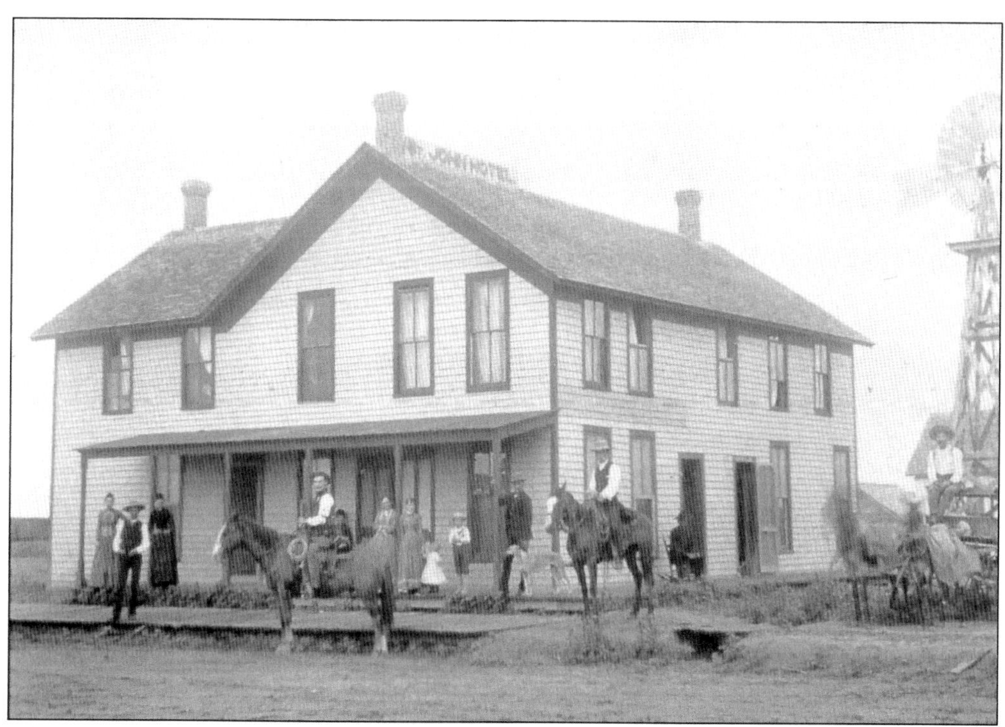

The Farnsworth Hotel was owned by the same family that chartered the first school in Fort Morgan. The two-story hotel was said to have a sliding wall that could be moved in order for the main level to be used for community dances and other social events. It was later called the St. John's Hotel.

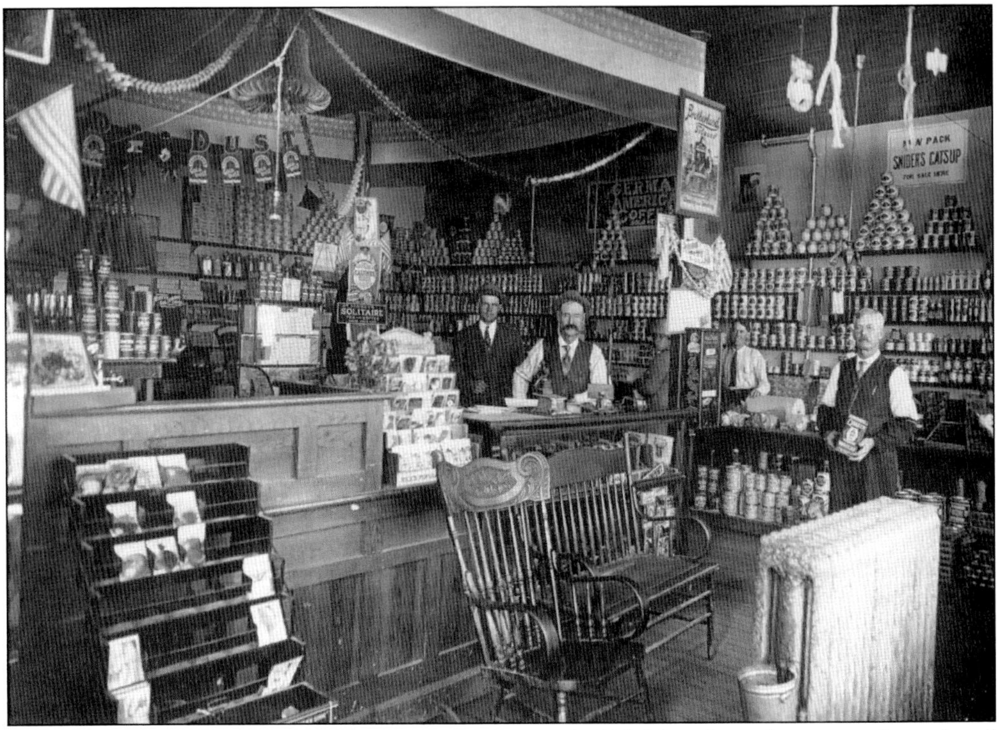

Pictured here is a grocery store in Fort Morgan around 1920. Note how the store is heated and the prices of various items: canned goods, corn, barley, beans, pears, and jams 10¢; staples and coffee 15¢; 100 pounds of sugar $5.80; eggs 12¢ a dozen; butter 18¢; and Swiss cheese 25¢.

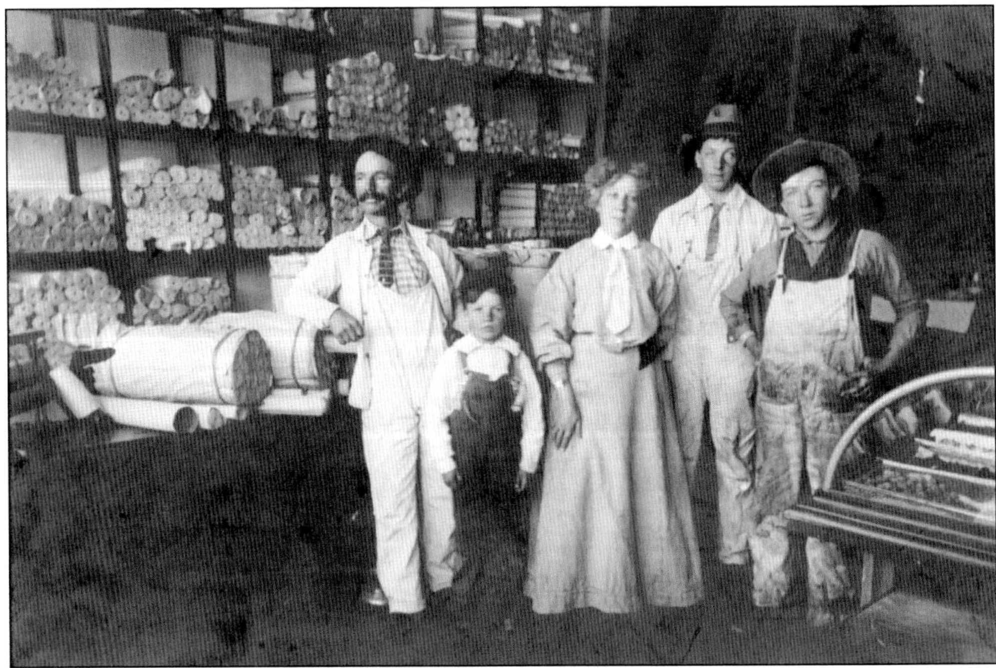

Pictured here in 1910 is the interior of Bellmore's Wallpaper Shop, located south of the railroad tracks in Brush.

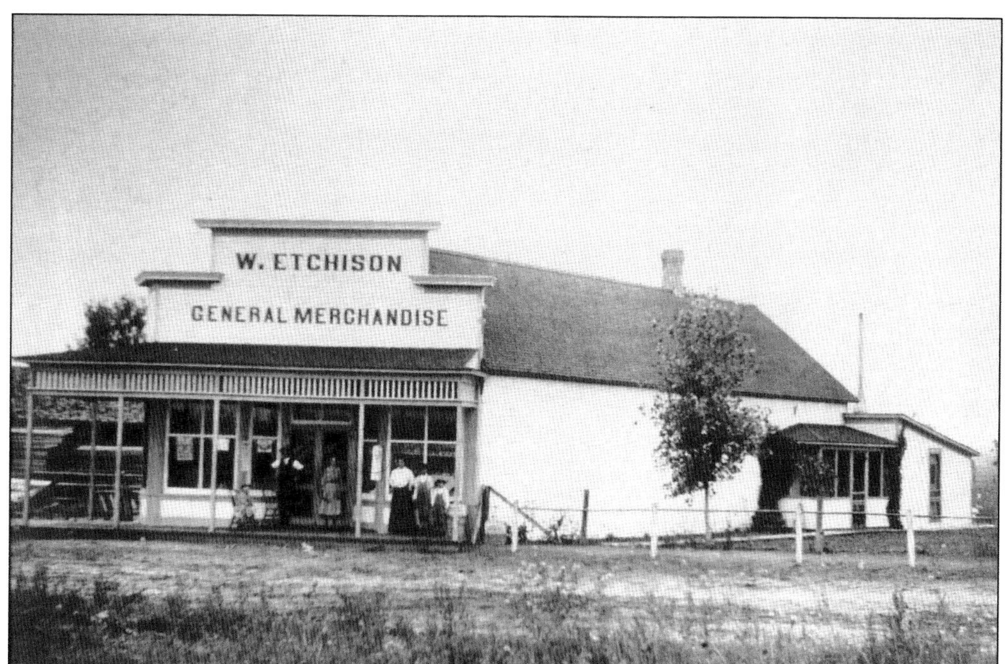

The Eli Etchison Dry Goods building, erected in 1894, was purchased in 1905. A new covered porch with wide plate-glass windows for the storefront and a hitching bar for customer's horses were added.

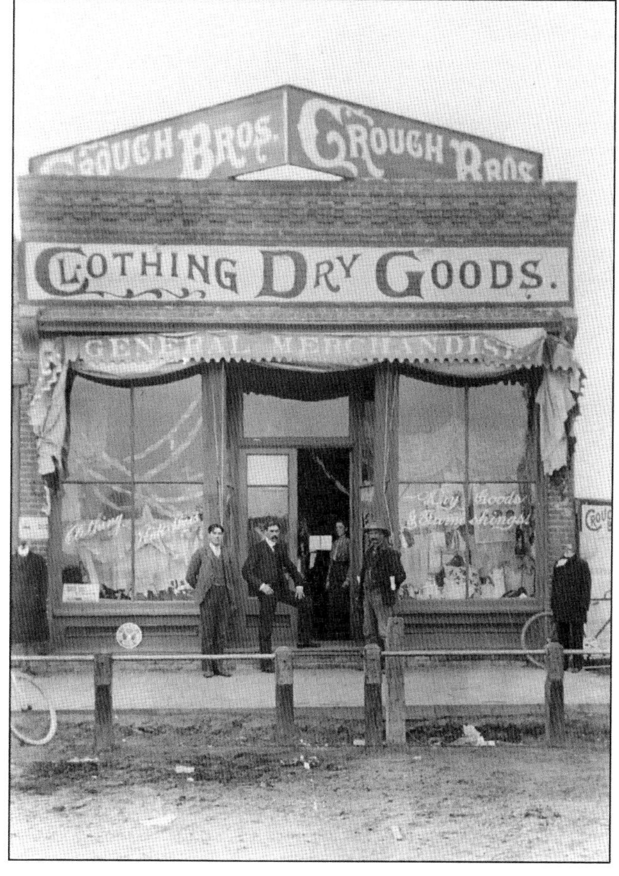

The Crouch Brothers Clothing and Dry Goods store was doing business in 1901. The company located in Fort Morgan sold ready-made clothing for men, women, and children as well as fabric and other cloth goods. The brick building has a glass front with a canvas awning, and on top of the building, "Crouch Bros." is painted on a triangular sign.

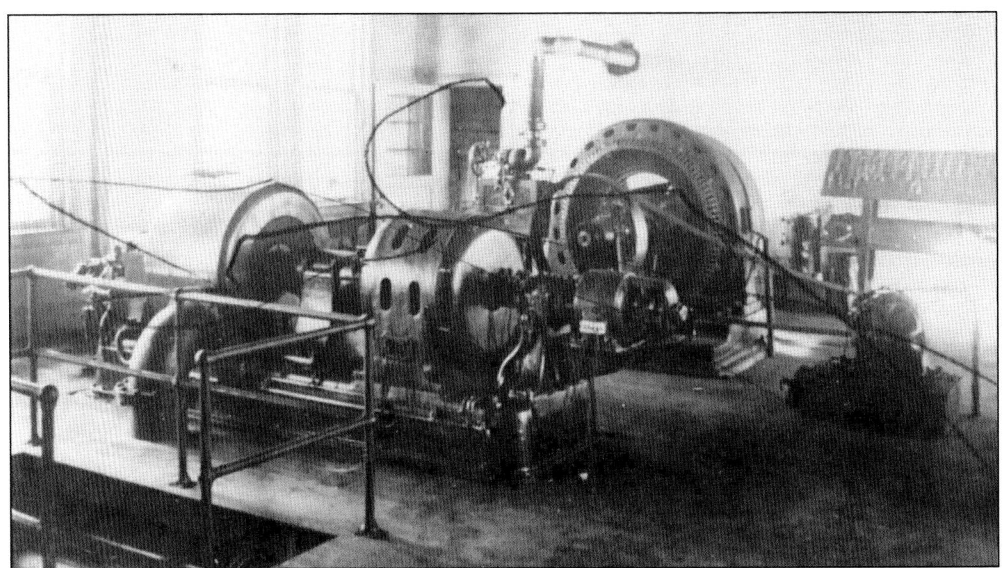

Pictured here in 1912 is the original Fort Morgan light plant, located in city hall, under the supervision of George G. Cox. At this time, Orlo More was chief engineer of the Fairbanks Morse Company, where he designed and patented the revolutionary squirrel cage induction motor.

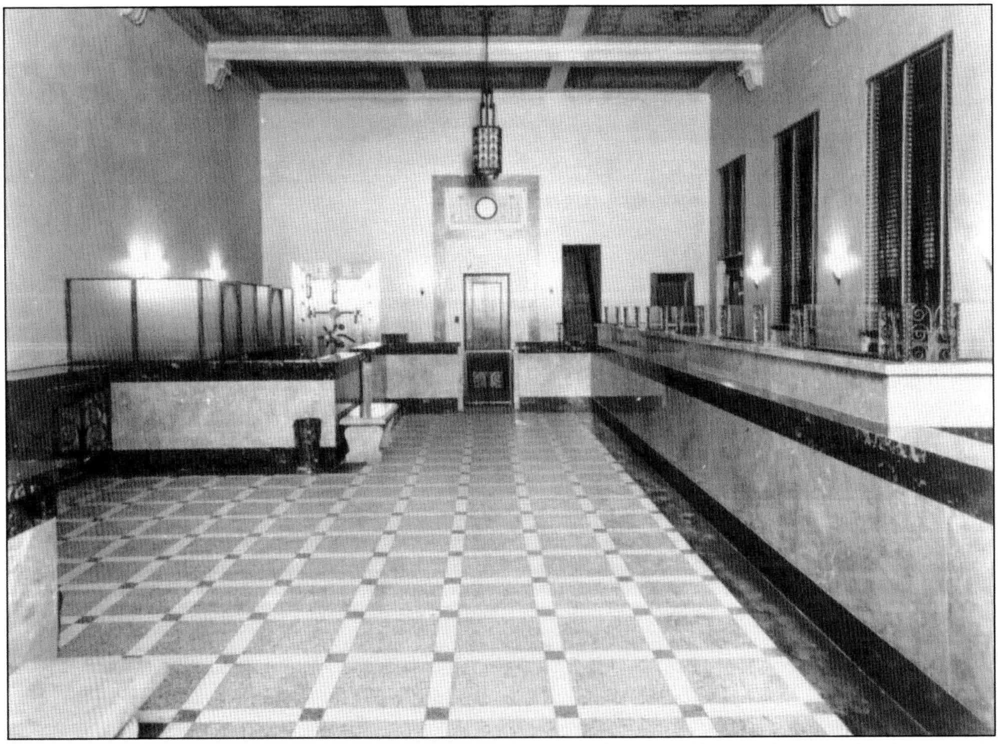

When the Farmers State Bank of Fort Morgan opened its doors in 1915, it shared a building with the *Fort Morgan Times*. The bank moved to 300 Main Street in 1920 after being purchased by the Bloedorn brothers in 1919. The building pictured here was erected in 1930. It is currently used for community offices. The bank moved again to 123 East Kiowa Avenue in 1966. It was later acquired by Wells Fargo.

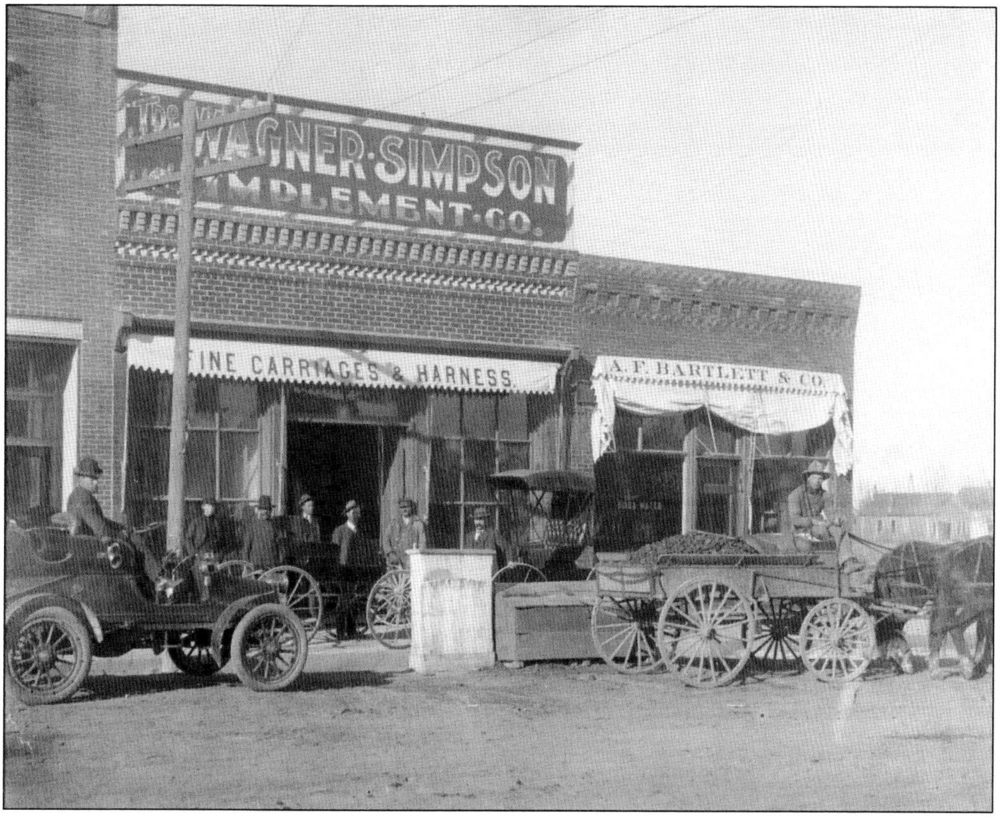

Farming brought business to Fort Morgan merchants, one being the sales of farm machinery and equipment. The Wagner-Simpson Implement Co. began in 1890.

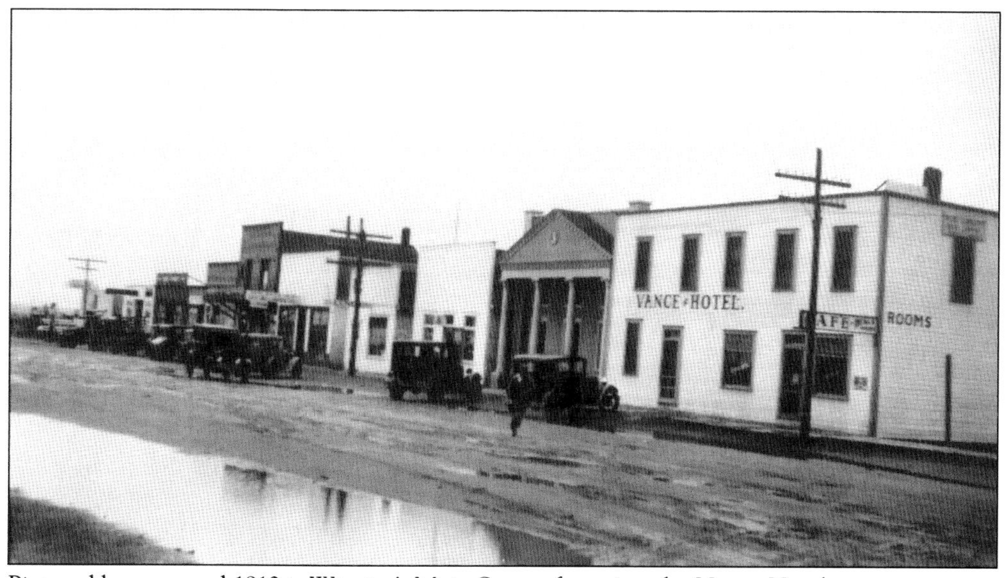

Pictured here around 1910 is Wiggins's Main Street, featuring the Vance Hotel.

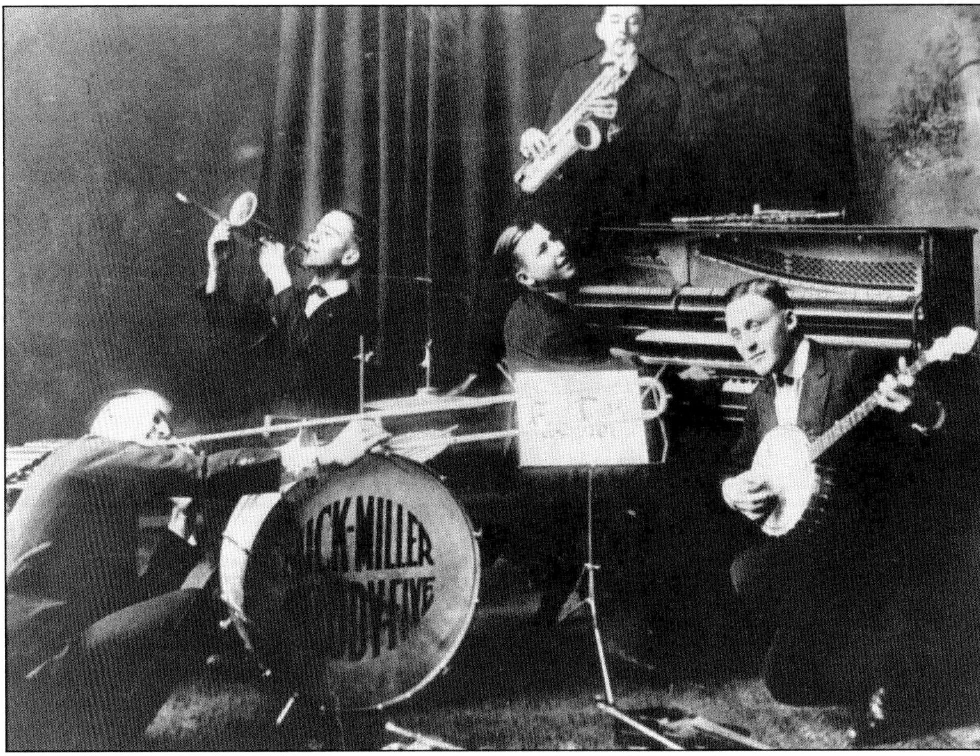

The Mick Miller Melody Five was the first band that Glenn Miller organized while attending high school in Fort Morgan. Glenn Miller is on the left with a trombone. Although not pictured, Alice Spencer was an original member of the band.

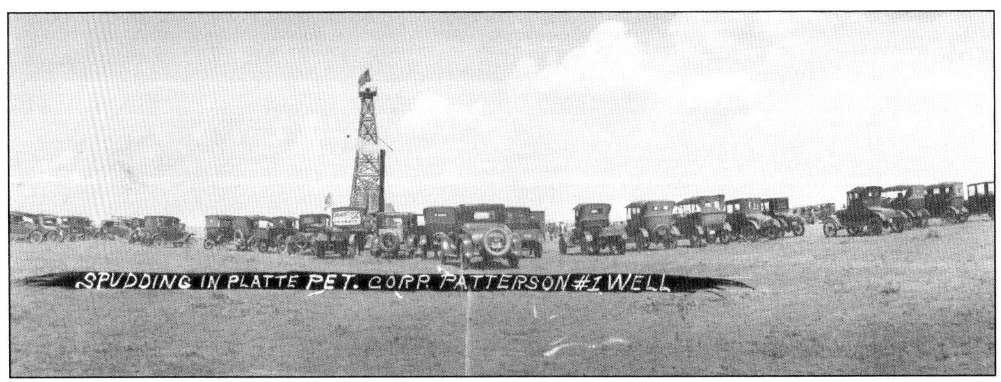

"Spudding in the Platte Pet. Corp. Patterson Well #1" is the caption written on the photograph. This was the first successful oil well in Morgan County. North of Orchard, the derrick is made of wood and has a US flag on top.

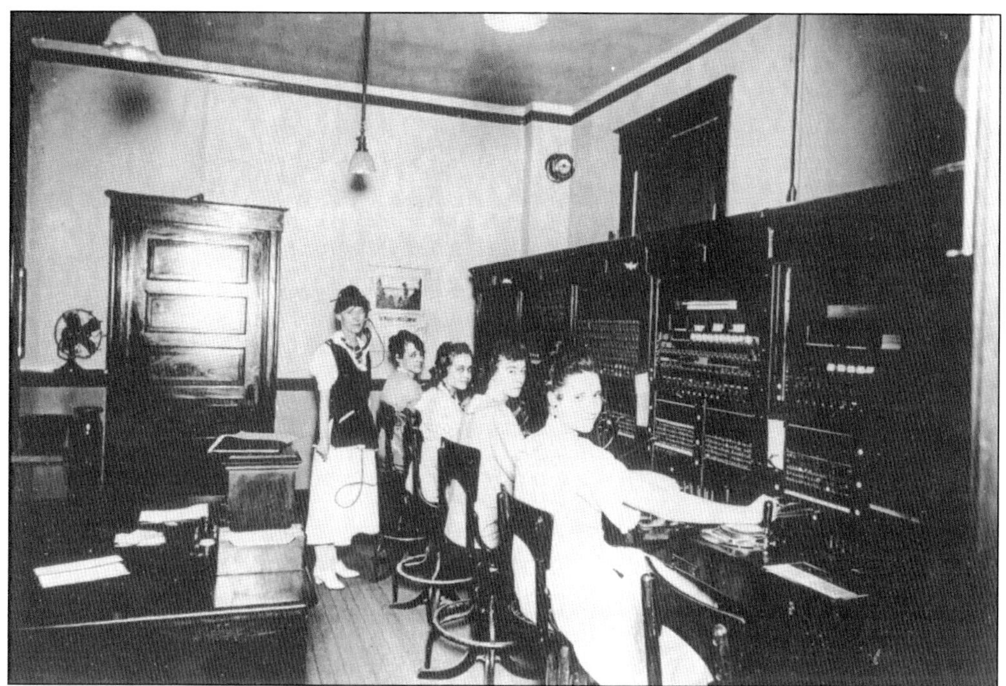

Mountain States Telephone Company, located in Fort Morgan, is pictured here 1917. Four operators sit in front of the telephone switchboard. The employees are, from left to right, Maybelle Anderson (chief operator), Fredona Clawges, Mildred Cooper, Jesse Headrick, and Lorene Clawges.

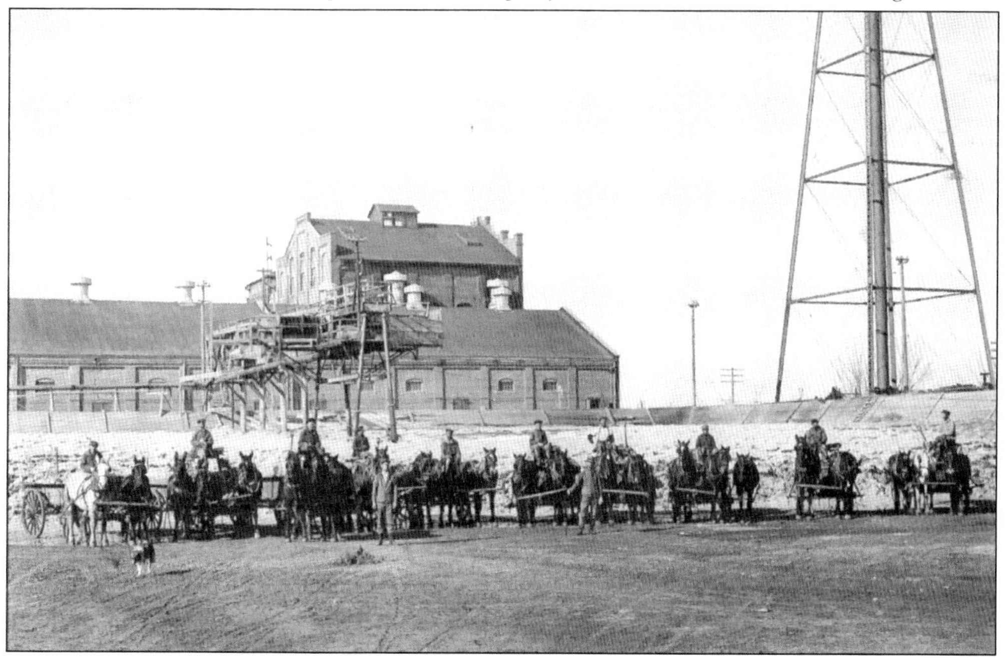

Recognizing the economic growth Great Western sugar factories brought to communities where they were located, Brush farmers and businessmen united in 1904 to build Jackson Reservoir, bringing irrigation to beet fields. The farmers pledged to grow 5,000 acres of beets for three years, and finally Great Western built this factory in 1906.

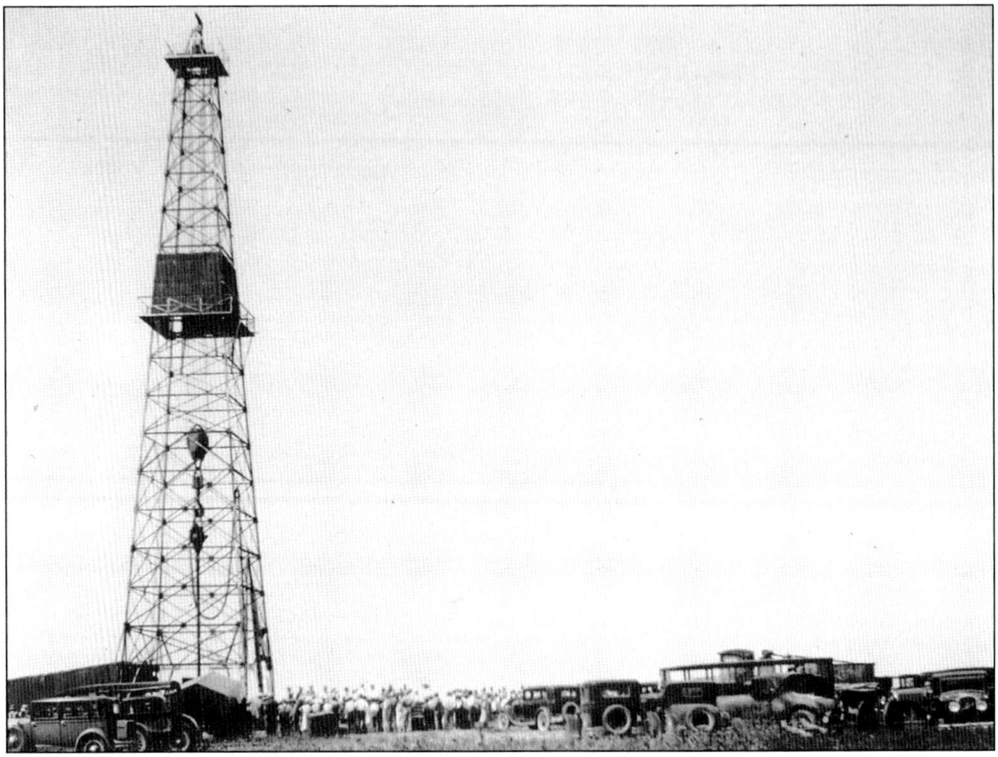

The Platte Valley Petroleum Company was organized in 1926. One of the early wells, approximately 10 miles north of Orchard, blew in in 1930. An estimated 2,500 people came to see the gusher. By the end of the 1930s, the first oil boom was over. Others followed and were scattered across Morgan County, including at one point the third-largest oil field in Colorado—the Adena Field.

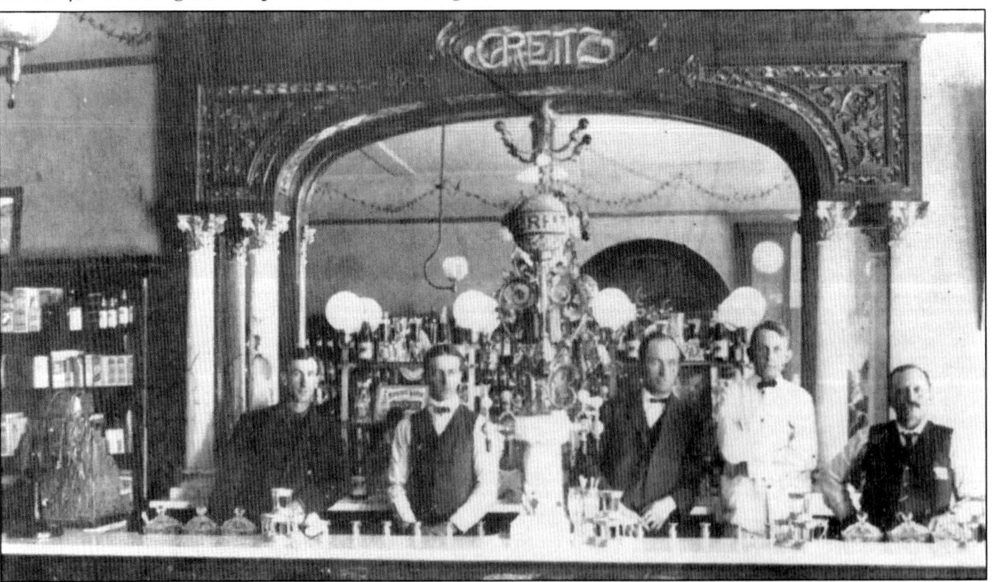

Soda fountains or ice-cream saloons were often found together with a pharmacy. The soda fountain counter served as a meeting place for people of all ages to enjoy carbonated beverages and ice cream.

The smoke in this photograph is coming from Fort Morgan's first municipal light plant, located in the basement of city hall, on the east side of 100 Main Street. It operated from 1908 to 1923, when it was moved to a much larger building in Riverside Park. The total cost of the city hall power plant was $11,500, which was $4,000 more than approved by the voters. Local citizens volunteered to make up the difference by subscription (they were not charged for their initial electricity use).

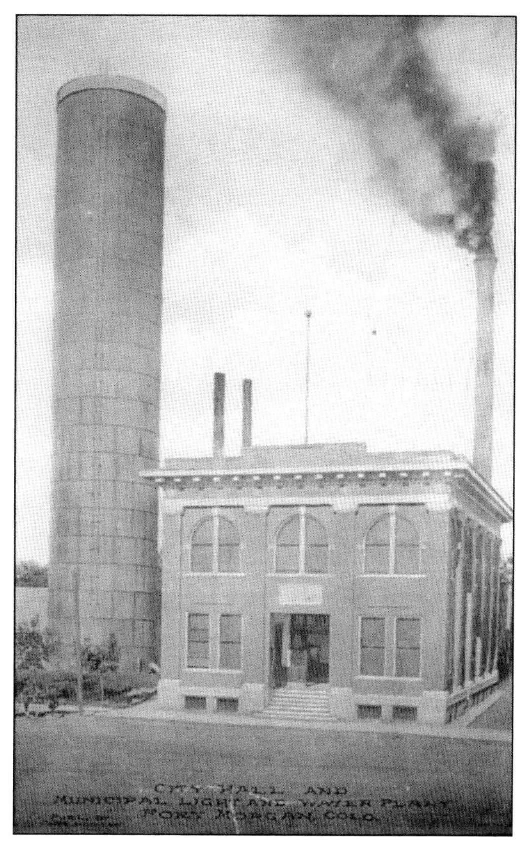

The Curry Hotel, located at 300 Main Street in Fort Morgan, was constructed around 1898. It was named after James P. Curry, who contributed the land the hotel was built on. Curry was a very prominent man who built up his fortune by farming, ranching, stock exchange, and founding the First National Bank. The Curry Hotel building stood until 1930, when it was torn down to make way for the Farmers State Bank.

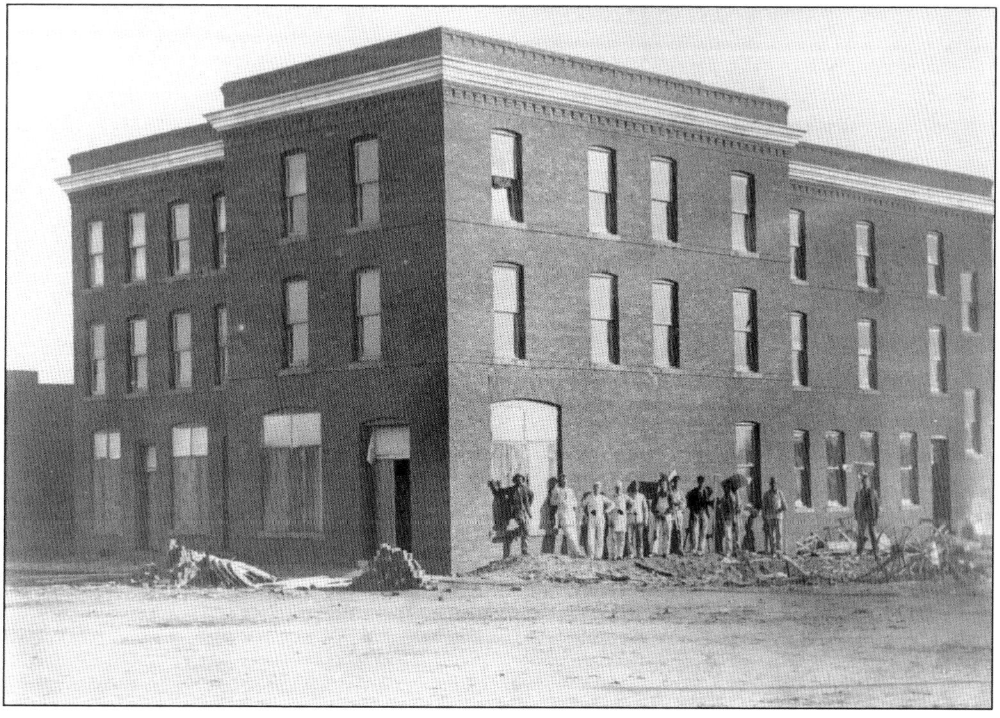

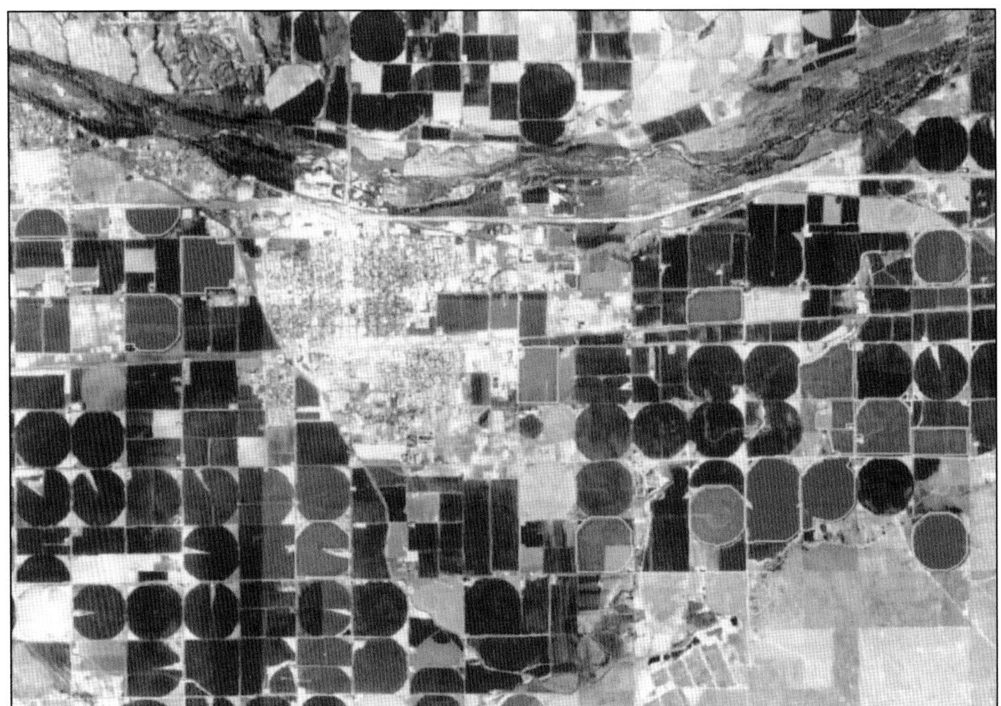

This is a recent photograph of pivot irrigation in Morgan County. The town of Fort Morgan can be seen in the center of the image. (Courtesy of Keith Bath Farms.)

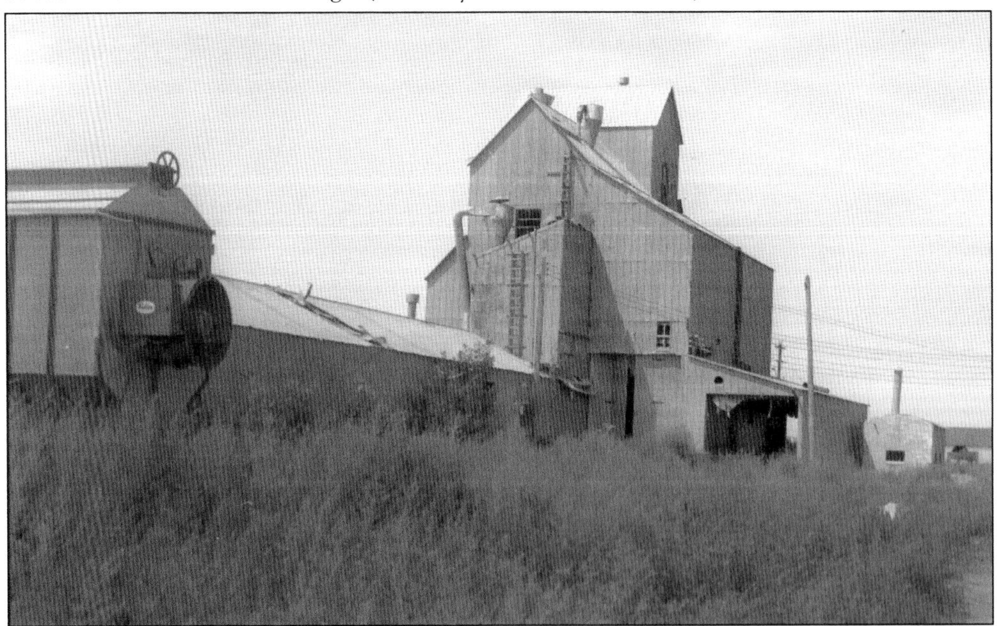

Grain elevators were invented in 1843 as a way to easily lift grain to storage silos. As grain dust is very explosive, fires were common to elevators such as the Roman Elevator. Located at the southeast corner of Sherman Street and Railroad Avenue in Fort Morgan, the elevator burned down around 1974. In 1978, the property was renovated for its current purpose, the Fort Morgan Senior Citizen Center.

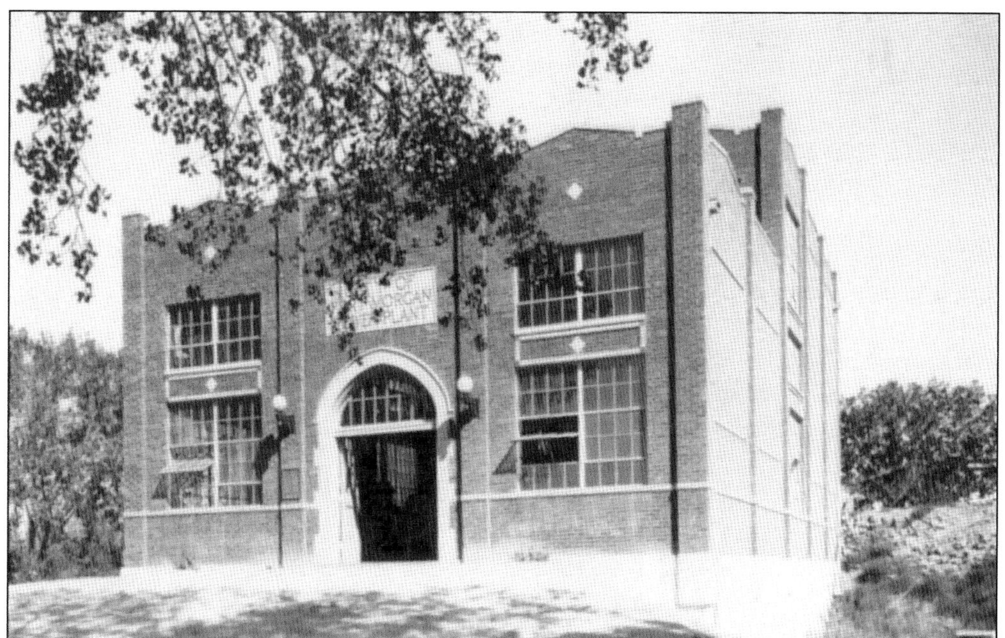

From 1923 to 1952, Fort Morgan's power plant provided electricity to the homes within the city limits. However, it was not the first electricity in town. Starting around 1905, power was generated by a boiler and generator inside city hall. Fred W. Carruth, an early town trustee, was instrumental in bringing electricity to Fort Morgan.

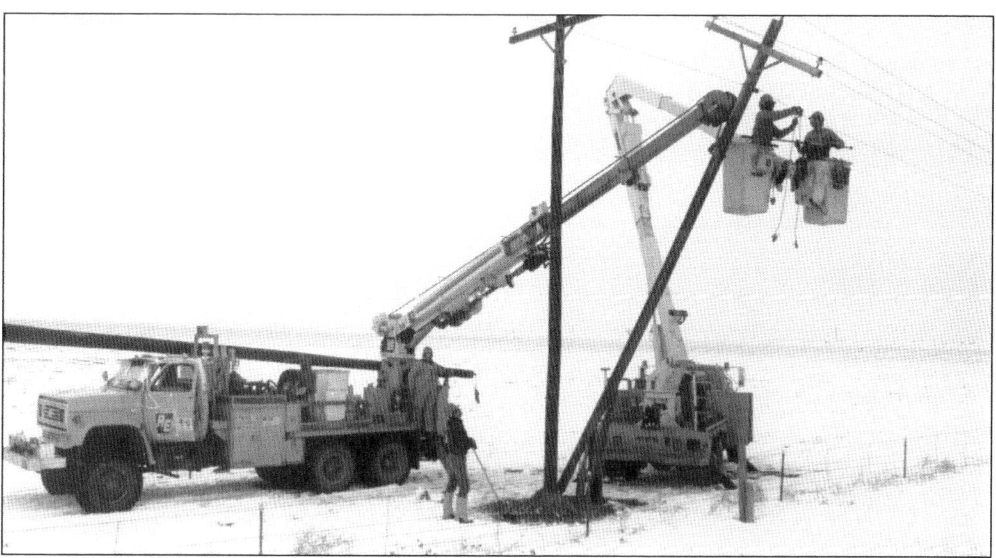

REA lineman work a line following a storm. The organization of Morgan County REA in 1937 brought electricity to rural Morgan County. It made significant changes in the darkness and drudgery of pre-electricity rural life. In addition to electric lights and refrigerators, it has allowed the ranchers and farmers to use electrical machines, greatly easing their work. Electricity pumps water from deep wells to irrigate marginal and arid land, increasing their productivity. Today, Morgan County REA services over 8,000 electric meters throughout its area.

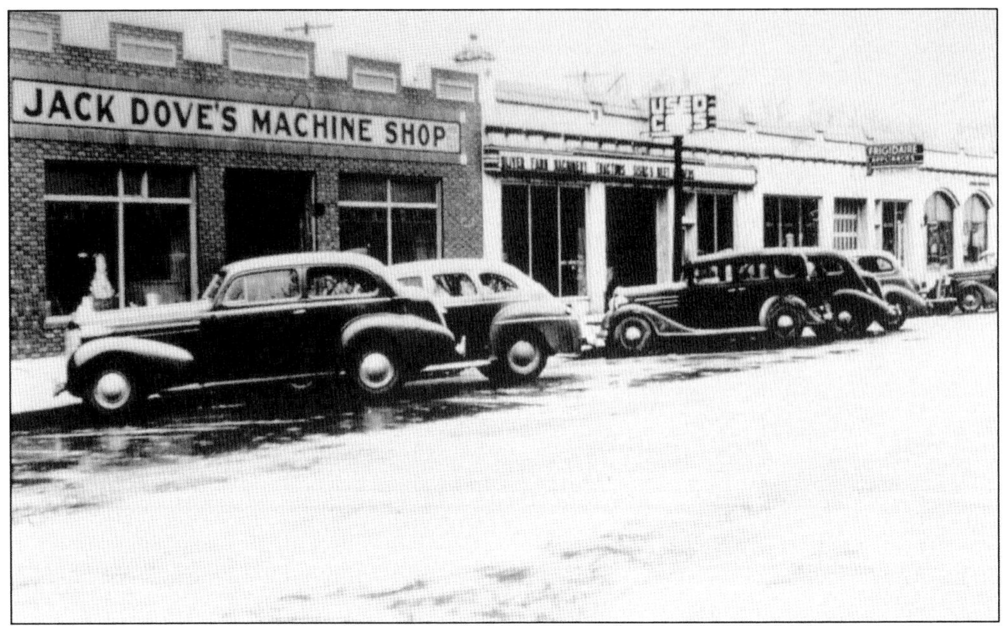

In 1916, Aaron Monroe "Jack" Dove purchased Paxton Machine Shoe and renamed it after himself. Dove's motto was "Yes, we can fix it!" Dove was a repairman as well as an inventor. Possibly his most notable invention was the reverse circulation water pump, which he designed in collaboration with Les Canfield. Dove also worked on designs for valve lifters and cylinder grinders. The shop pictured above was his fourth of five locations, 509 Main Street in Fort Morgan.

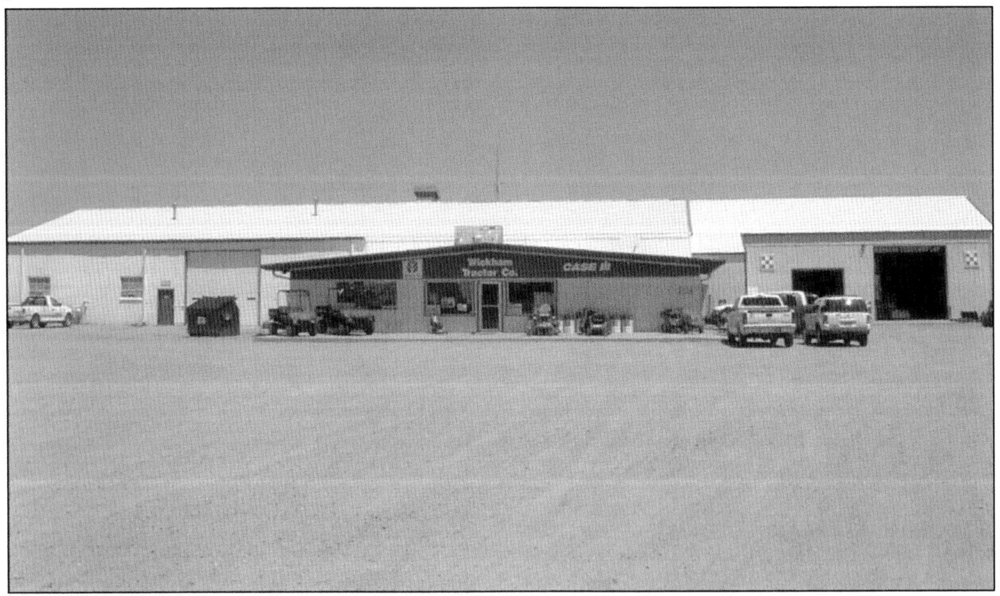

Wickham Tractor Company has been serving the equipment needs of Northeast Colorado farmers and ranchers since 1960. It has two locations, Fort Morgan and Sterling, and is proud of its heritage as a family-owned and -operated business. It is presently owned and managed by brothers Jason and Bradley Wickham, who are the fourth generation of Wickhams to run the business. As agriculture evolves in the 21st century, Wickham Tractor Co. stands poised and ready to provide the solutions required for its customers' success.

The Pawnee Power Plant was completed in 1980. Located between Fort Morgan and Brush on County Road 24, it operates a coal-based steam turbine generator. It is powered by coal mined in Gillette, Wyoming. The power plant is owned by Xcel Energy.

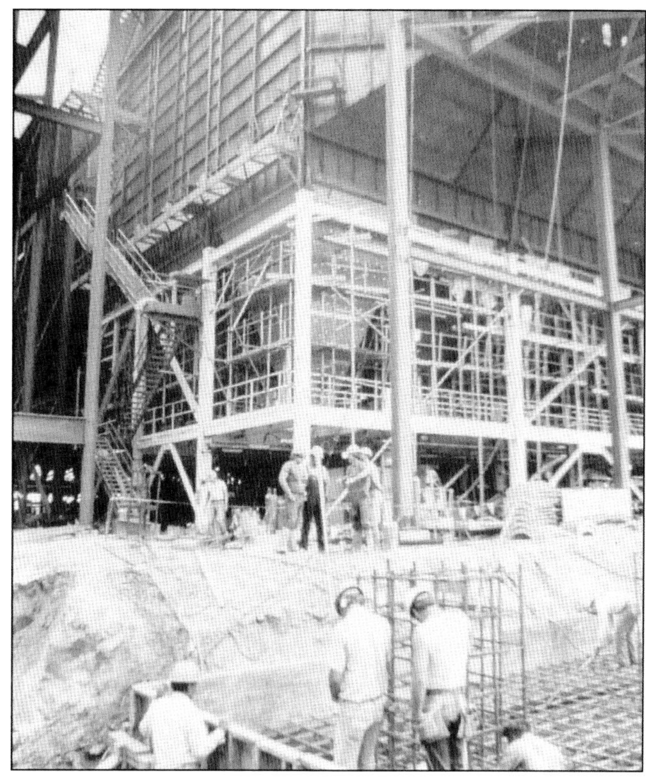

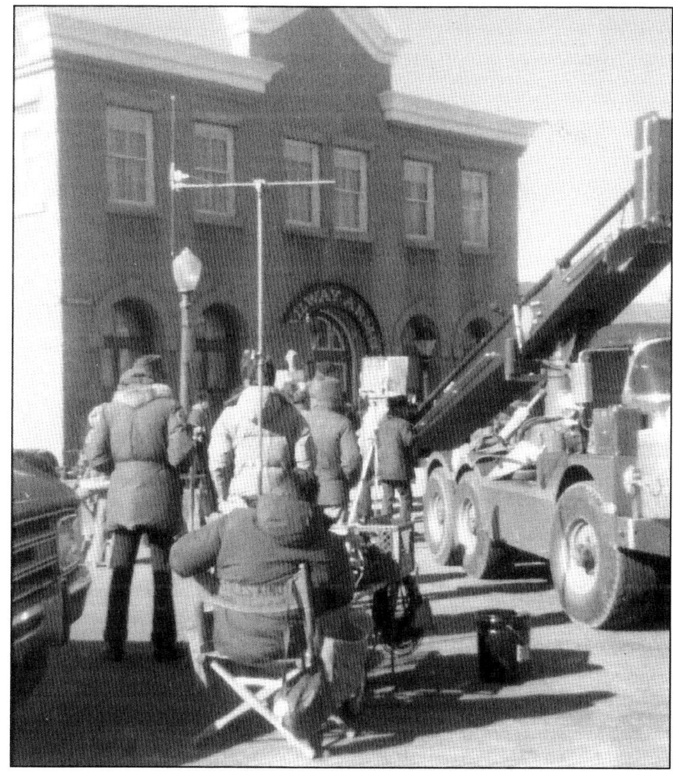

Centennial is a 12-episode television miniseries that originally aired from October 1978 to February 1979. It was based on the novel of the same name by James A. Michener. Part of the filming for the series occurred in Orchard.

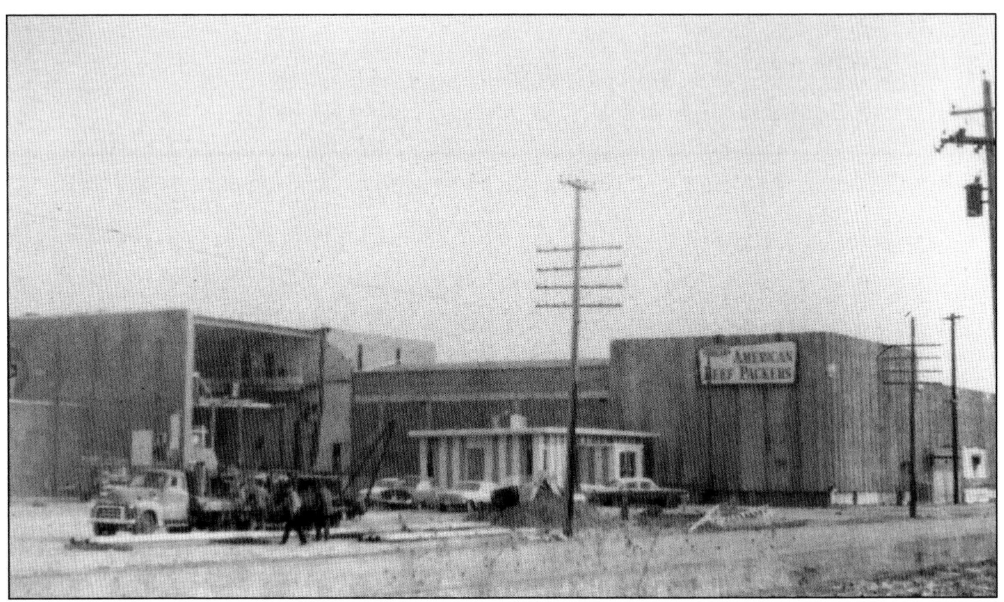

The American Beef Packers plant opened in 1966 east of Fort Morgan on Burlington Avenue. The plant has only grown since then. When purchased by Sterling Beef in 1983, it employed 980 workers. The plant has been owned by Xcel and currently operates as part of Cargill—a multifaceted corporation that runs food-production operations the world over.

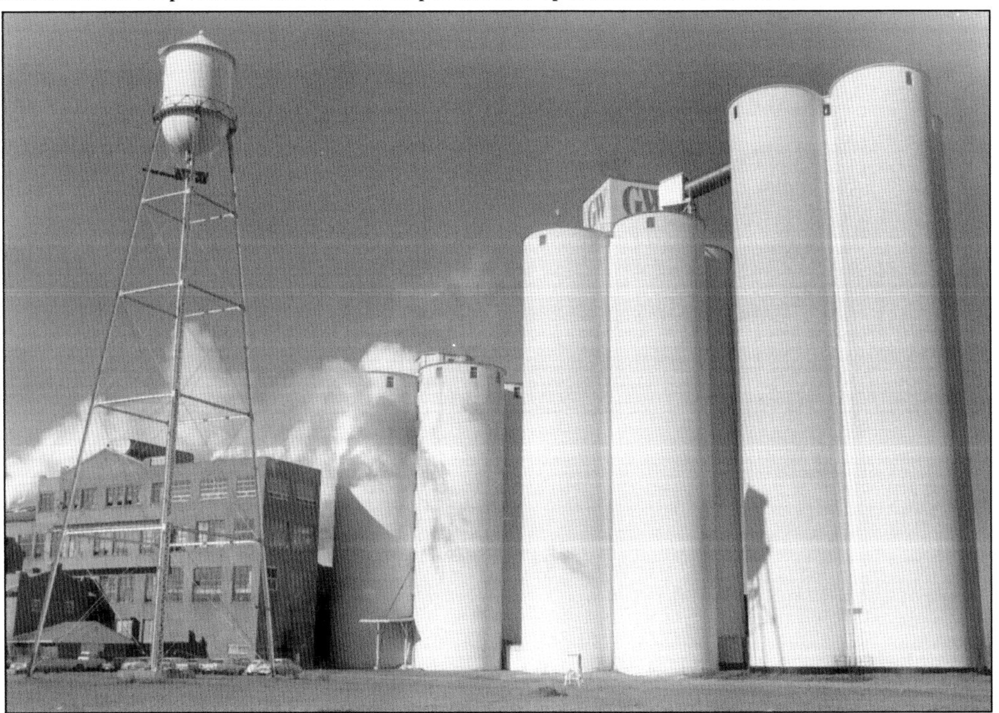

Great Western's small silos were built in 1940. The tall silos were in existence from about 1970. By 1975, the tall silos would be strong enough to support the weight of the sugar, and at that time they went into service. Cement dries slowly and continues to dry for decades. Once concrete is completely dry, it becomes weaker and weaker.

Six

ETHNIC GROUPS

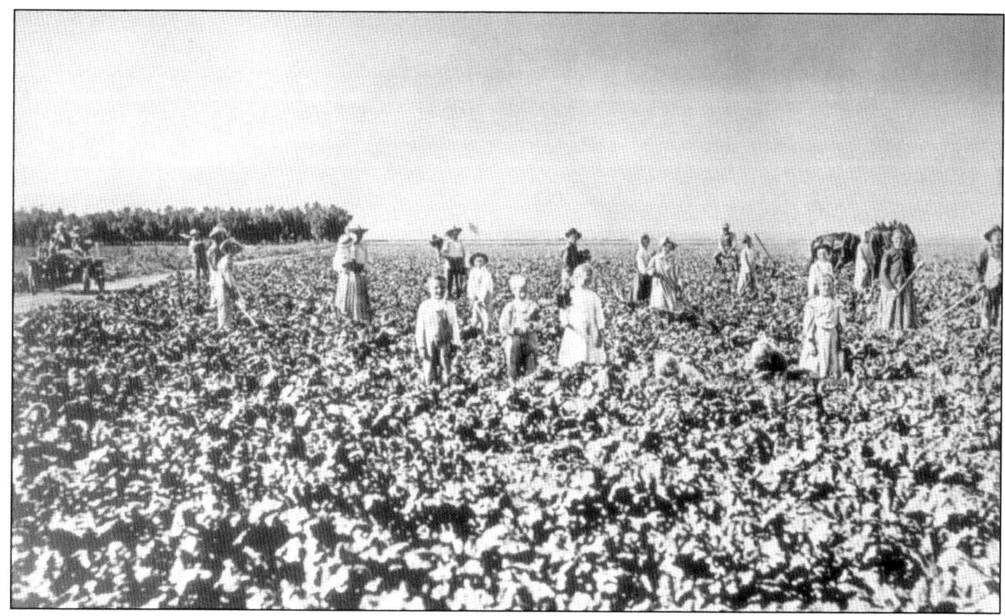

German Russians work a sugar beet field in Morgan County. Life in most German families revolved around work, church, and socializing with fellow German immigrants. The entire family functioned as a unit, with earnings contributed to the advancement of the family. Often, the monetary earnings were given to the head of the household, who would dole out dollars and cents in response to needs. Locally, Germans were beet workers, then renters of farms, and finally owners of frames. Today, many of the best farms in Morgan County are owned by people of German heritage.

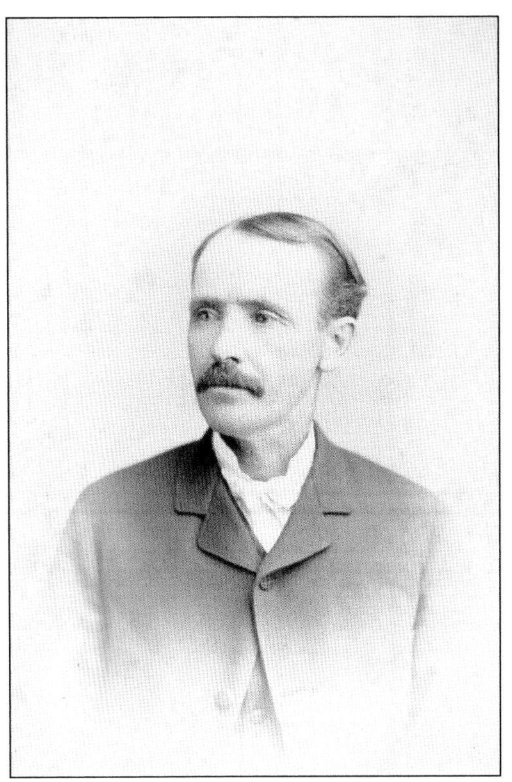

Many of the founding families of Fort Morgan were related to Abner S. Baker. They were old-stock Americans whose ancestral roots were predominately English, Scottish, and Scots Irish. They shared common Protestant religious traditions, conservative Republican political views, and economic entrepreneurship. Abner Baker came to Colorado in 1870 as a member of the Union Colony in Greeley, where he learned the techniques in constructing irrigation canals. Realizing the future of the development of the fertile but arid land of the lower South Platte River valley required water, he was involved in the construction of the Platte and Beaver, the Fort Morgan, and the Bijou Canals. He secured a large part of the land around Fort Morgan and platted the townsite, which was filed on May 1, 1884. He named the site Fort Morgan in honor of the old fort, which was well known at the time.

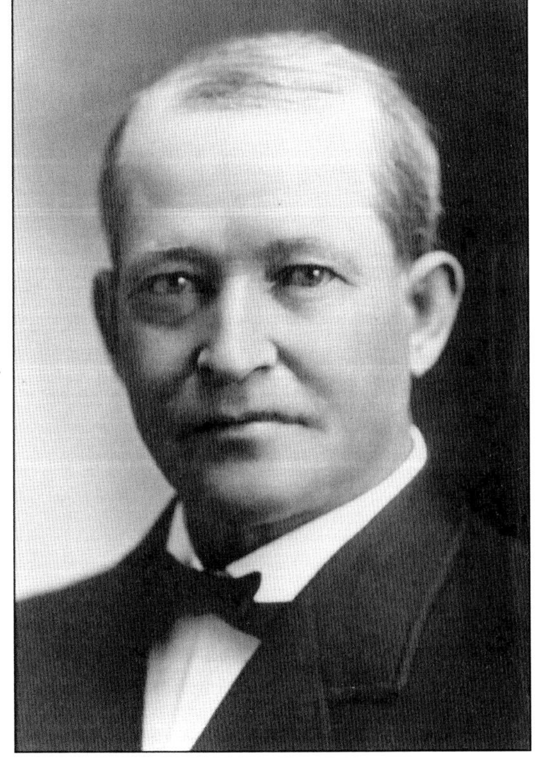

Lyman was a brother of Abner Baker. He and G.W. Warner founded the *Fort Morgan Times* on September 1, 1884. For several months, he boarded a Union Pacific train and printed the weekly paper in the *Greeley Tribune*'s office, which he had formerly run. Finally, his father's claim shanty, a 12-by-24-foot structure in the middle of Main Street south of Platte Avenue, was ready. Baker moved in an old Army press that printed one page of a six-column paper at a time and a boot full of secondhand type. He sold the paper to James A. Ide in May 1901 and devoted the rest of his life to farming and raising sheep.

Kate Clatworthy was a sister of Abner Baker. She was married to William Henry Clatworthy. The family came to Fort Morgan in the spring of 1884 to take charge of Abner's general store. Kate was instrumental in naming the first streets of Fort Morgan. She helped initiate the need for trees in the cemetery and aided in the care of them. She was serving as president of the school board when the first class of four graduated in 1896.

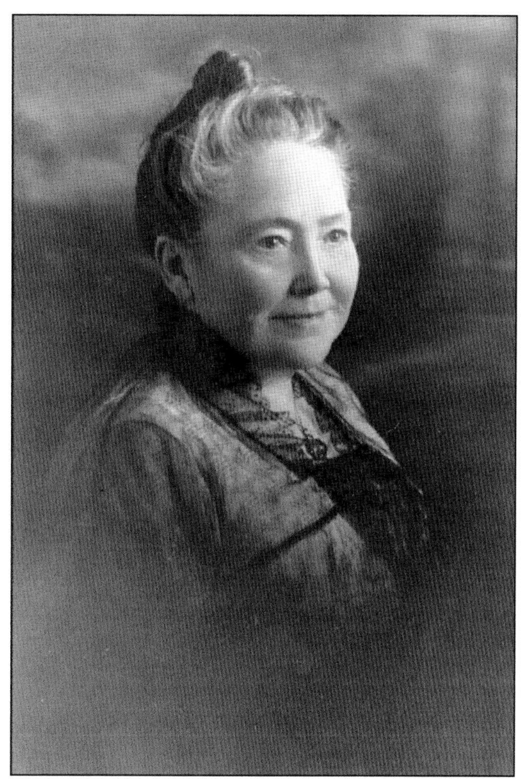

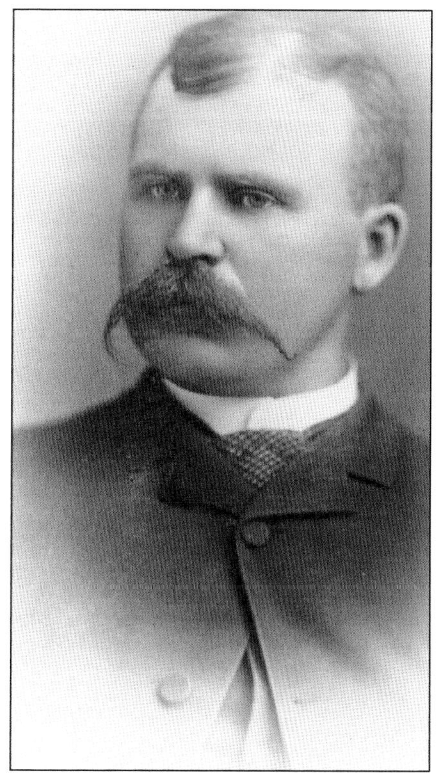

George Warner came to Colorado at the invitation of Abner Baker to become the secretary and treasurer of several companies formed to build the canals. In addition to cofounding the *Fort Morgan Times*, Warner promoted the development of the new town. In 1895, he published a real estate pamphlet, *An Oasis in the Desert*, for the purpose of attracting outside investors. He filed preemption and tree claim in the town on what is today the southeast corner of Sherman Street and Platte Avenue. His charming brick home still stands at 508 Sherman Street.

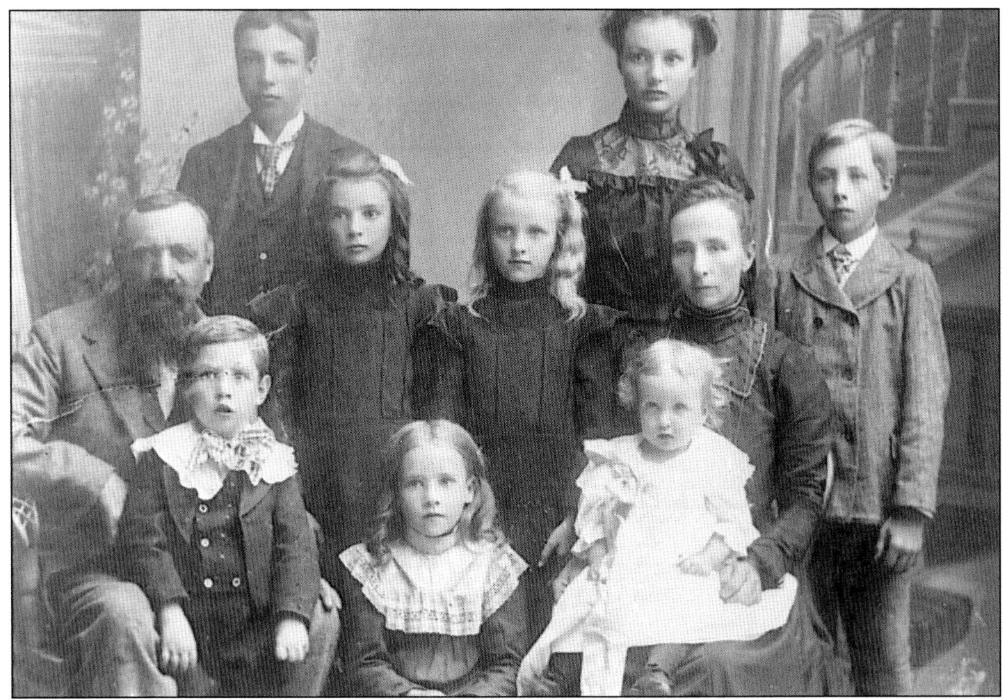

Danish settlement in Brush included the Danielsen family, along many others. Daniel Alfred Danielsen, born in Denmark, and his wife, Anna Martha, born in Norway, are shown here with their eight children, all born in the United States.

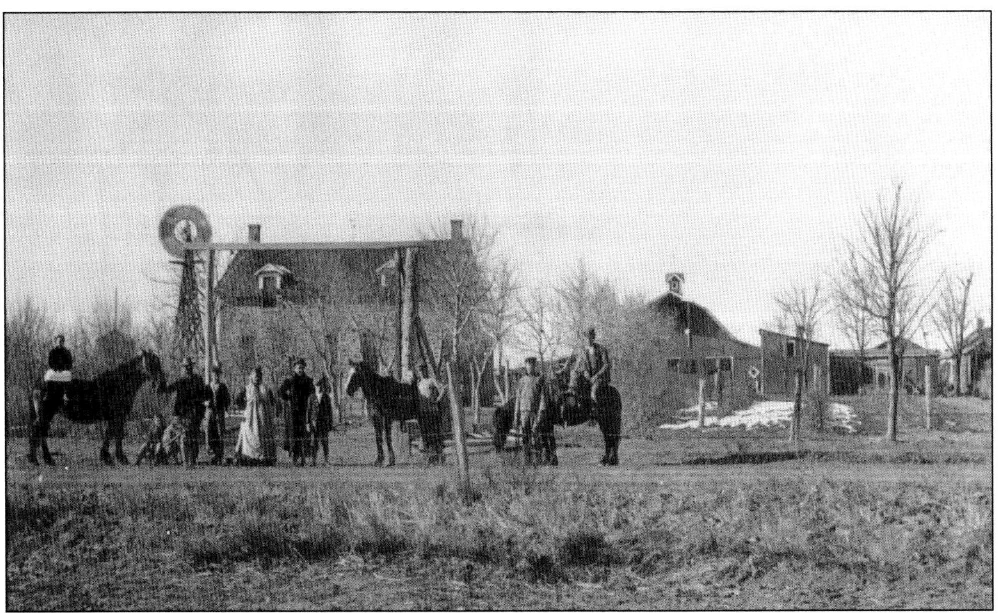

The Danish family of John C. Christensen settled a very productive farm near Brush, three miles west and have a mile north. This property features rock quarried by hand from south of Brush to build a two-story house.

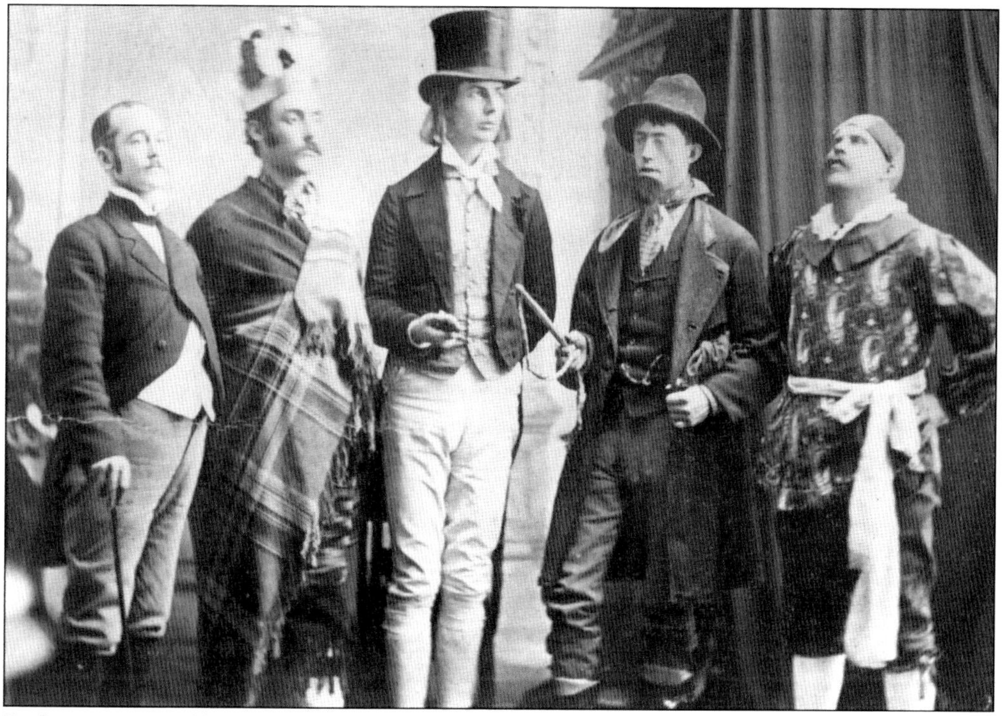

Each man pictured here is dressed in a costume for Stunt Night in the Farnsworth House around 1884–1885. From left to right are Frank Baker, Chase Luce, Harry Flint, W.H. Clatworthy, and George Warner.

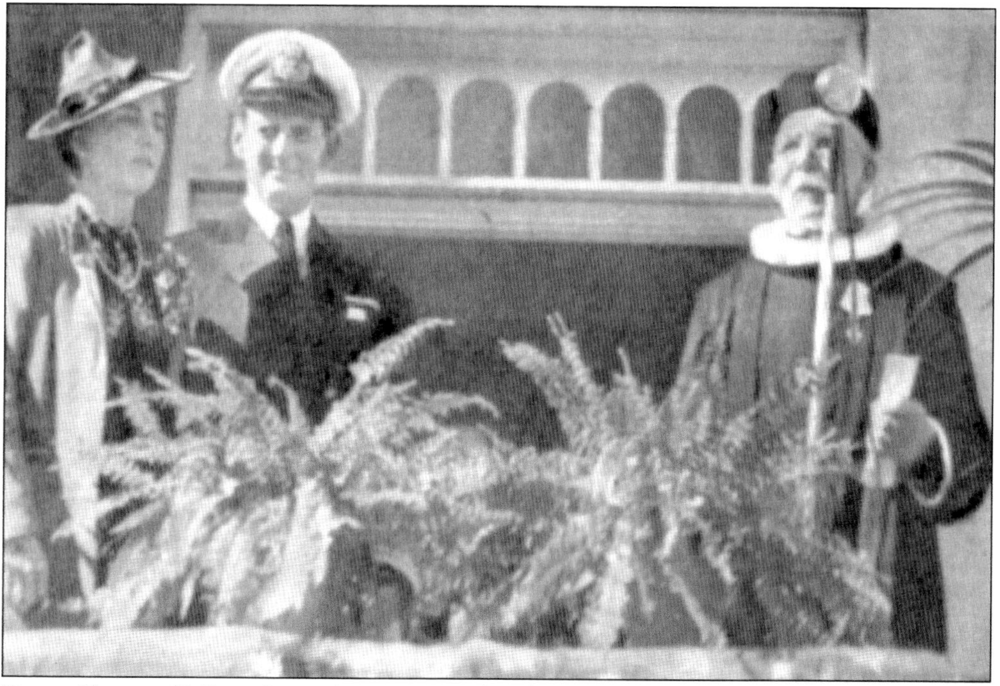

Pictured here in 1947 are Crown Princess Ingrid and Crown Prince Frederik of Denmark standing beside Rev. J. Madsen at the Eben-Ezer Institute of Brush, Colorado.

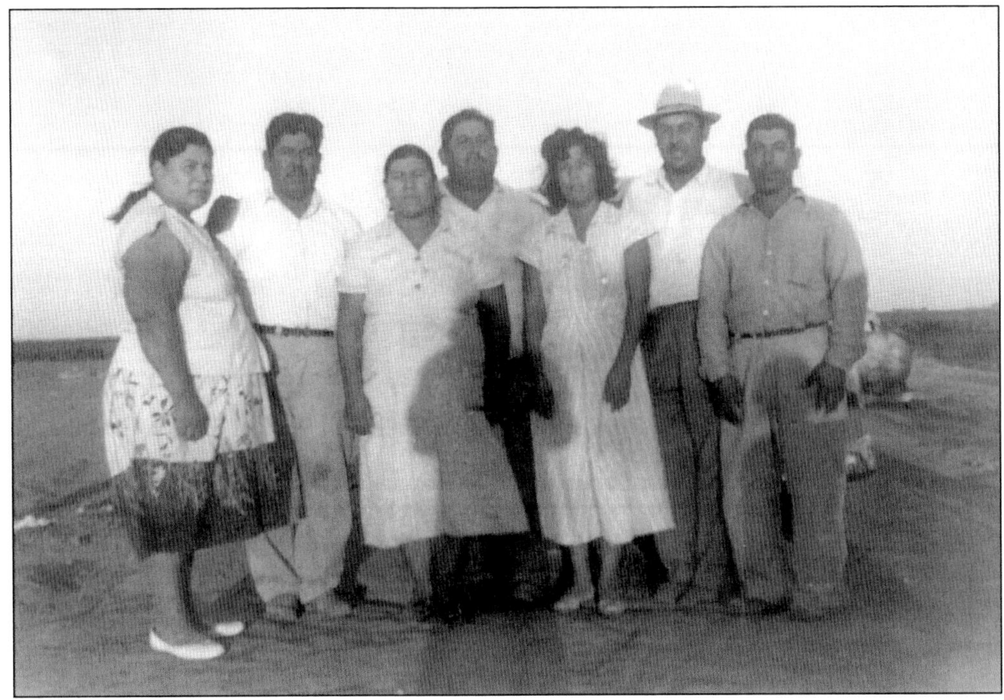

The Canalas family is a part of one of Morgan County's largest ethnic groups. The Hispanics arrived in the early 1900s, coming mostly from Texas or Mexico. They were considered excellent workers on the ranches, farms, or factories.

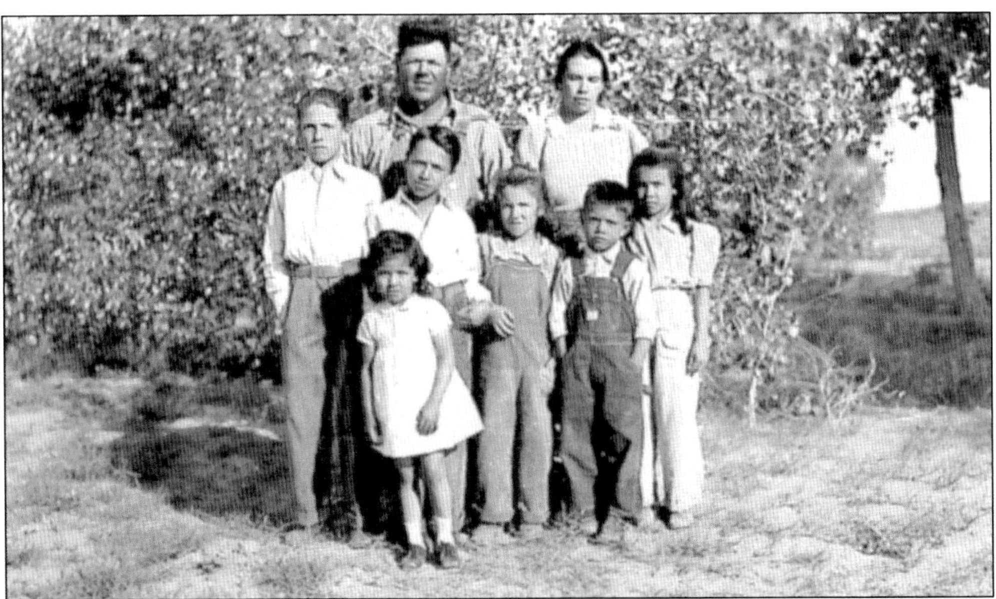

The Gonzales Baltazar family, pictured here around 1945, was one of the earliest Hispanic families in the Fort Morgan area. They owned and farmed their irrigated farm north of Fort Morgan.

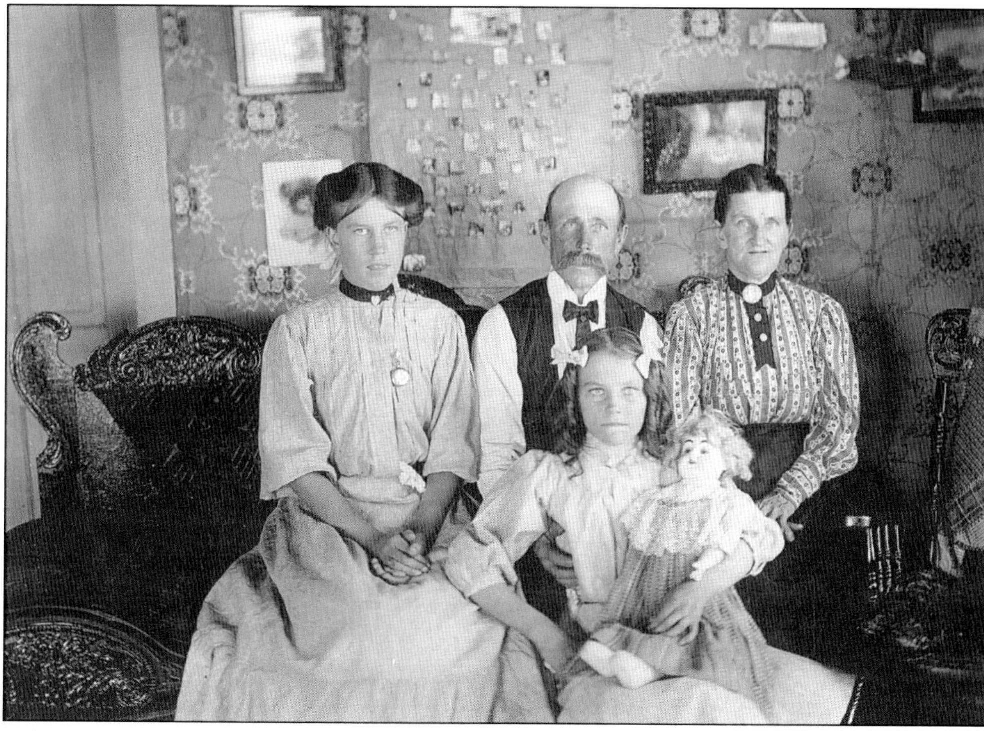

Others from Scandinavia came to the Brush area as well as elsewhere around Morgan County. Shown in the parlor of their home half a mile south and east of Brush are Mr. and Mrs. Edward P. Henderson and their two daughters, Sphena (left) and Ruth May.

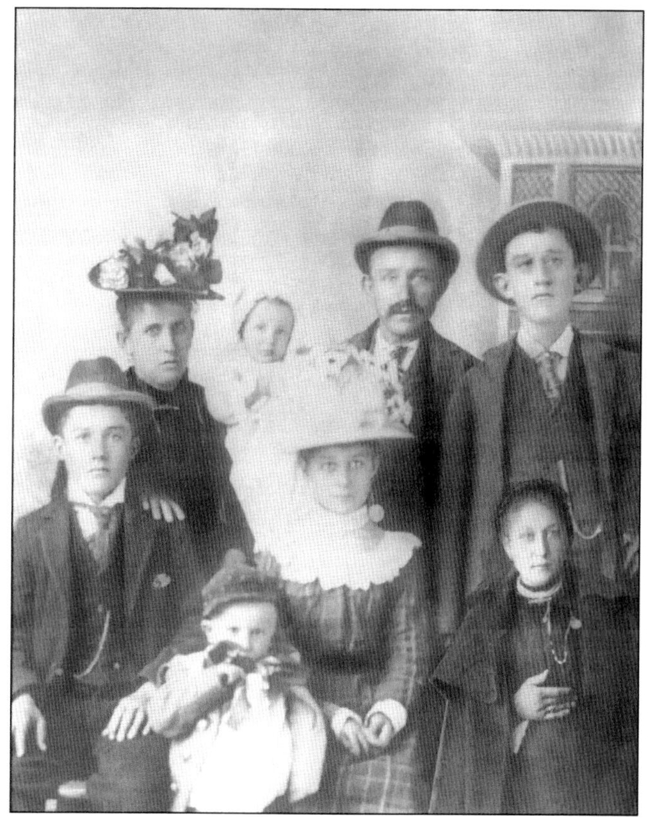

Italian settlement in the Weldona area dates back to the 1880s. After first working for established farmers, they eventually owned their own land and worked at raising cattle and sheep and planting and harvesting sugar beets and potatoes. Shown in this photograph is one of the prominent families, the Lorenzinis.

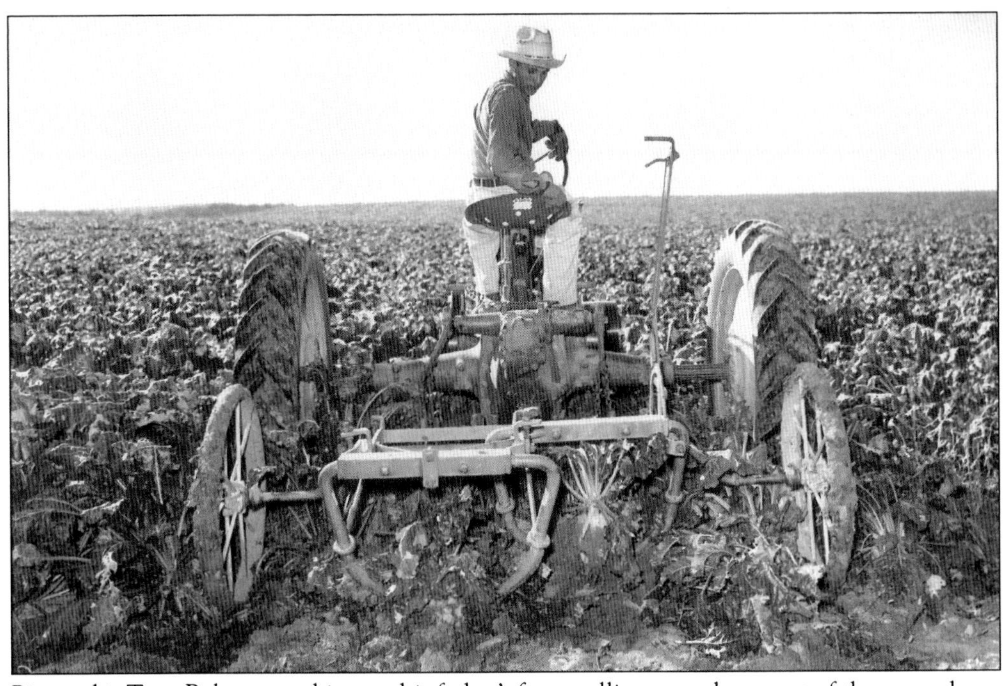

Pictured is Tony Baltazar working on his father's farm pulling sugar beets out of the ground.

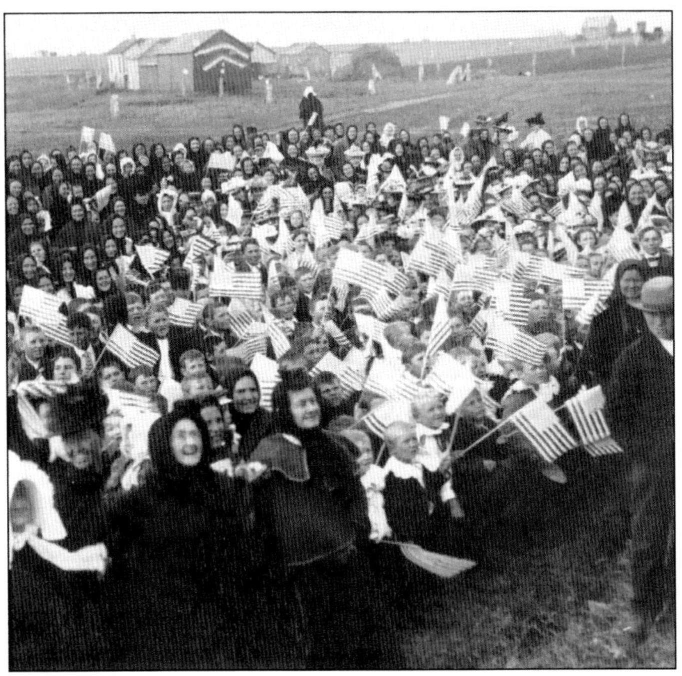

When the Russian Germans arrived in Morgan County around 1906 as beet laborers, their dress, language, and behavior caused them to be regarded by the locals as peculiar. They were very frugal and thus quick to own their own farms, which forced the men to learn English and become naturalized citizens in order to become owners. (Courtesy of the Library of Congress.)

Seven

Architecture and Community

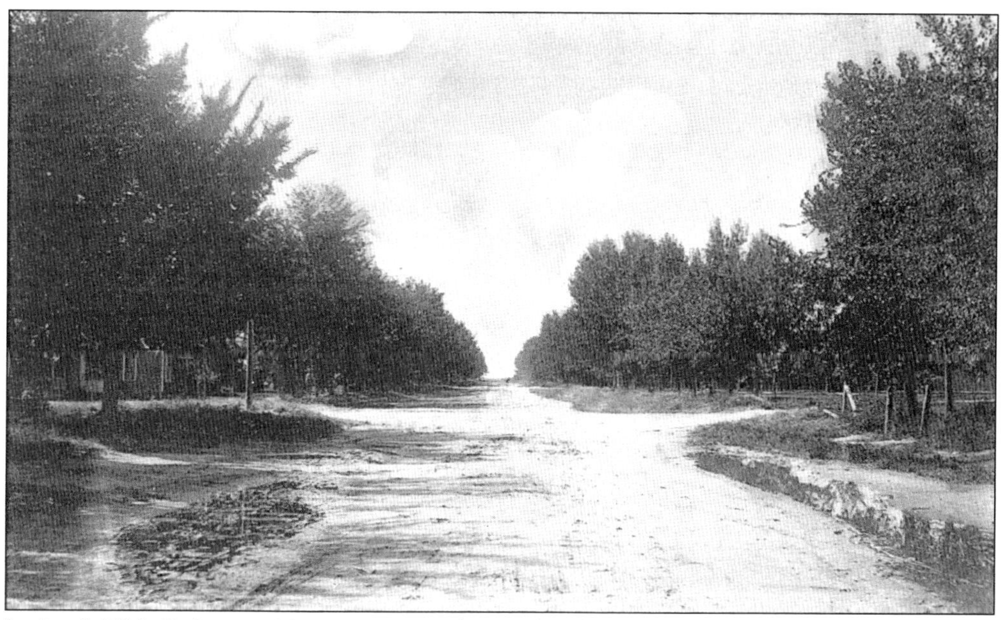

In April 1888, Ordinance No. 10 was passed. It read as follows: "Every able-bodied male resident of the town of Fort Morgan over the age of 21 and under the age of 60 years shall be required to labor upon the streets and alleys of the town under the direction of the street supervisor two days in each year or in lieu of such labor may pay to the street supervisor of said town the sum of $1.50 for each day's labor required, provided such payment be made within two days after demand of such labor by the street supervisor."

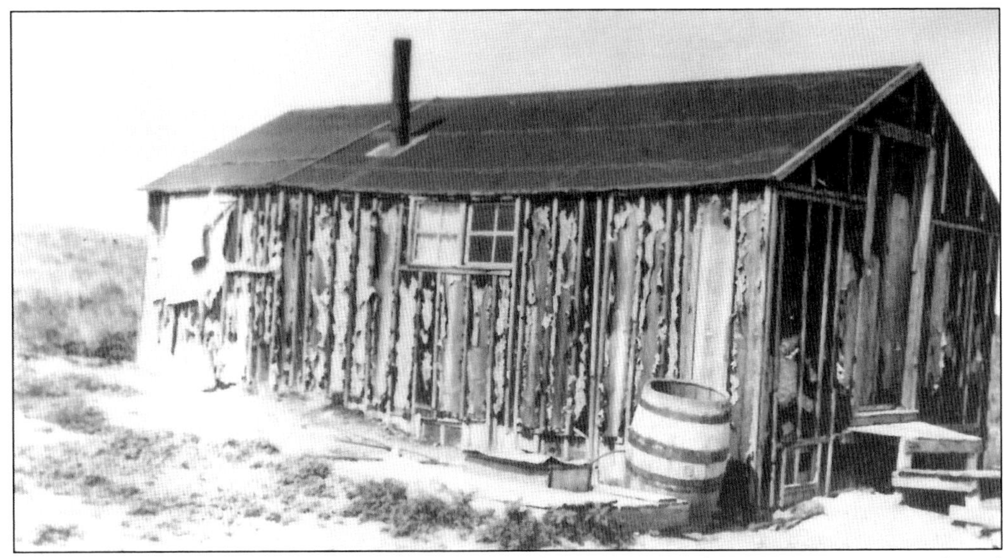

Many new settlers made do with a small one-room house, putting their money into animals and equipment. This tiny house was known as a tar paper shack.

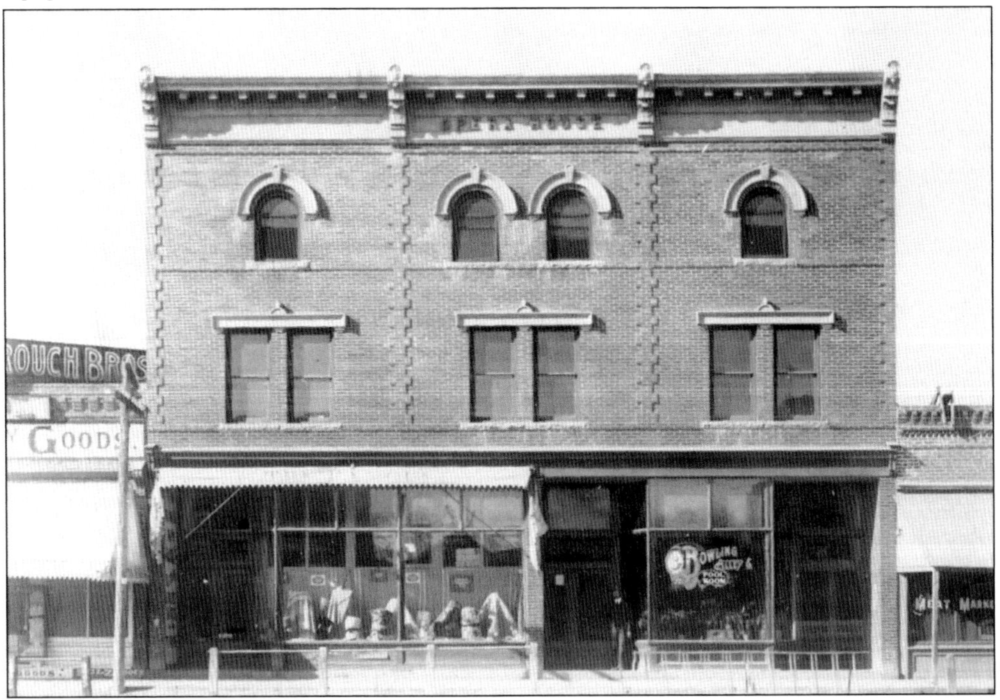

Built in 1902–1903 by Thomas F. Grace, the Grace Opera House is one of the outstanding landmarks in Fort Morgan's downtown streetscape. The upper level contains a large auditorium space or opera house. With such large spaces rare in early Fort Morgan, the opera house was used frequently for dances, high school commencement ceremonies, and other town functions; it was rented by members of the Elks Club as their first meeting hall. Downstairs on the first floor, Tom Grace operated a pool hall and bowling alley, renting the other half of the space out. The building, typically, has housed a variety of businesses, including the Schwartz Women's Wear Shop, Reithmann Grocery, and later a Montgomery Ward and Gambles.

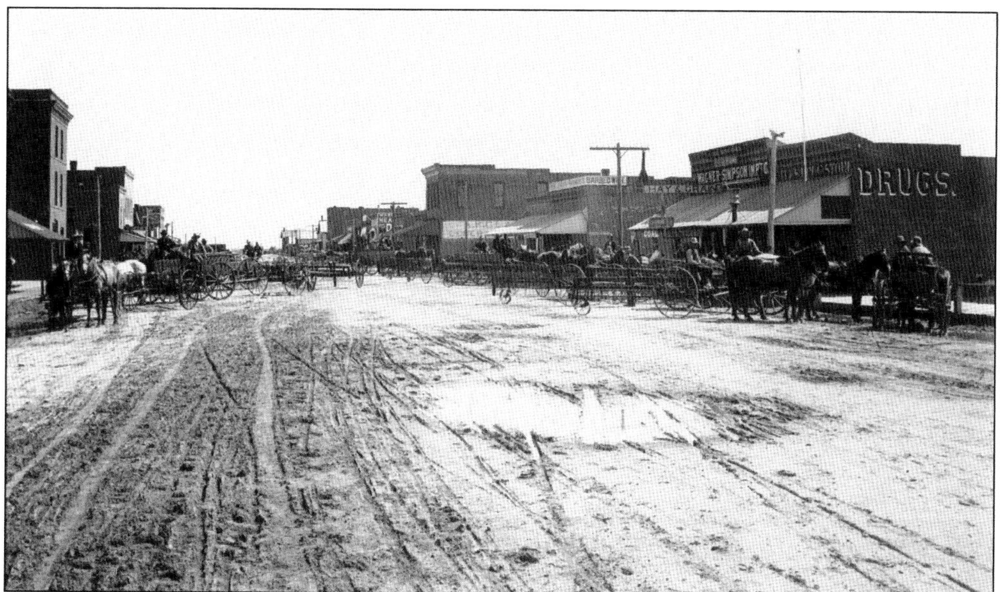

Pictured here is Fort Morgan's Main Street in 1897.

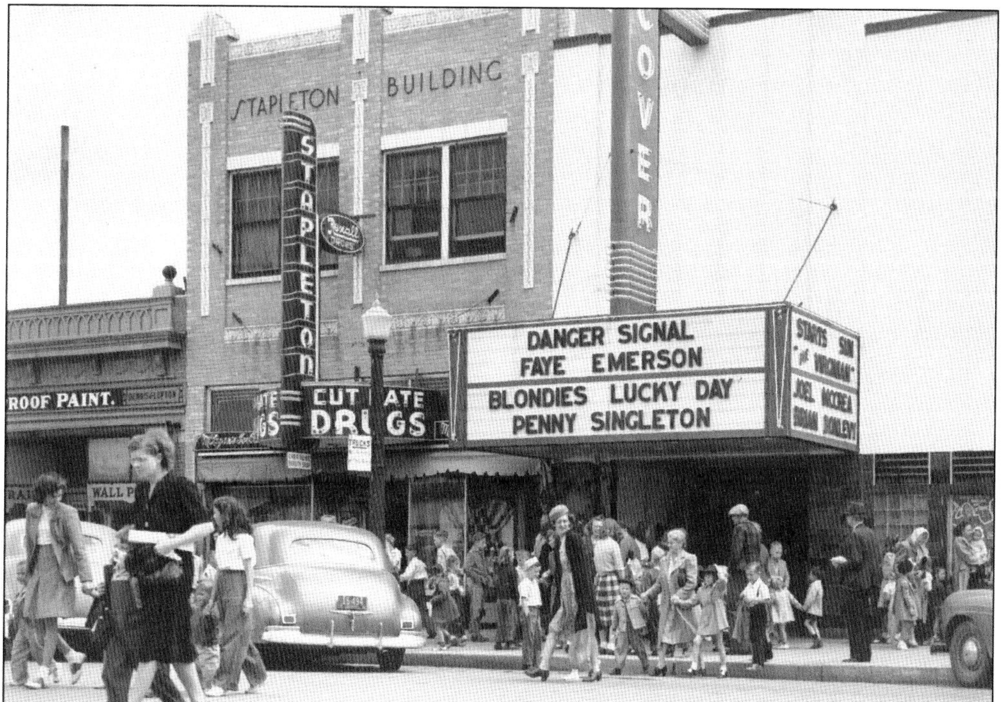

In 1894, a frame building was erected by J.P. Looney. In 1916–1917, U.G. Cover tore down the wooden building and built the Cover Opera House. This opera house was a blend of 20th-century Functional and Gothic Revival. On January 18, 1944, the original building was destroyed in a massive fire. The structure was rebuilt, totally fireproof, but it bears no resemblance to the original Cover Opera House. Marquees come and go; remodels and expansions occur. The Cover Theatre remains a site for community entertainment.

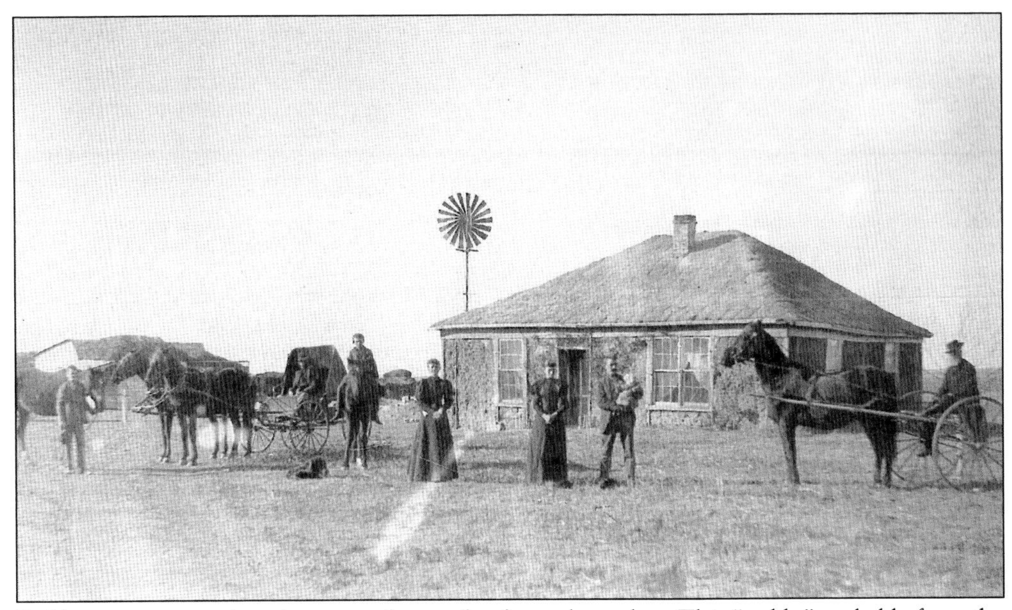

Sod houses were not just short-term homes for the early settlers. This "soddy," probably from the Orchard area, sports glass windows with curtains and a real roof. With the windows and curtains, it is probable it also had a real floor.

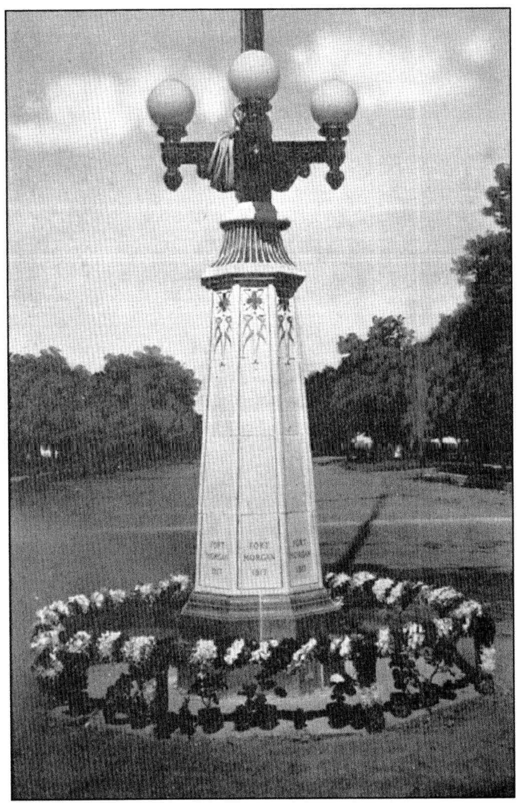

In 1917, a rather elaborate flagpole was erected in the middle of the Beaver and Main Streets intersection. In the early 1920s, an out-of-town visitor struck it with his car and filed a lawsuit against the City of Fort Morgan. Afterward, Mayor Gill and the city had the structure removed. Also removed was the marker for the site of Old Fort Morgan, which sat in the middle of Riverside at Grant Street; however, it was saved and relocated. In the early 2000s, when the downtown area was being remodeled in a massive project, the cement footing of this flagpole was uncovered and finally removed.

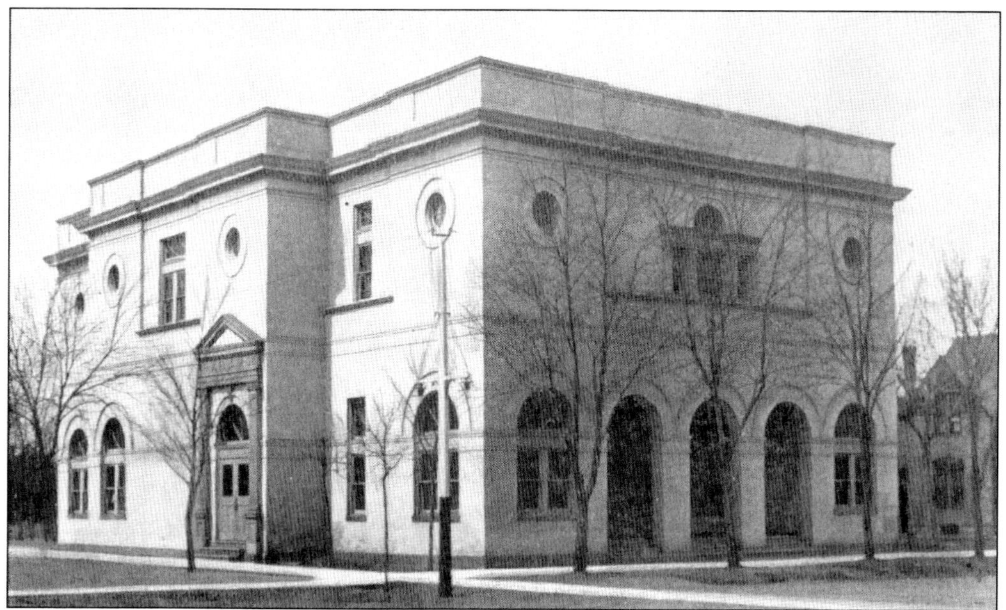

The Masonic temple was originally built in 1906 with an addition constructed in 1926. The 1906 portion of the building was destroyed in a fire on April 20, 1971. However, the 1926 part of the structure was saved and remains today.

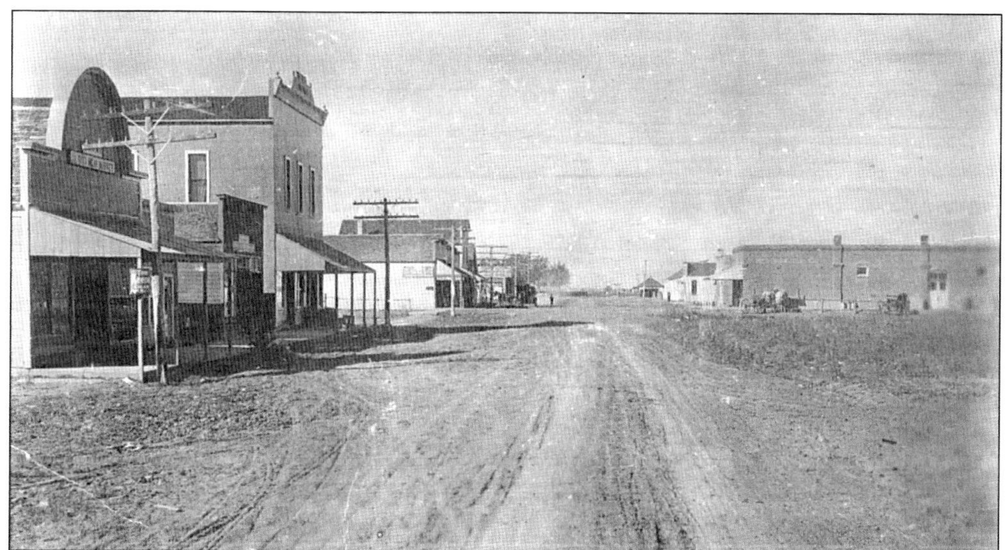

Hillrose, on the eastern side of the county, was named by Kate Emerson of Denver, the original landowner. Her sister was Rose Hill Emerson, and Kate revered the name. Hillrose, shown here in about 1911, has faded as a business center, but it remains an active community of homes.

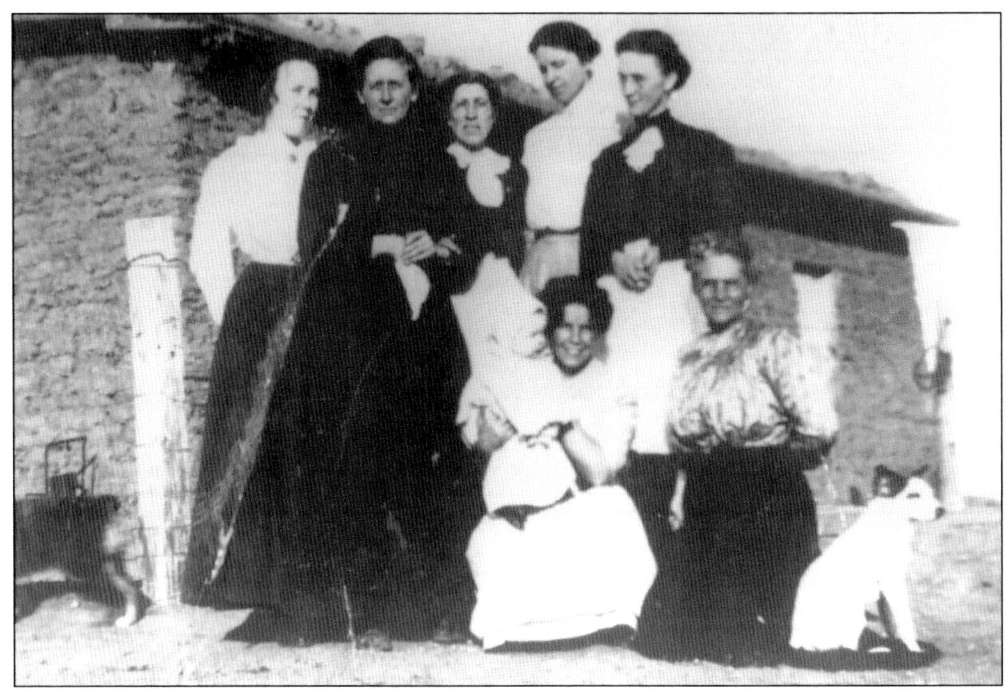

Pictured in this 1912 photograph of a sod structure in Adena are, from left to right, Edna Hawthorne, a Mrs. Shauermann, Mrs. E.H. Groves, a Mrs. Neveill, a Mrs. Fyar in front of a Mrs. Tompkins and baby Gale, and a Mrs. Schnetiman.

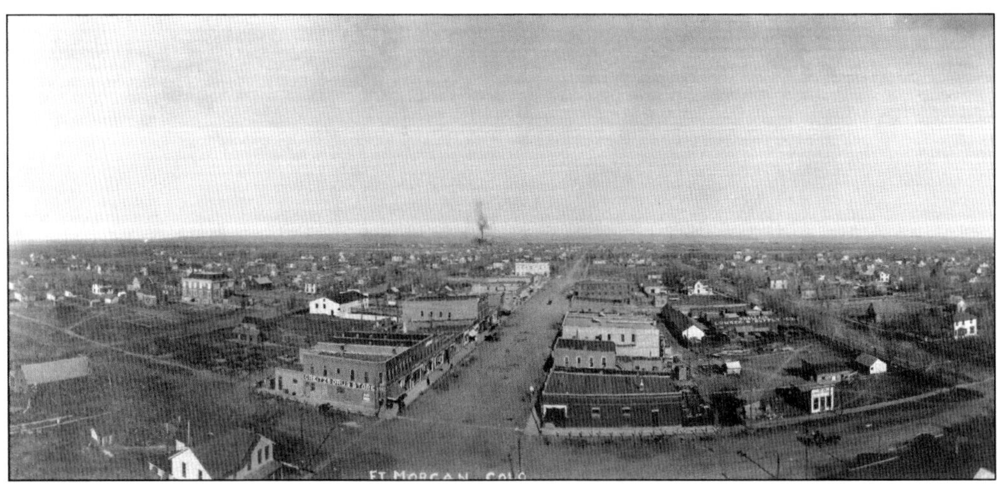

This is a panoramic image of Fort Morgan captured in 1910.

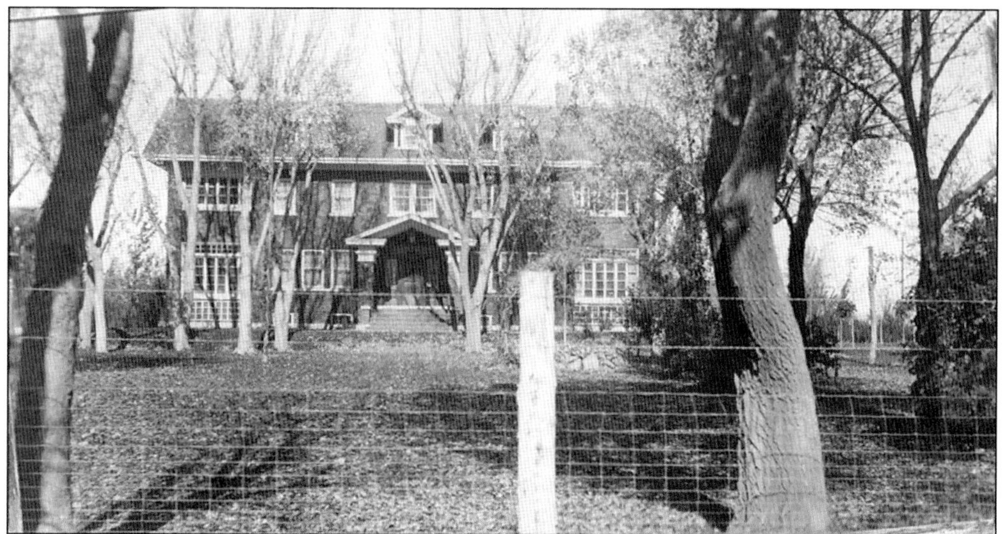

This Classical Revival–style house, popular in the early 1900s, was built in 1926 by J.H. Roediger. Roediger was a prominent banker and sheep and cattle feeder in early Fort Morgan.

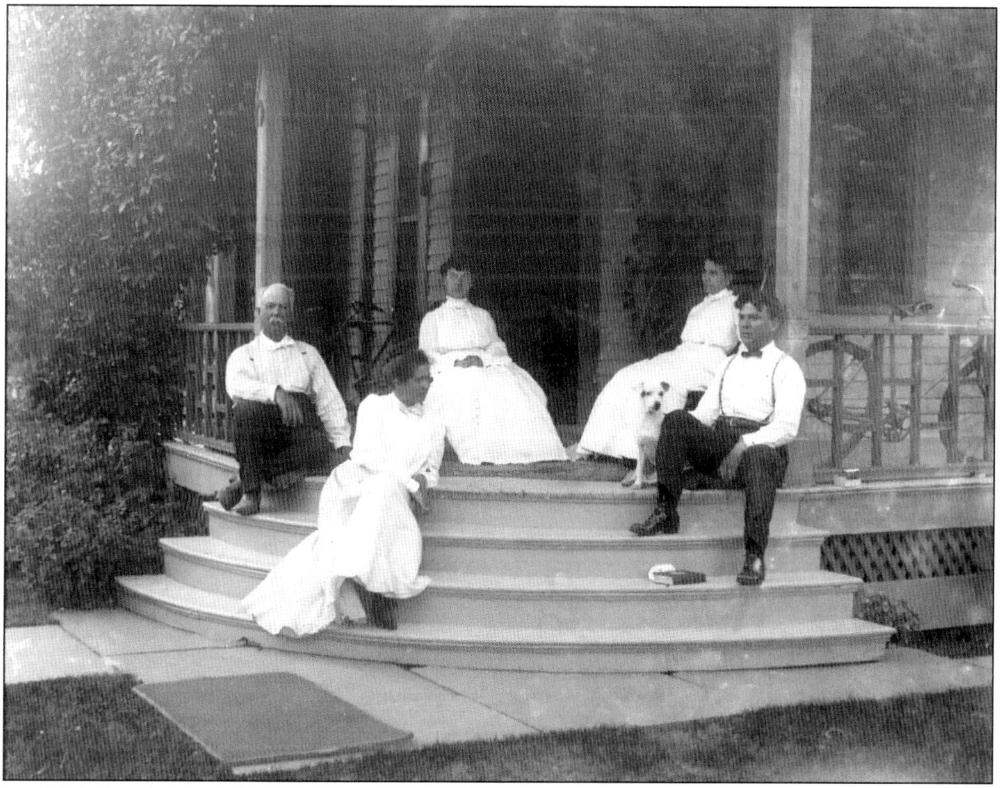

In 1908, Fort Morgan became unique by offering free to each customer of electricity an eight-candlepower (40-watt) porch light. This allowed the city to glow at night, thus earning the nickname the "City of Lights." Two prominent Fort Morgan bankers, M.L. More (left) and his son-in-law Julian Herman Roediger (right), relax with their family on the front porch of the More home, located at 423 East Platte Avenue.

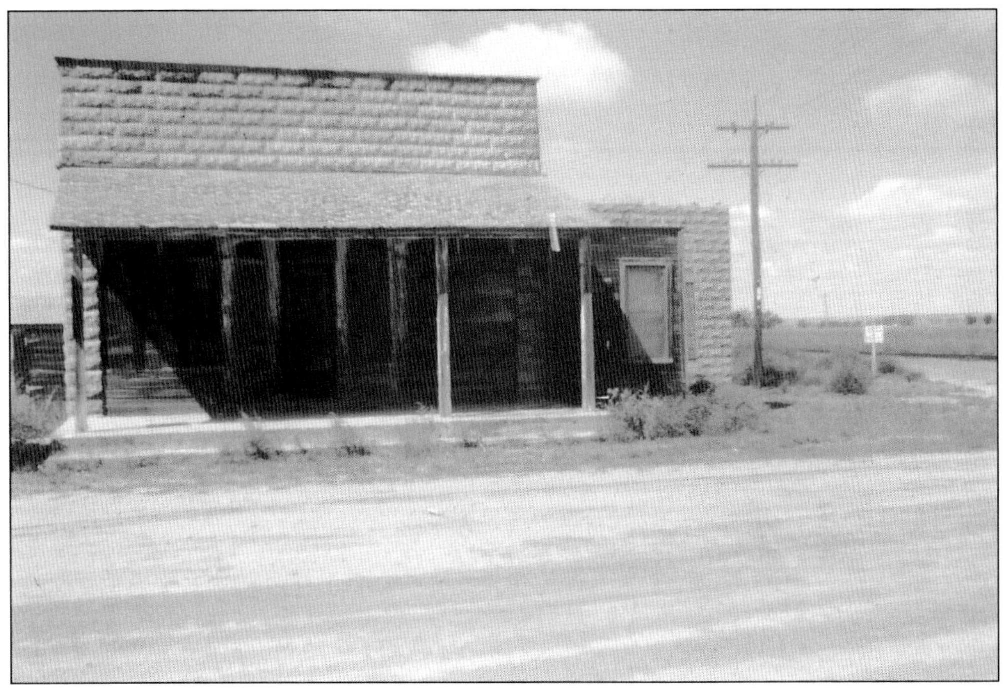

As the area became more settled and prosperous, many buildings were constructed of cement blocks instead of wood or mason bricks. As evidenced by the passing of time, these edifices were durable. This building was constructed about 1909. Harry Greenley was manager of the Goodrich Lumber yard, owned by the Riverside Lumber Co. and later sold to Warren Lumber Co.

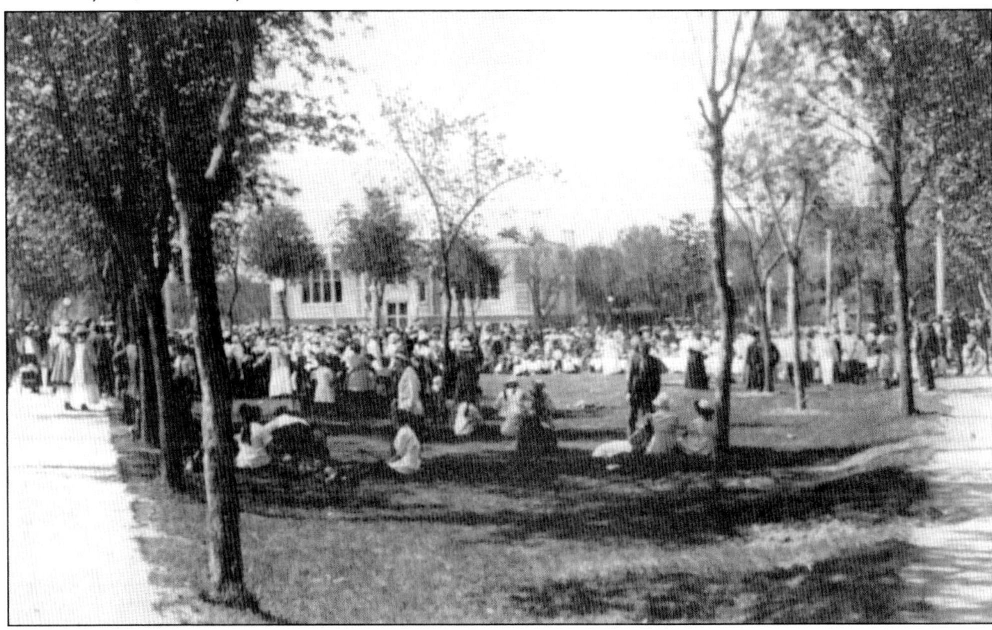

In 1891, a group of 16 women organized the Ladies Library Association. The members raised money for books and bookcases and made books available to the community. In 1906, a 900-book collection was mailed to city hall. The Carnegie Corporation gave $10,000 in 1914, and on February 25, 1915, the library was opened. The Ladies Library Association disbanded in 1915.

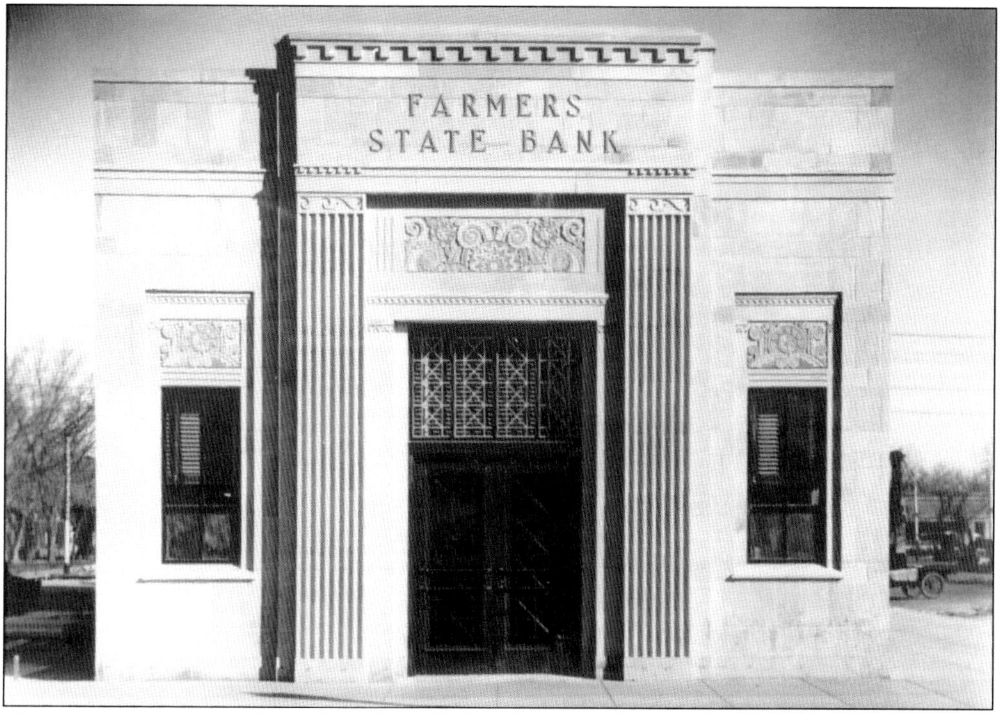

The 1930 Farmers State Bank building is listed in the National Register of Historic Places. The building is a finely articulated example of classical Modern and Art Deco style with its smooth surfaces, carved stone panels, and stylized decoration emphasizing the geometric form. The Farmers State Bank building is one of the most classical buildings in the downtown business district. When the bank was completed and opened to the public in 1930, it was one of the most modern and up-to-date bank buildings in the state of Colorado. The Farmers State Bank is also significant for its association with John H. Bloedorn Sr., the founder and president of the bank from 1919 until 1967.

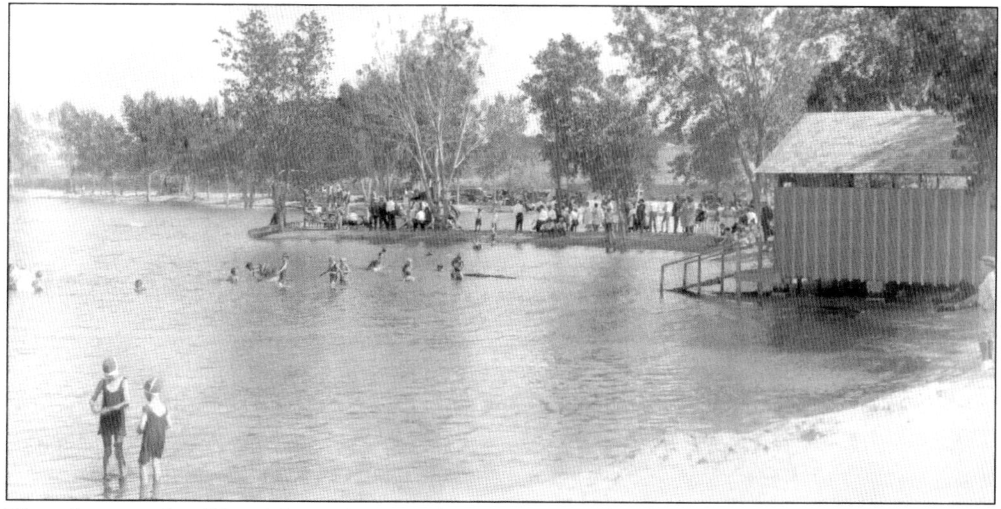

This photograph of Fort Morgan's original swimming pool, taken in 1930, shows the bathhouse and a portion of the swimming hole. The old swimming hole was replaced by a cement pond. One can still see parts of the old pool—it is the duck pond at Riverside Park.

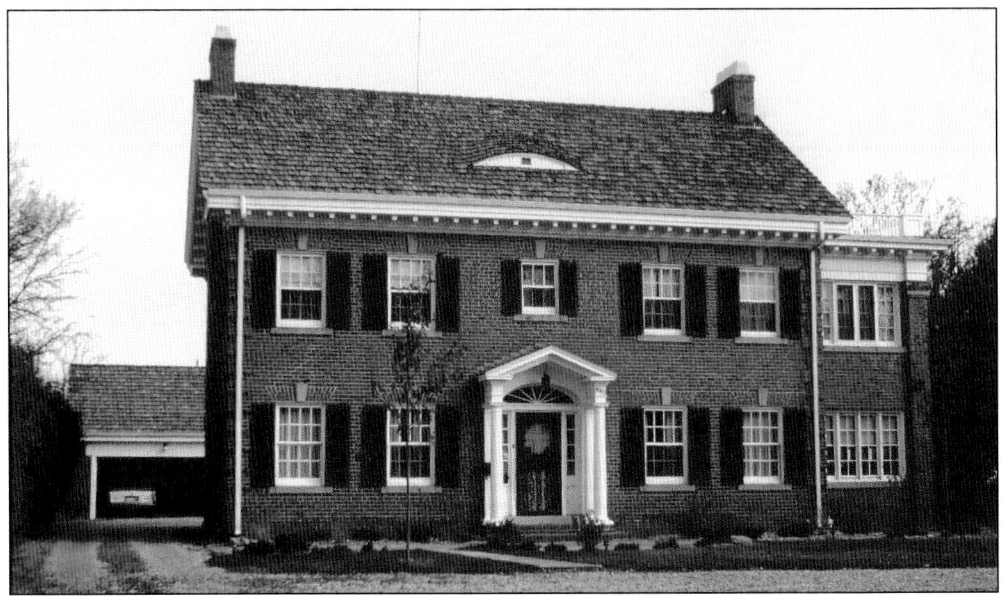

Built in 1926 by John and Corliss Bloedorn in a combination of various styles, this house was the scene of many parties, club meetings, dances, and literary and bridge meetings. John bought Fort Morgan State Bank in 1919 and changed the name to Farmers State Bank. He was also involved with the school board and board of directors for Great Western sugar.

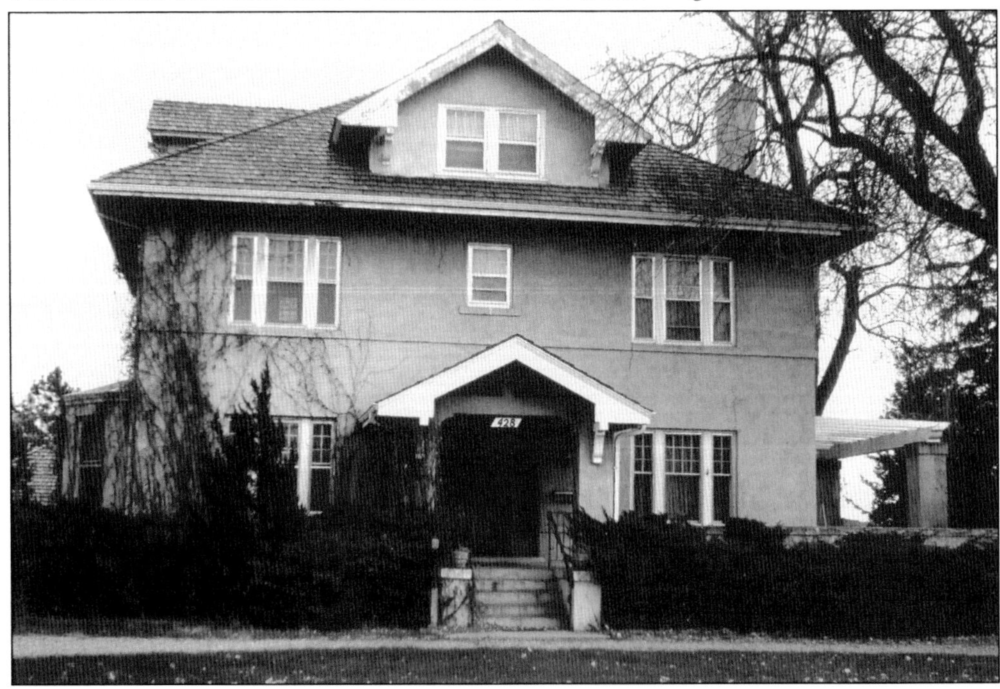

This home was built by Ralph and Olivia Graham in 1914. They owned the Bijou Ranch, and Ralph was active at the local and state levels in Morgan County Lamb Feeders Association and Nebraska Lamb Feeders Association. Olivia was an heiress to Gilmer Lumber Co. fortunes. She brought new varieties of vegetation to Morgan County from Texas, including the first gum oak trees.

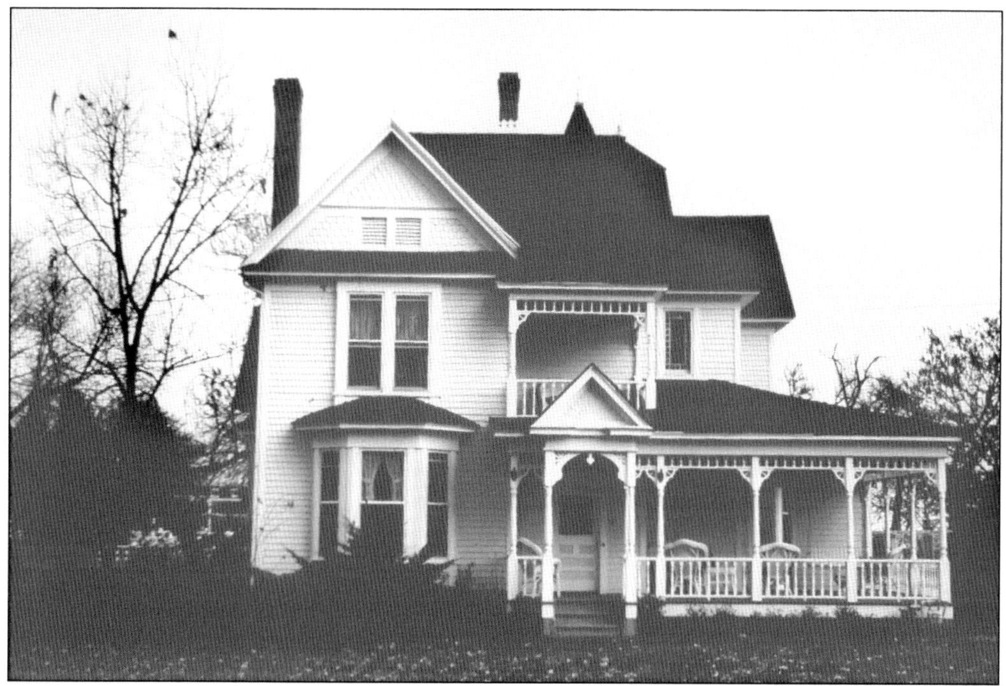

Built by James P. Curry in 1898, this Queen Anne home served as the meeting place for many clubs; church and private dinners were also held here. Curry and his wife, Alma, homesteaded south of Fort Morgan in 1888. He became active in banking and directing irrigation projects.

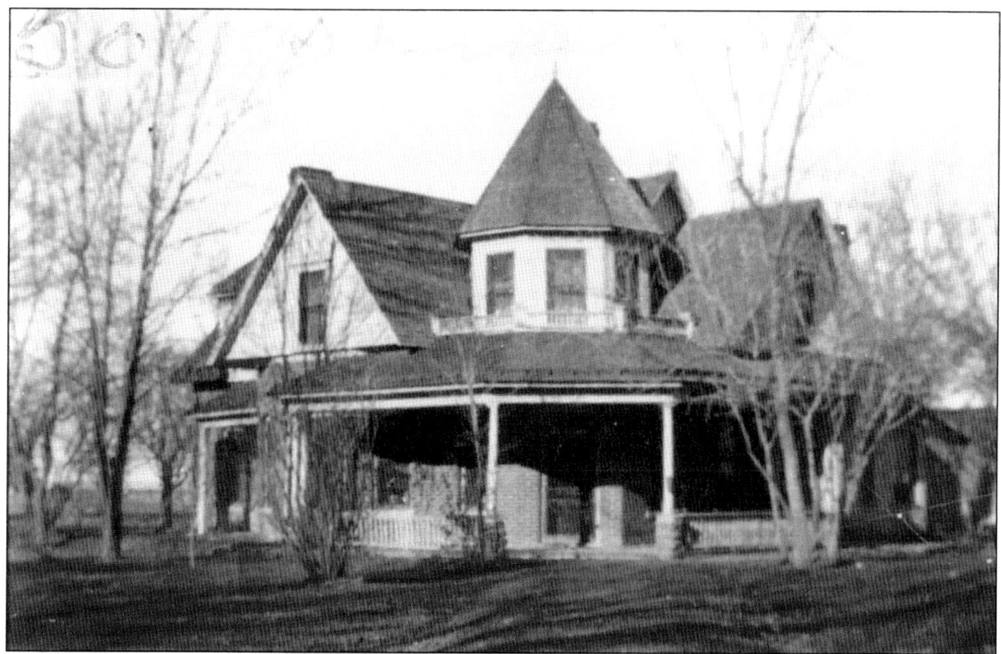

Warner House, part of the Sherman Street Historic District, was built by George Warner in 1889 for his bride, Hannah Louise Farnsworth. The home was used as a community center for plays, and an ice-skating rink was created in the yard in the winter.

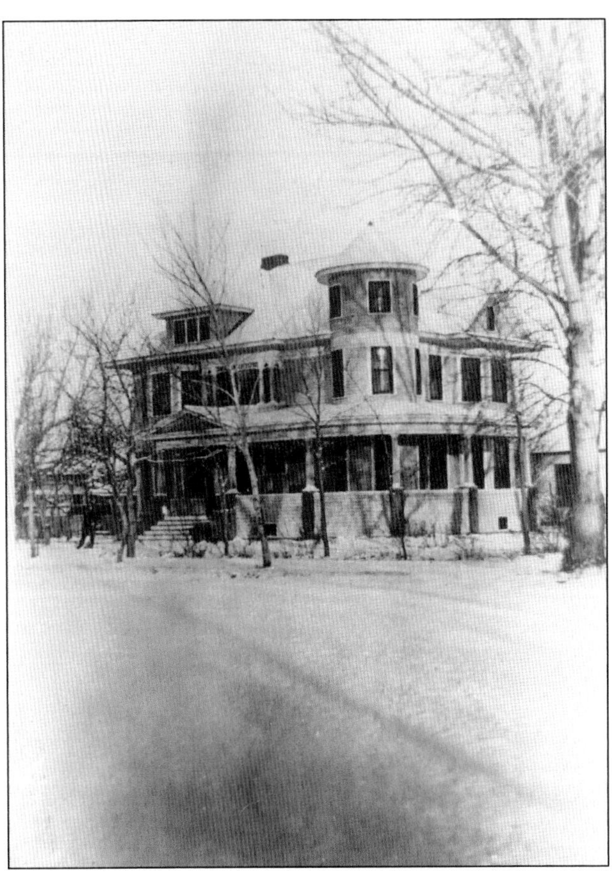

The Edwards home, located 325 East Beaver Avenue, was known as the Castle.

Clatworthy Hardware Co. was begun in 1927 by W.H. Clatworthy. He felt that hardware stock was the only merchandise that would not spoil or go out of style. Clatworthy eventually added McCormick farm equipment to his inventory.

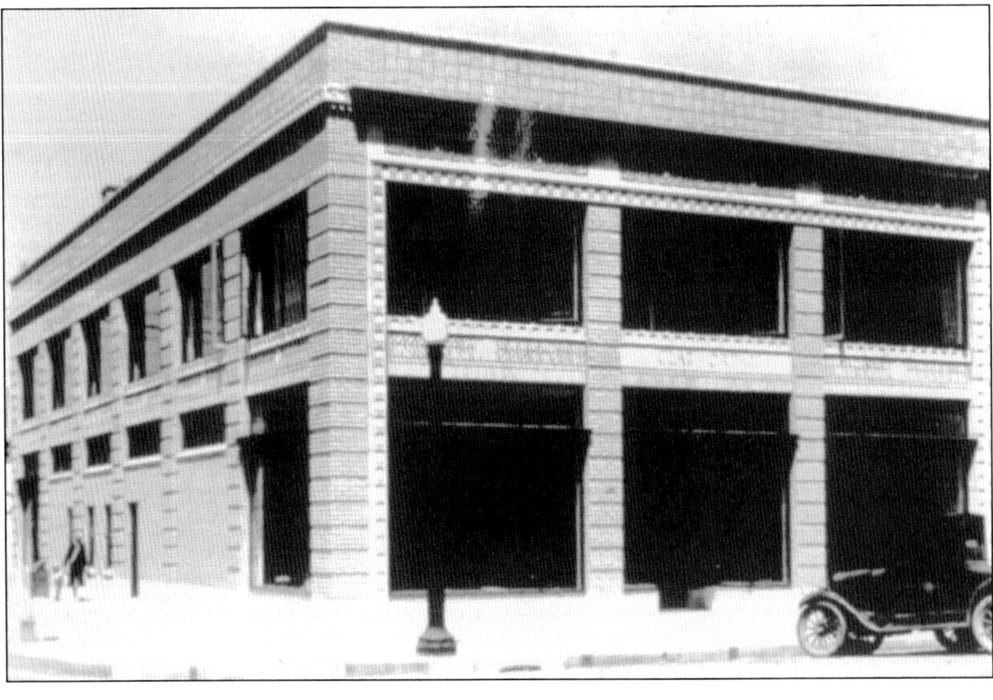

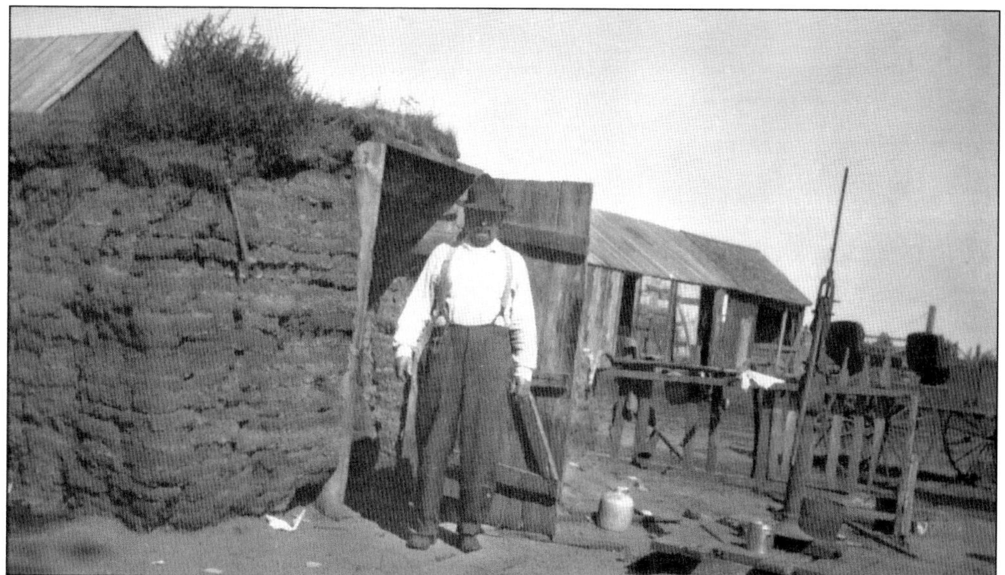

Tyler Heiskell stands here at the entrance to a old sod house, probably at his ranch near Weldona. In the background are barns and other outbuildings. At this point, the old soddy was probably just a storage building.

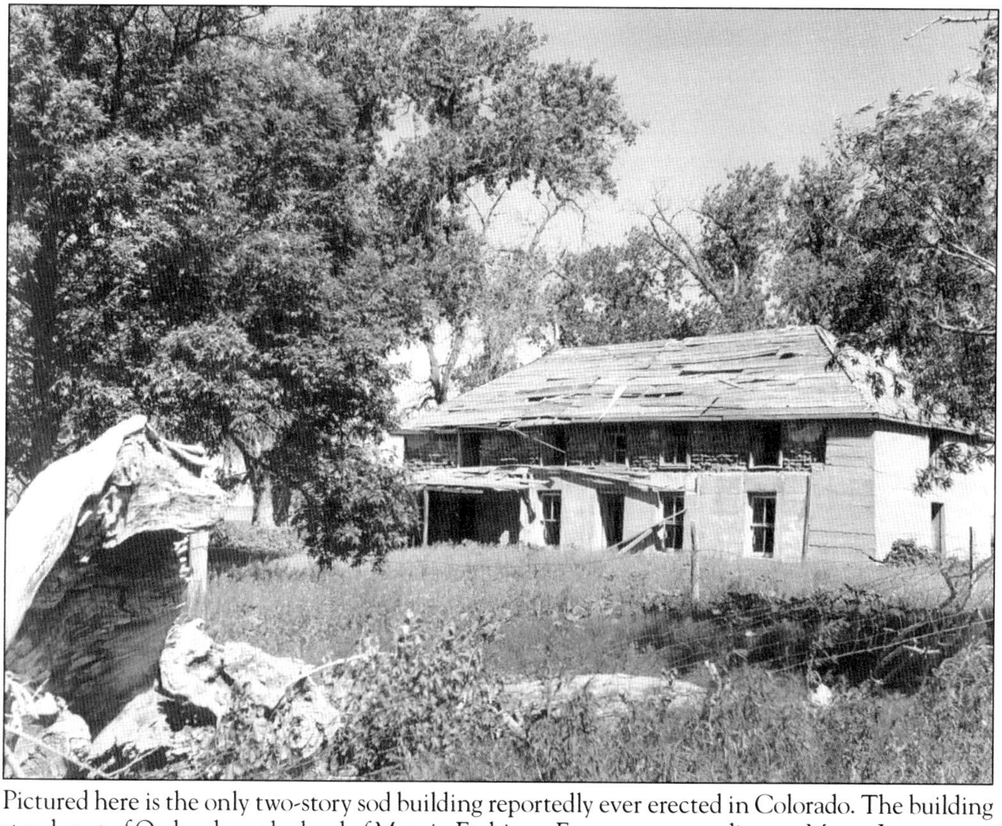

Pictured here is the only two-story sod building reportedly ever erected in Colorado. The building stood west of Orchard, on the land of Marvin Etchison. Former museum director Marne Jursermeyer and assistants made a casting of the sod walls prior to the building's destruction.

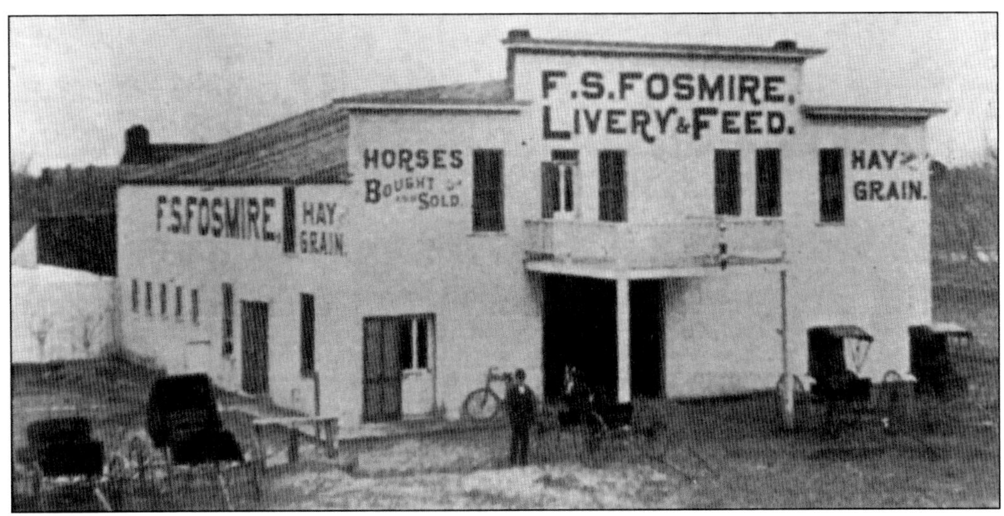

When the country was settled, horses were the source of most power. Frank S. Fosmire, an early settler of Fort Morgan, owned on of the many stables in town. Fosmire was also listed as the police magistrate. In 1897, he died at his home, located on Meeker Street.

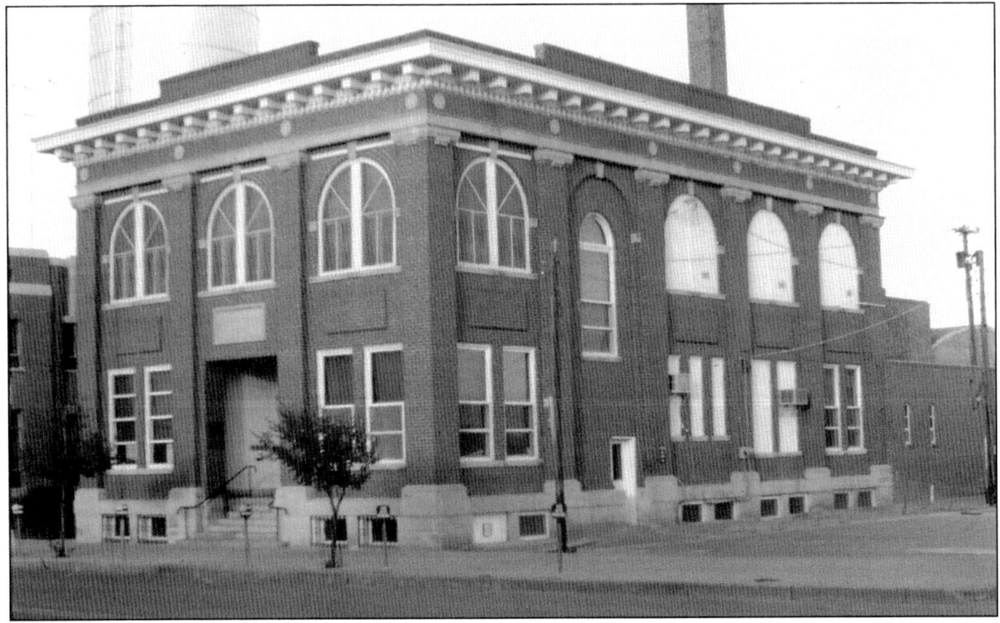

The 1908 Fort Morgan City Hall building is listed in the National Register of Historic Places for its associations with events that made an important contribution to the development of Fort Morgan. With its monumental proportions and dignified details, this striking example of the Classical Revival style at the original head of Main Street represents the beginning of Fort Morgan's municipal history. The city hall building symbolizes the growth, prosperity, and maturity of the Fort Morgan community. The building became the focal point in the civic development of Fort Morgan and served as a center of municipal government and community life for 75 years. The building is also significant for its association with George Cox, who was the city's first, most influential, and most productive superintendent. Cox was responsible for Fort Morgan's planning, establishing and operating the growing range of city services and public amenities during the first four decades of the 20th century.

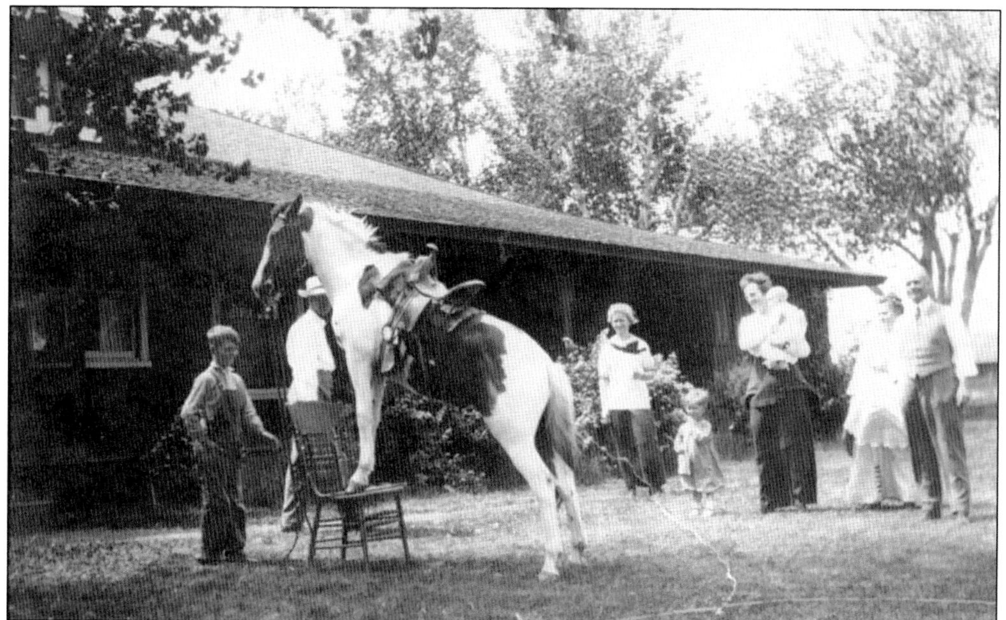

The house pictured here around 1912 is typical of a one-story ranch house. This is a photograph of the Hogsett family on the Moore Ranch. The photograph shows a paint horse with its front hooves on a chair. Robert Hogsett is standing in front of the horse doing the trick.

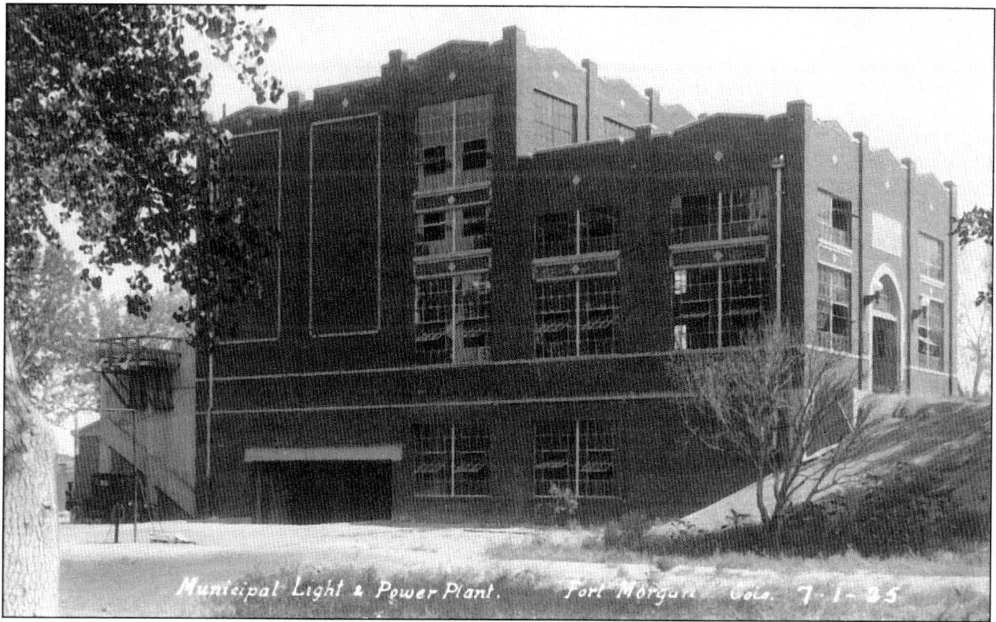

The 1923 Fort Morgan Power Plant building is listed in the National Register of Historic Places for its distinguished example of technological and industrial development as well as an architectural design for an early-20th-century industrial building. Under the leadership of Fort Morgan's first city superintendent, George Cox, the power plant building represents the first, most sophisticated exercise in publicly owned electrical power generation plants. In addition to housing the complicated coal-fired power-generating equipment, the unique architectural design was intended to be pleasurable to work in and enjoyable to look at.

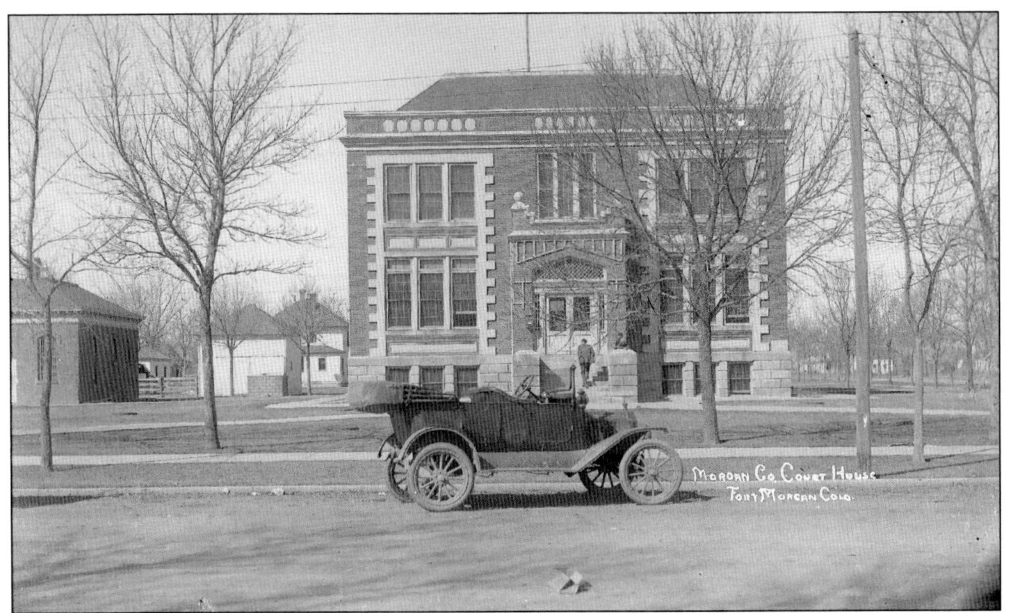

This photograph shows an earlier courthouse, but the 1936 Morgan County Court House is listed in the National Register of Historic Places for its association with the political and governmental development of Morgan County. In the midst of the Great Depression, the county commissioners took advantage of the federal construction grant from the Public Works Administration (PWA) to match county funds toward the erection of a new courthouse to replace the 1907 building. The 1936 courthouse is a good example of the Modern style with Art Deco elements. The 1921 jail building replaced the original facility built in 1898. The new 1936 courthouse and 1921 jail formed the two-building complex, which operated as the county's judicial and administrative center. The jail served as the county's processing and holding facility for 65 years.

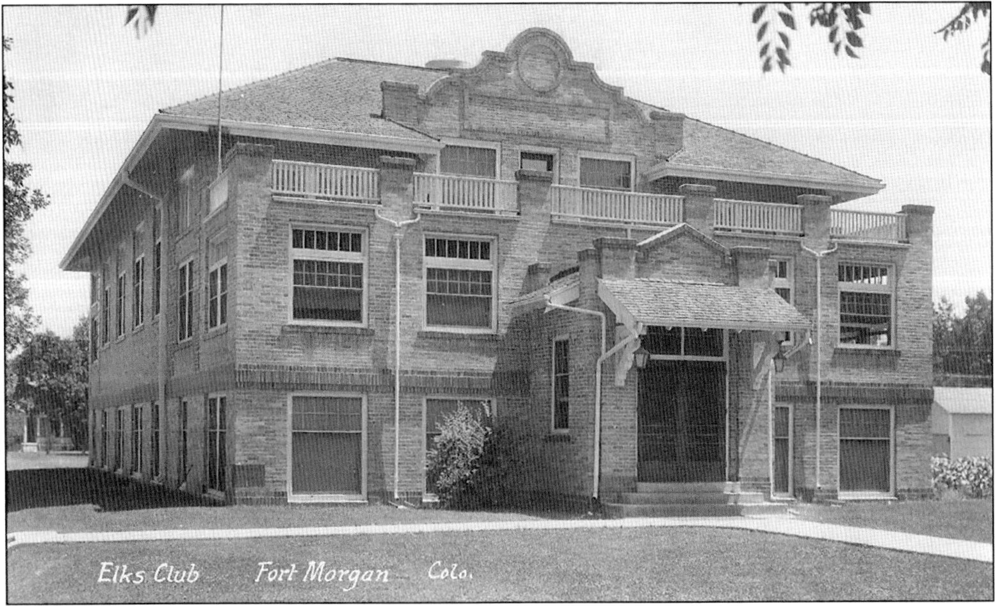

The Fort Morgan Elks Club, pictured here in 1925, was founded in 1884. To this day, members meet in this building.

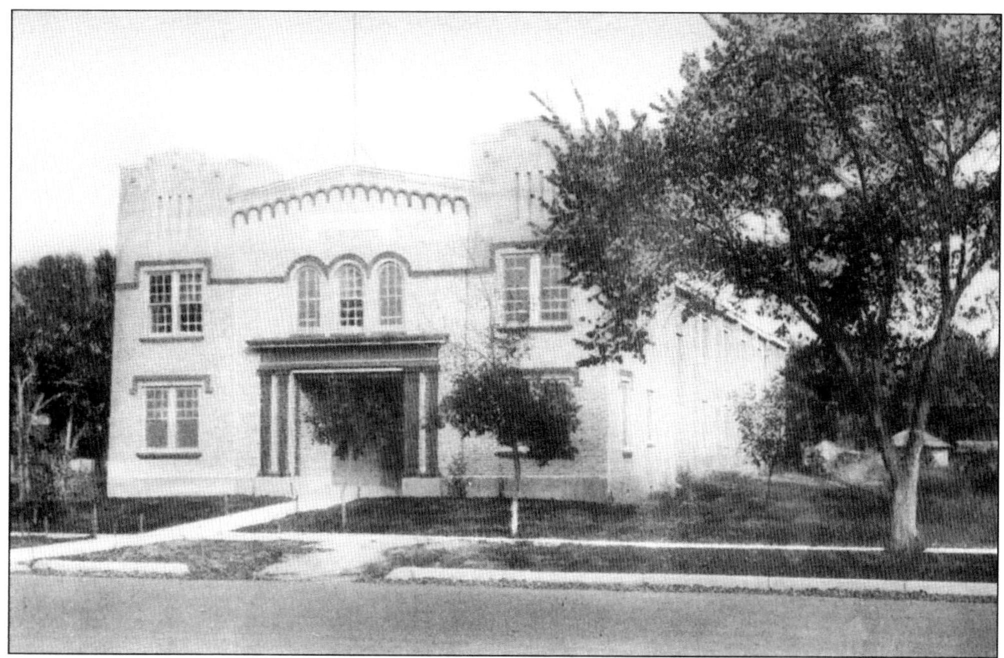

The 1922 Fort Morgan State Armory is listed in the National Register of Historic Places for its association with the community's military and recreational development. The construction of the building represents the initiation and maintenance of the National Guard unit in Fort Morgan. The armory's dual purpose of serving as a community center fostered the growth of entertainment and recreational opportunities in the town. The armory was built on a standard plan designed by Denver architect John Huddard.

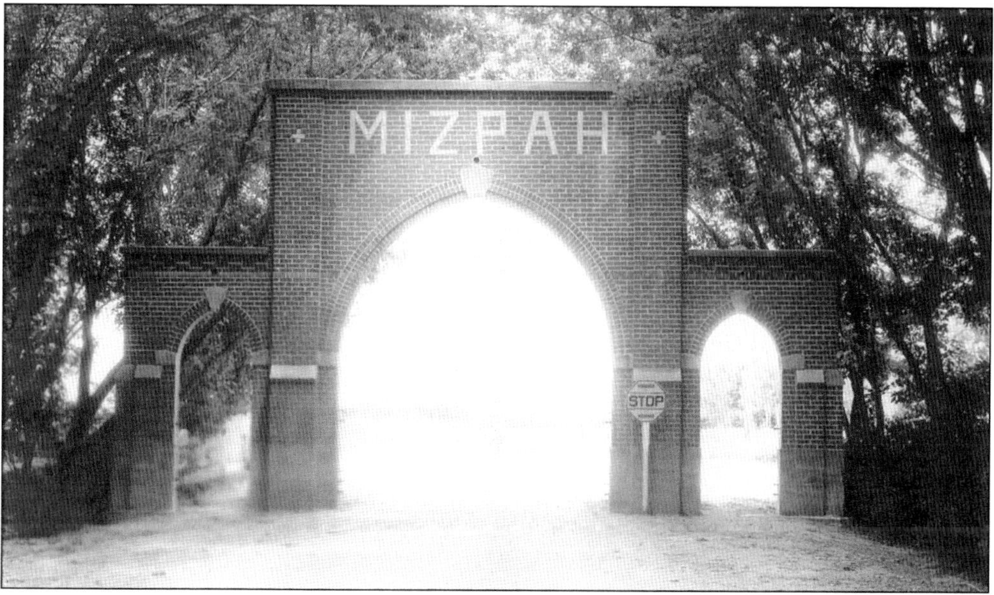

The gate at Eben Ezer in Brush has brickwork forming the word "Mizpah." The Hebrew name, which means "watchtower," is included in Genesis 31:49, which states, "May the lord watch between us when we are apart from one another." Another translation reads, "The LORD watch between me and thee, when we are absent one from another."

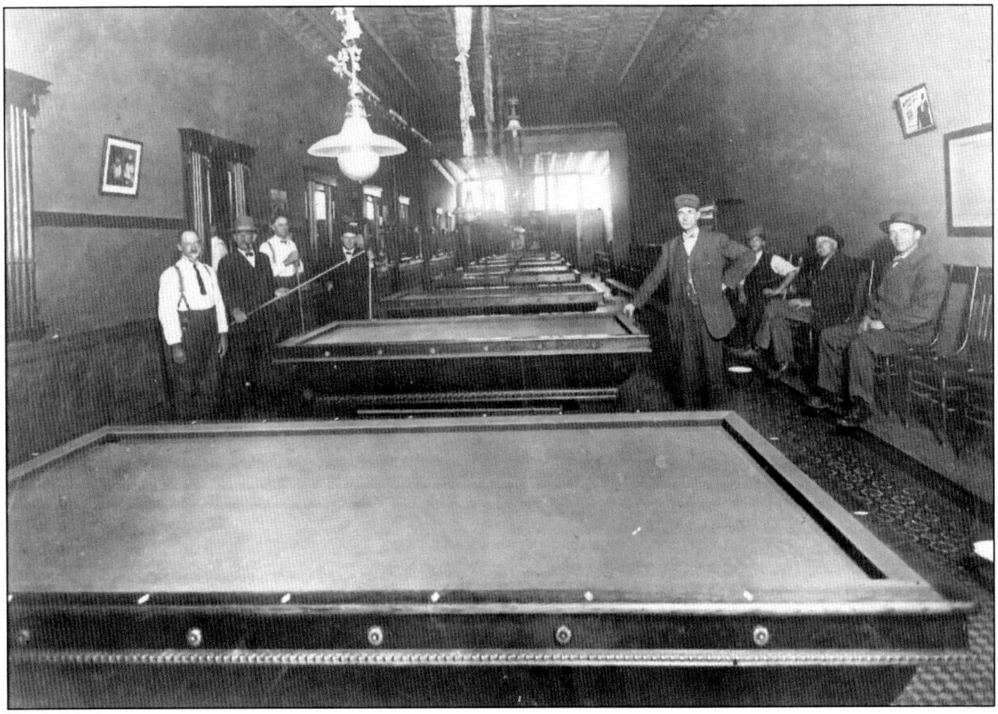

This pool hall was located in Fort Morgan at 223 Main Street.

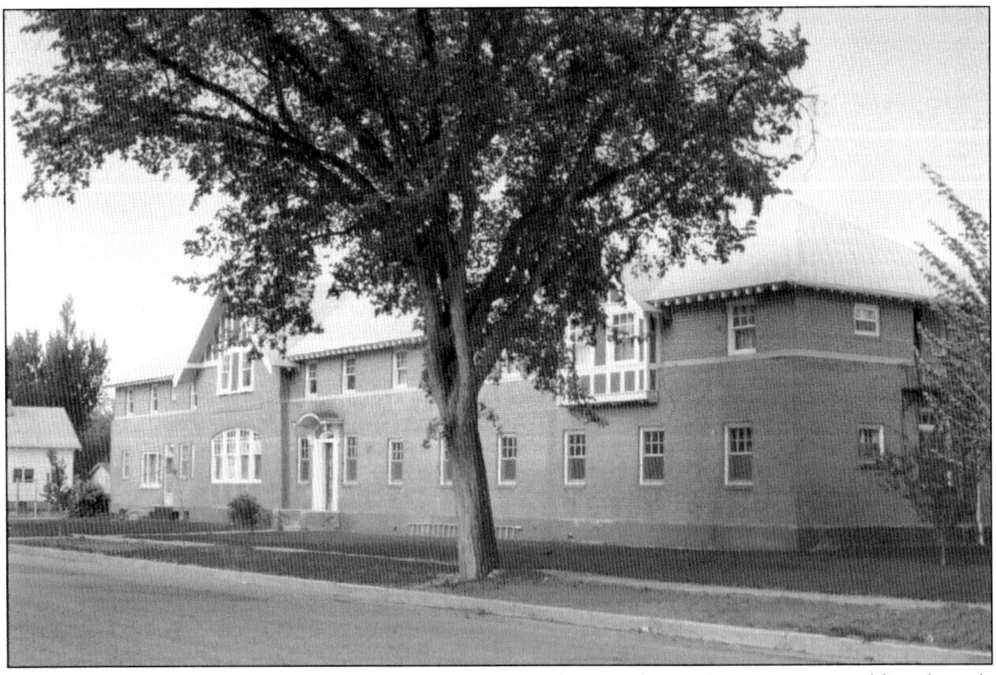

Pictured here is a Great Western dormitory converted around 1953 by Ivo Dyar and her friends for use as Fort Morgan's hospital.

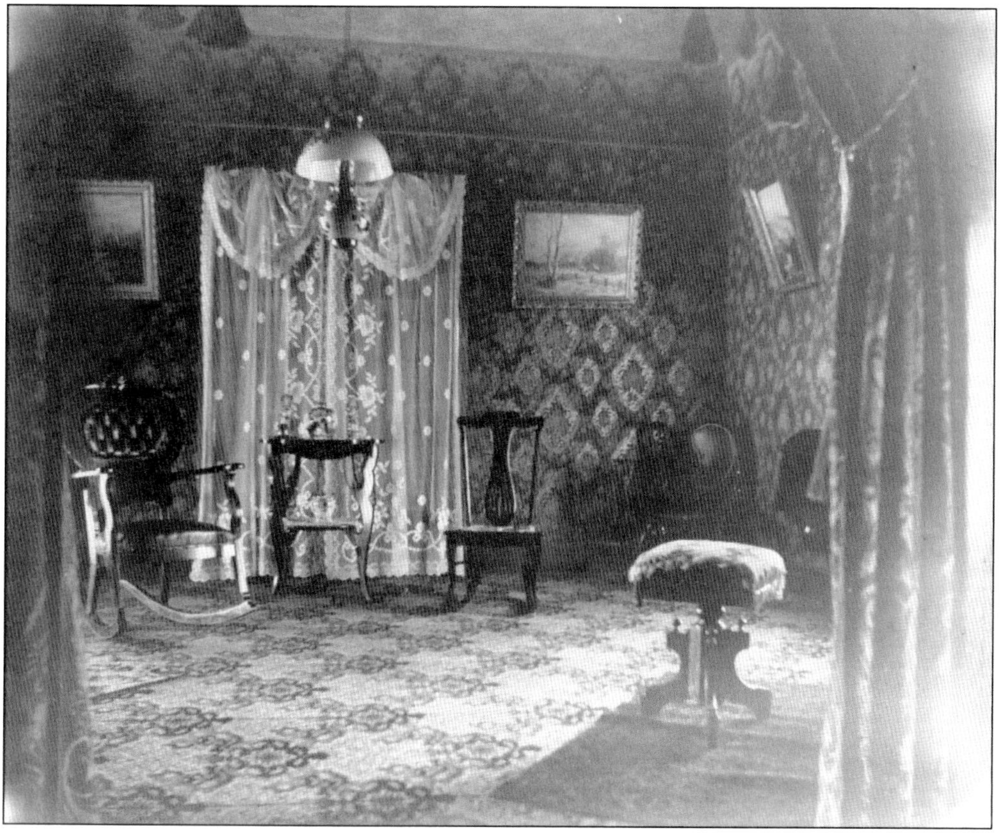

An early-20th-century living room is pictured here. The wallpaper has floral shields with a border of shields and garlands. One window is covered with shears and the other window has a heavy velvet drapes with ties and tassels. The center ceiling lamp is probably kerosene, and the chairs are a variety of wooden styles, with a leather rocking chair and a piano stool in one corner. There are three landscapes on the walls and a patterned carpet on the floor.

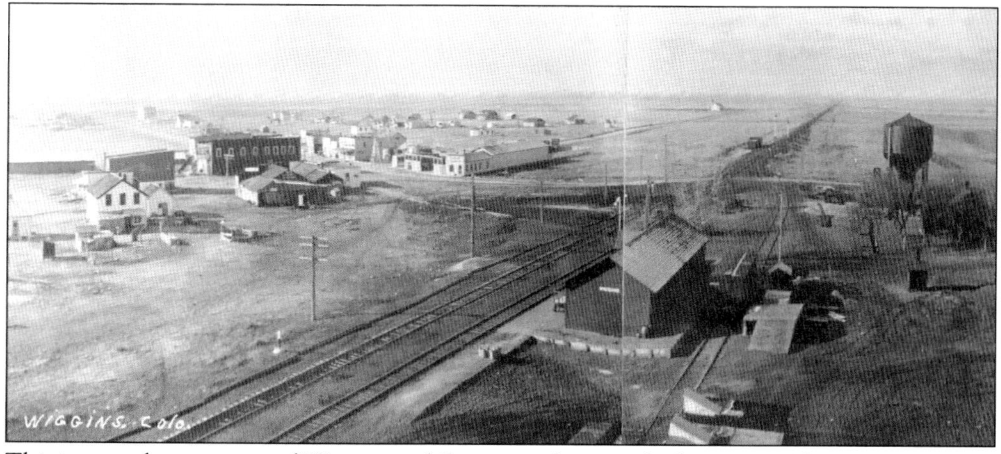

This is an early panorama of Wiggins and Corona with a view looking west. The water tower and depot are in the center of the photograph, with Wiggins to the left and Corona to the right; by this time, the entire community is being called Wiggins.

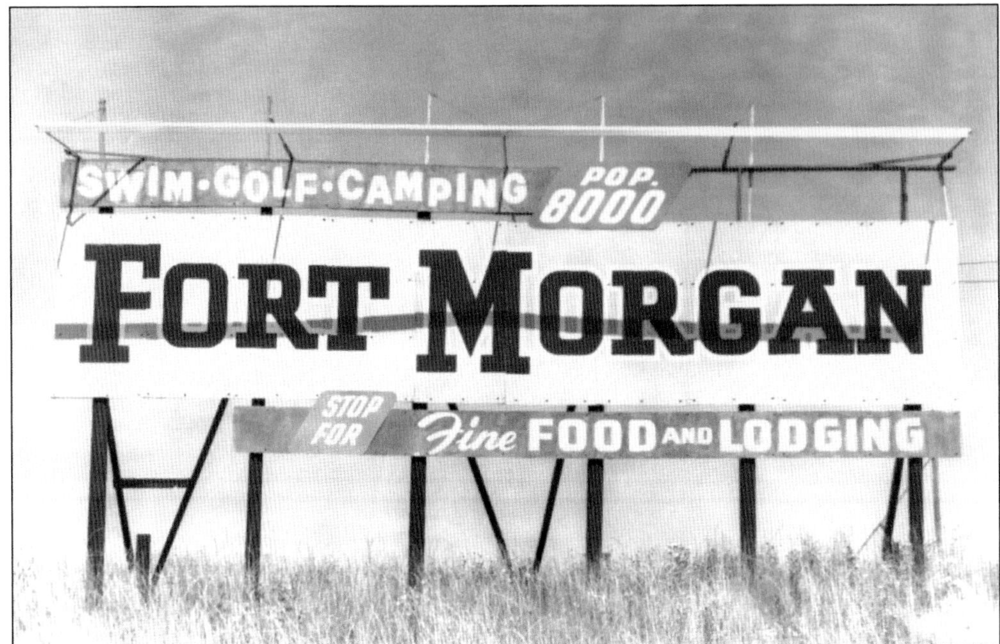

This 1967 illuminated billboard reads "Fort Morgan— Swim, Golf, Camping — Pop. 8000 — Stop for Fine Food and Lodging."

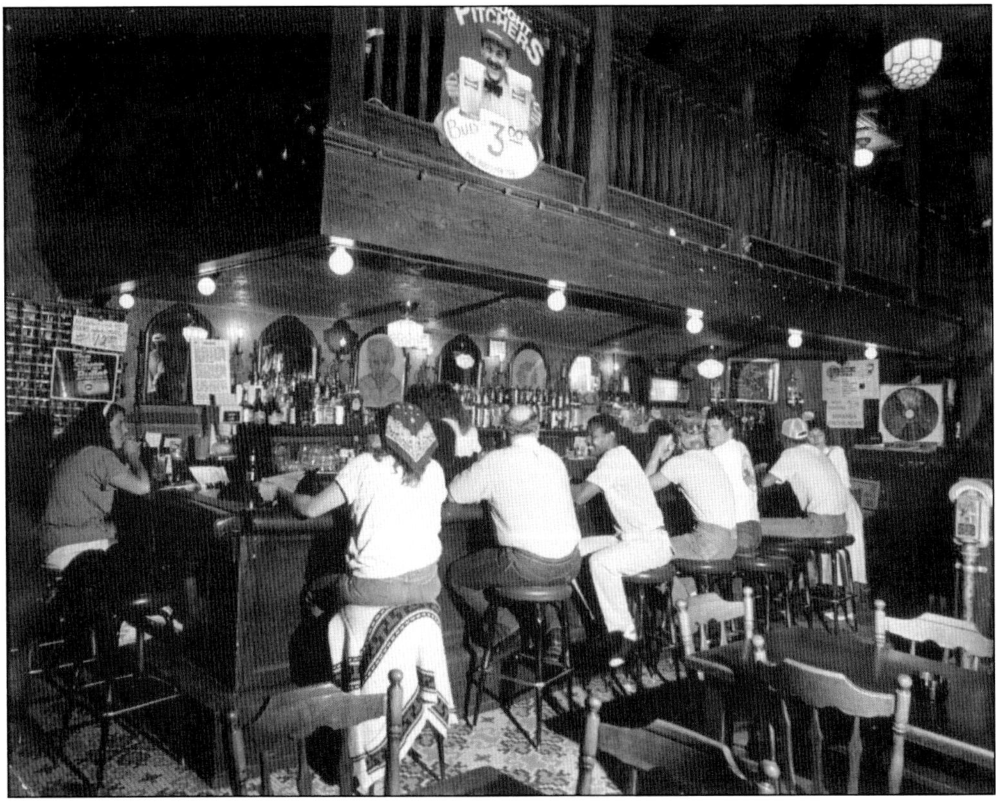

Pictured here in 1989 is the Queens Lounge in Fort Morgan.

Eight

NATURAL DISASTERS

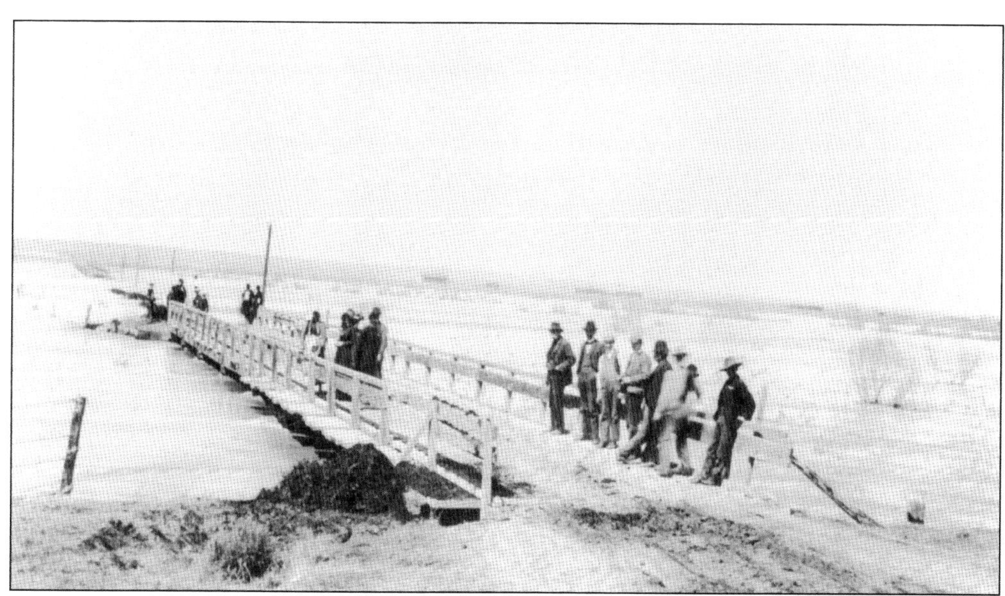

The first bridge over the South Platte River to the north side washed away in a flood. In the background is the Union Pacific station as well as ranch buildings.

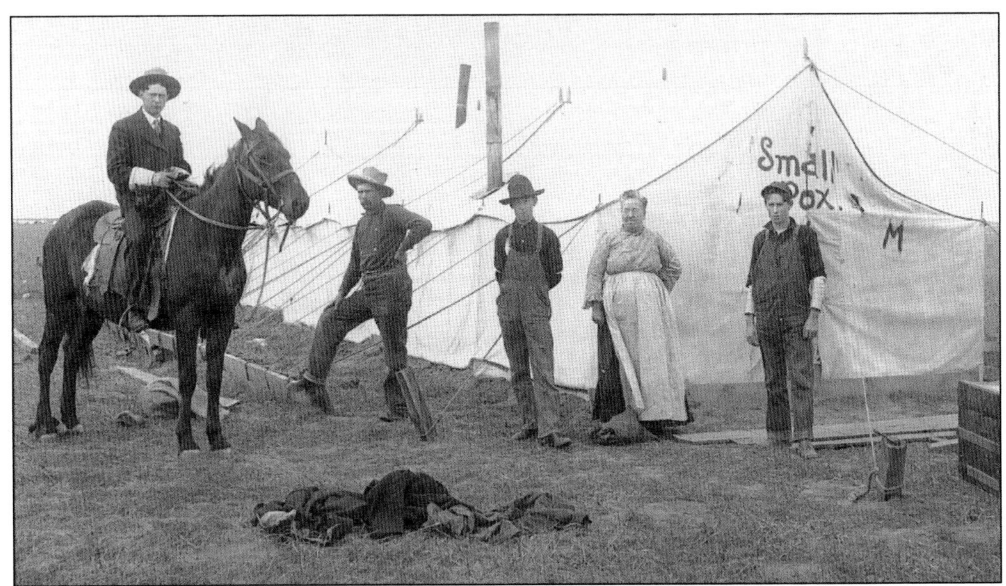

Dr. A.F. Williams sits on a horse next to a quarantine tent near Empire Reservoir on April 10, 1909. A mild form of smallpox was prevalent in Colorado that year. There were so few fatalities that no one believed it was true smallpox, leading to a decrease in vaccination rates. Smallpox was often misdiagnosed as chicken pox or "yaws" by inexperienced doctors.

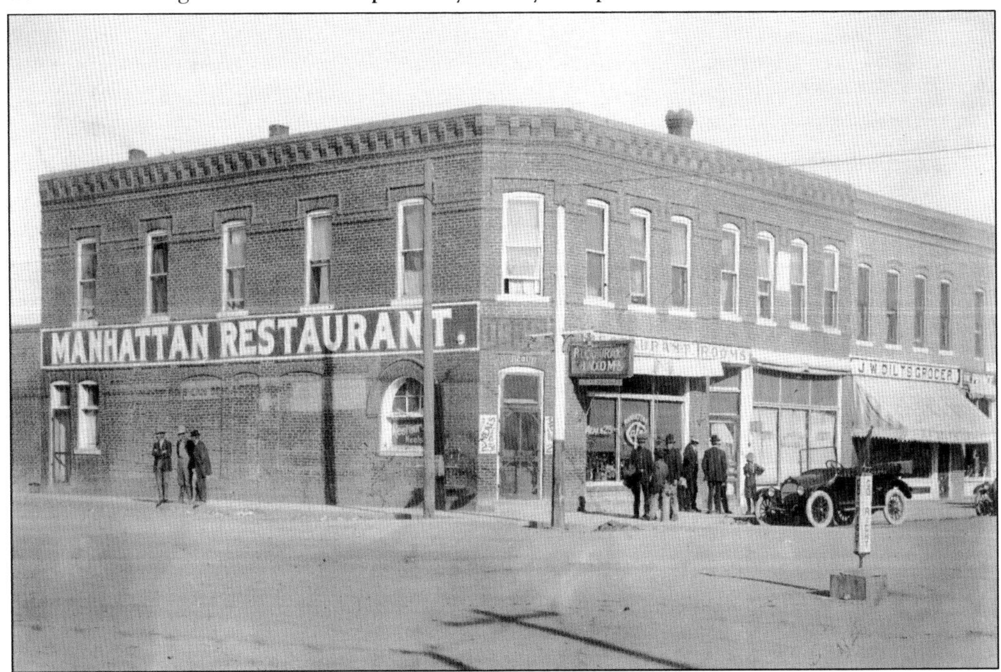

The Manhattan Café, in a structure originally built as the first bank in Fort Morgan, was the scene of the death of Fort Morgan marshal Charlie P. Eyser. On September 30, 1916, Eyser confronted bootleggers John Swan and R. "Happy" Wilcox at their apartment upstairs. A gun battle ensued; Eyser was shot and later died. The operator of the café, a Mrs. Weimer, was at her door in another apartment, watching through a keyhole, when a stray bullet killed her instantly. Swan and Wilcox were convicted of Eyser's death, but Swan escaped—and was never found.

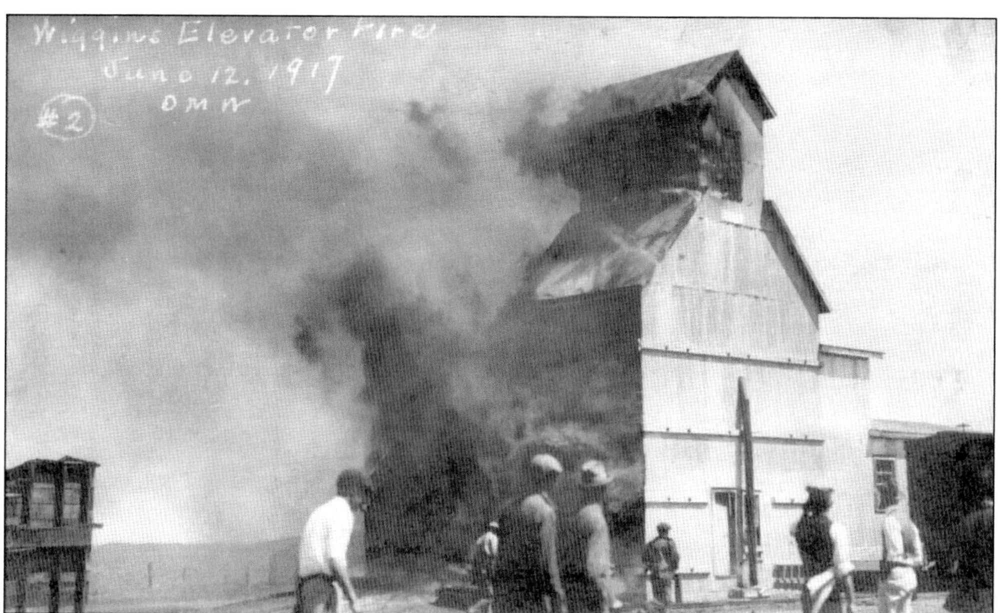

Pictured here on June 12, 1917, is the fire that beset a Wiggins grain elevator.

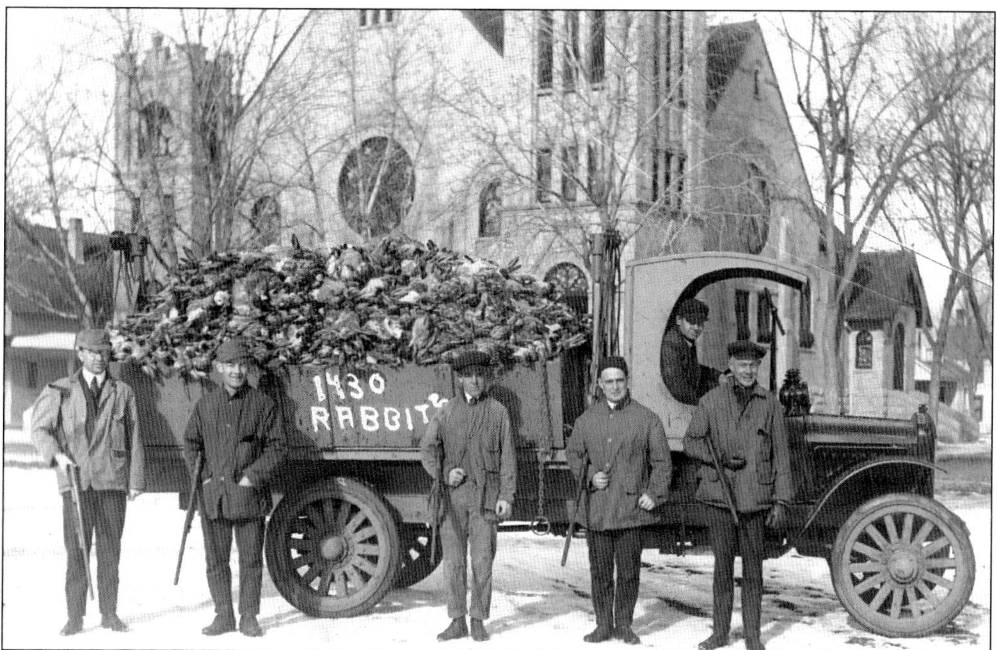

Rabbit hunts were held during the winter months in the mid-1920s. This particular hunt netted 1,430 rabbits. Sometimes, men skinned and dressed the dead rabbits and then put them into containers with ice. Then they were loaded onto a train car and taken to Denver to feed the poor. Other times, the dead rabbits were sold to farmers for hog feed. The sole purpose of the periodic rabbit drives held in Morgan County was to keep farms and ranches from being overrun by rabbits, which were eating alfalfa and other crops. It was calculated that eight rabbits ate as much as one cow, so if a rabbit drive was not held, the rabbits would end up eating the amount of feed needed for 1,000 head of cattle.

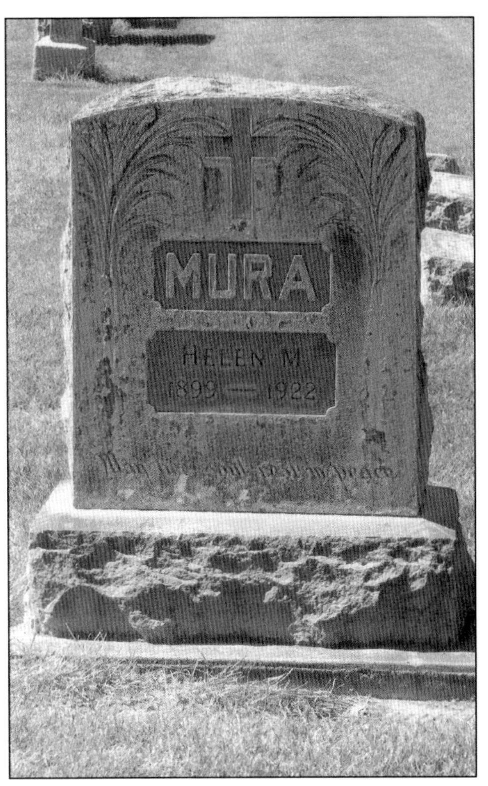

Helen Mura emigrated from Italy with her family, and they settled in Weldona. Helen became a schoolteacher and taught at the North Star School (seven miles northeast of Weldona). Her parents, Esnazio and Sabina, hired an Italian farmhand, Maggiorino Stabio. He was smitten by Helen; however, she did not return his feelings. On March 2, 1922, Stabio, in front of the students at the school, shot and killed Helen—he then turned the gun on himself. Helen was 23 years old.

Enid Marriott, a Wiggins schoolteacher, disappeared in the early winter of 1930. Two months later, in early 1931, her body was found frozen in an irrigation ditch. Six months later, after confessing, John Schopflin was arrested. For the first time in the history of the 13th Judicial District, a death penalty was requested. Schopflin was found guilty, but his life was spared. His sentence was committed and he was later paroled. A few months after his release, he committed suicide. Here, Clyde "Stub" Roberts of Wiggins shows where the teacher's body was found. Stub was 14 at the time and lived on the farm next to the ditch.

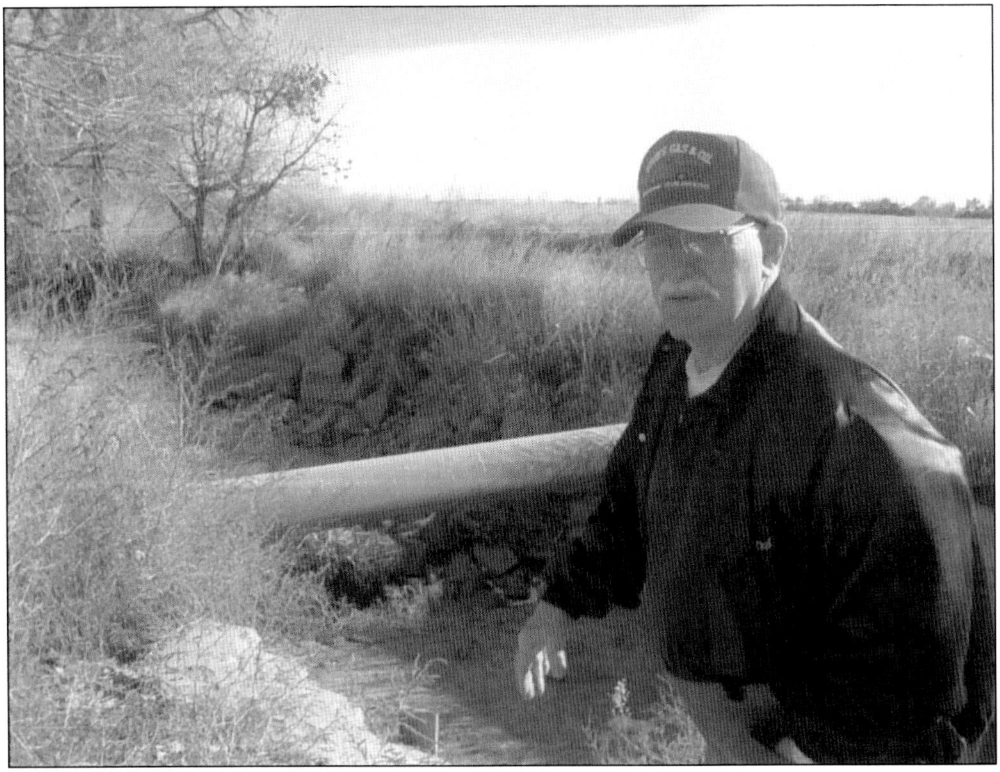

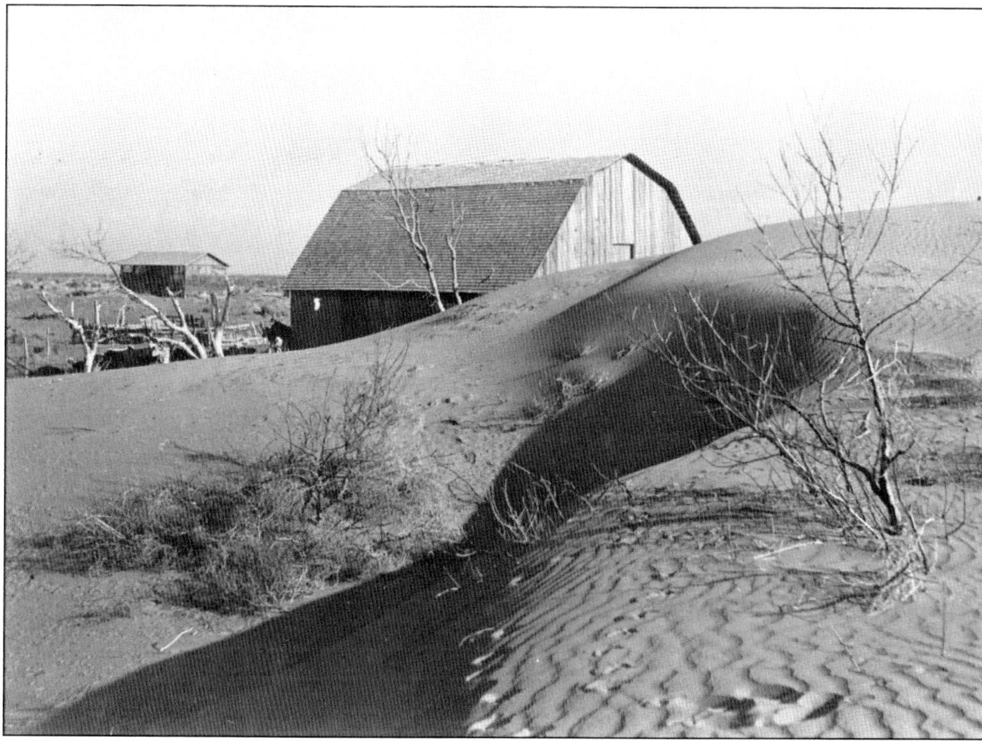

Dust storms rolled like wheels across the prairie, churning up the plowed topsoil. The storms often lasted for days, and people hung blankets in their windows to keep the dust out. On February 22, 1935, a major dust storm hit the Fort Morgan area, bringing traffic to a standstill. Sand had to be cleaned from carburetors and distributors, windshields were sand-pitted, and paint was torn off of the automobiles. (Courtesy of the Library of Congress.)

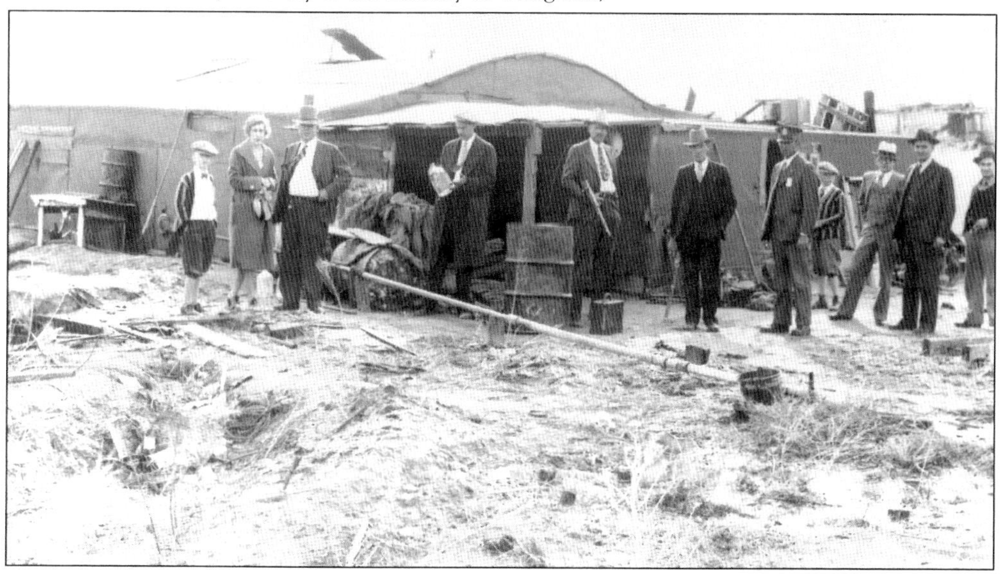

Raiding one of the largest stills in the state near Fort Morgan, around 1932, are, as identified from left to right, Wyllis, Nellie, Howard St., Tom Sigafoos, Loren Bates, Harvey Yokum, Jake Stroh, H.A. Anderson Jr., Byron Bashor, Rufus "Capt" Johnson, and Jimmy Scanlon.

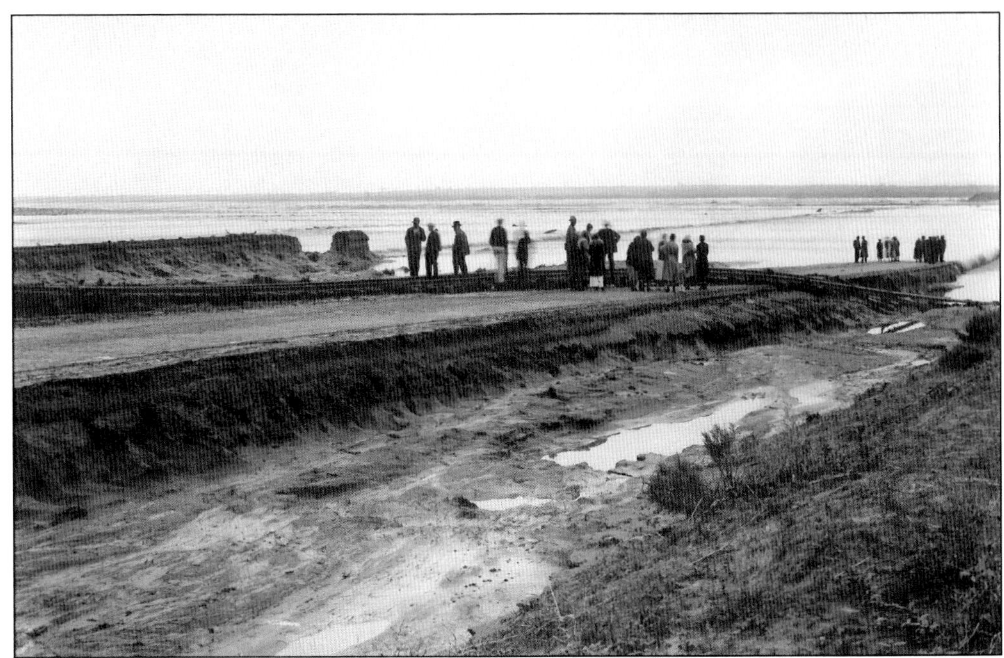

Pictured here during the 1935 flood is the Burlington Railroad and Highway east of Wiggins. Bijou Creek claimed over a mile of road and railroad. On May 31, 1935, a 10-foot wall of water crested at Fort Morgan, and the city's electrical plant flooded. Riverside Park was covered by water, and everything except for the Rainbow Bridge was swept away. Some 30 miles of lowlands were inundated by floodwaters.

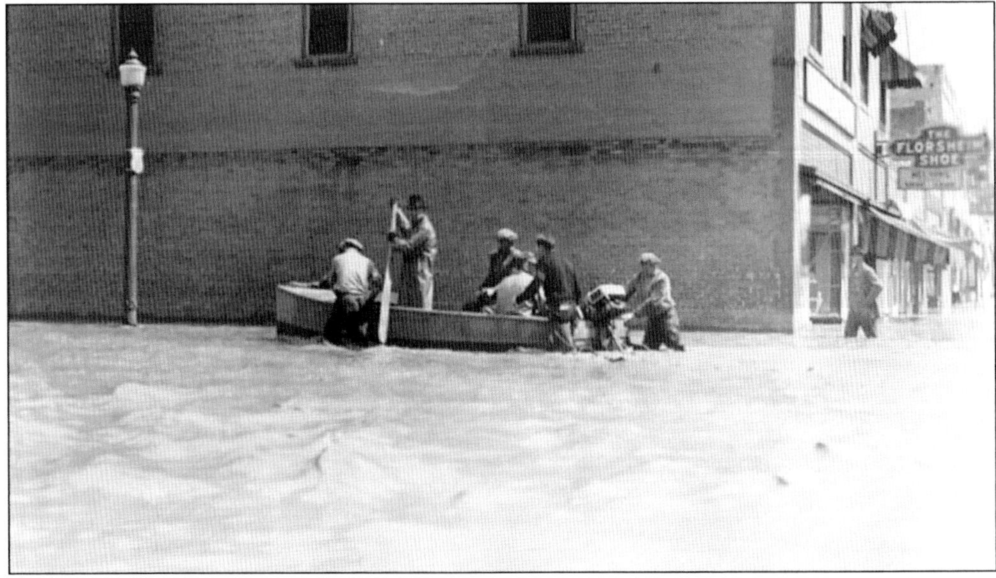

Unable to drive through the flood tide in the Platte River, the Beaver Creek backed up and turned the streets in the main business district of Brush into rivers during the Memorial Day flood of 1935. Following the flood, townspeople were instructed to boil their water and air out their basements in order to prevent disease.

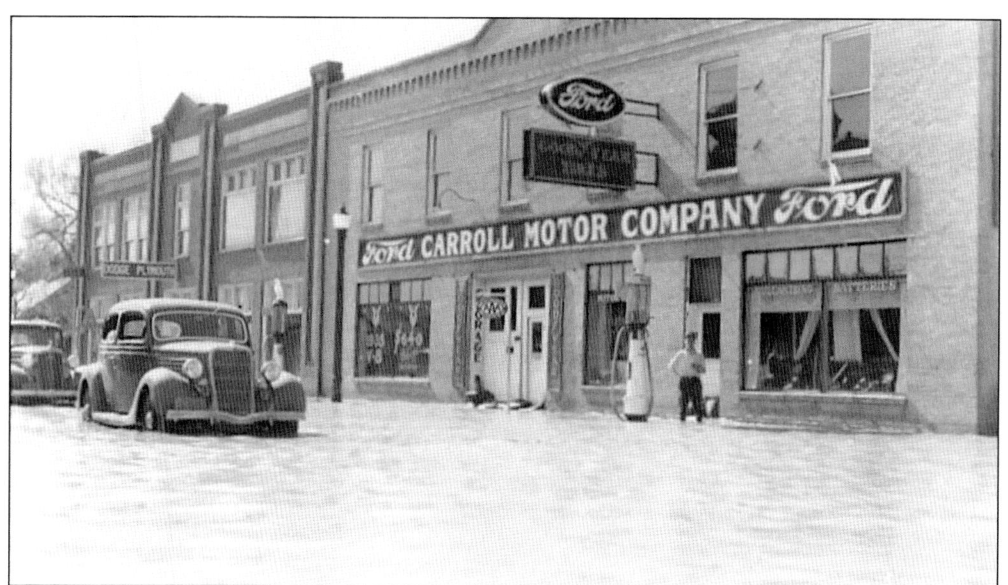

Pictured here are the aftereffects of the 1935 in Brush. L.A. Gray bought the Ford agency in 1915, and H.T. Carrol purchased the business in 1917. Ford's Model Ts were shipped by the railroad in boxcars. Seven chassis were stacked on one end and the bodies and fenders on the other end. The parts of the cars were assembled by the dealers.

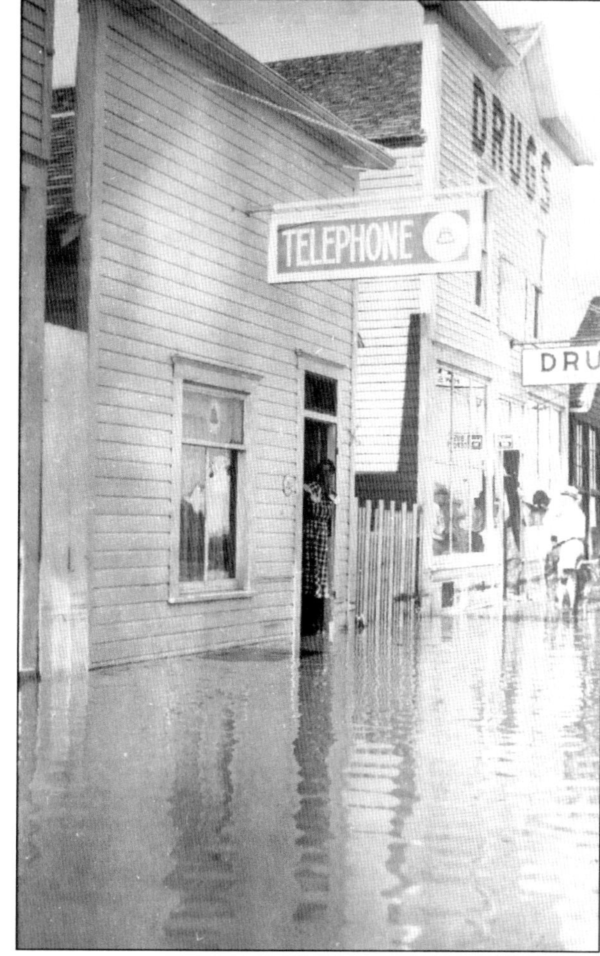

The 1935 flood is shown here in Hillrose.

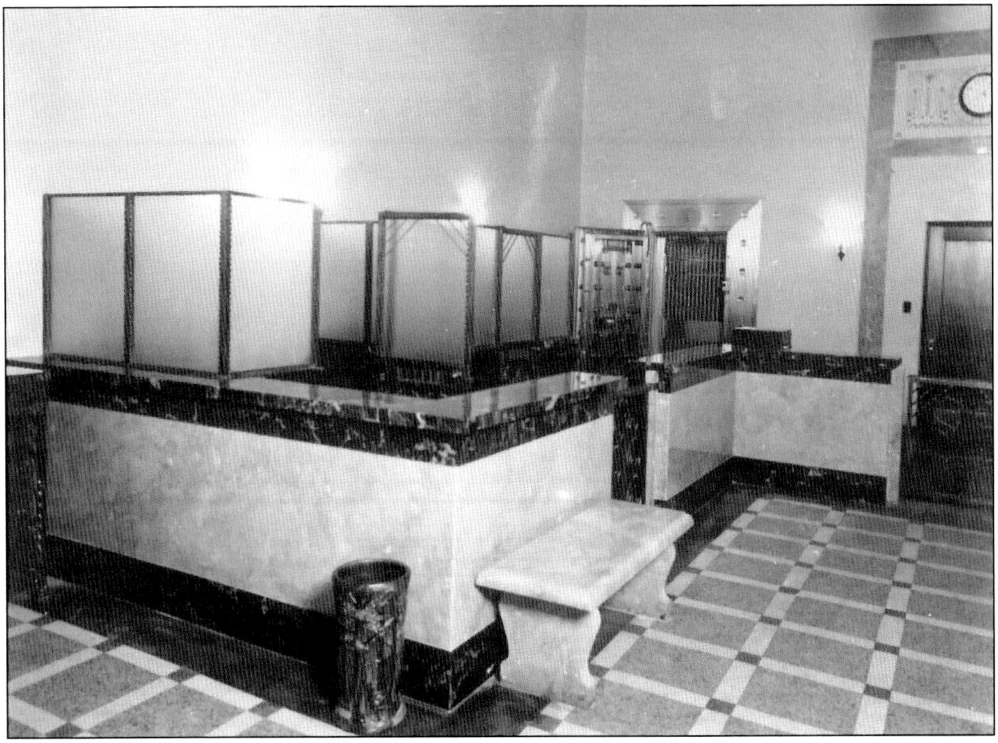

The first bank robbery in Fort Morgan history happened on July 8, 1939. Two goggled gunmen entered the bank and held employees and customers at gunpoint. The gunmen fled with all the cash not in the vault. They were stopped in Sydney, Nebraska, and one of the robbers was killed in a shoot-out with police. The second escaped to later die in a second shoot-out, in Garden City, Kansas. Most, if not all, of the money stolen was recovered, a total of $10,322.

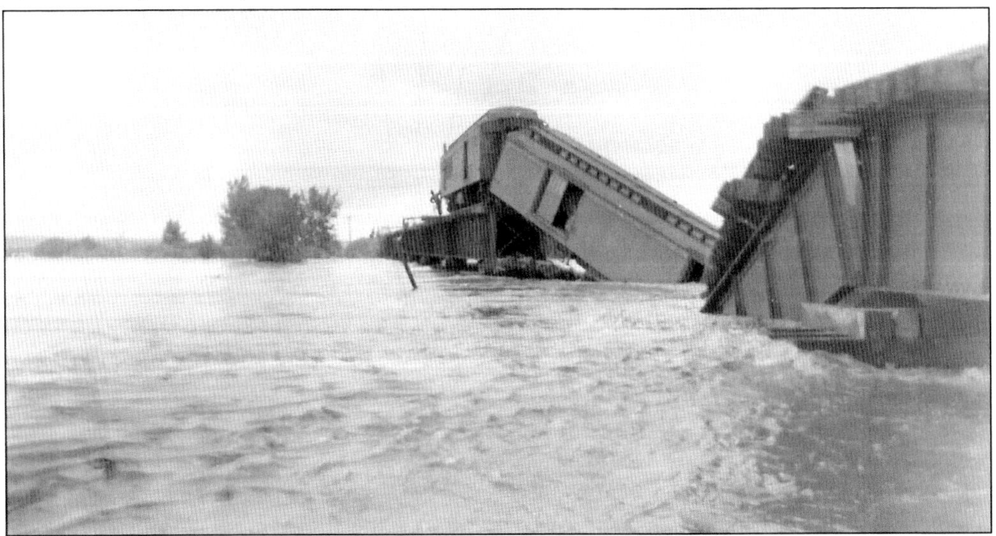

During May 1921, a flash flood washed out the railroad bridge at Union (located four miles north of Hillrose). Railroad officials were forced to cut the partially submerged coach loose a day after the disaster. Fireman Snedicker and Engineer Gouty, both of Sterling, drowned in the floodwaters. The coach of Burlington passenger train No. 303 is still buried in the riverbed to this day.

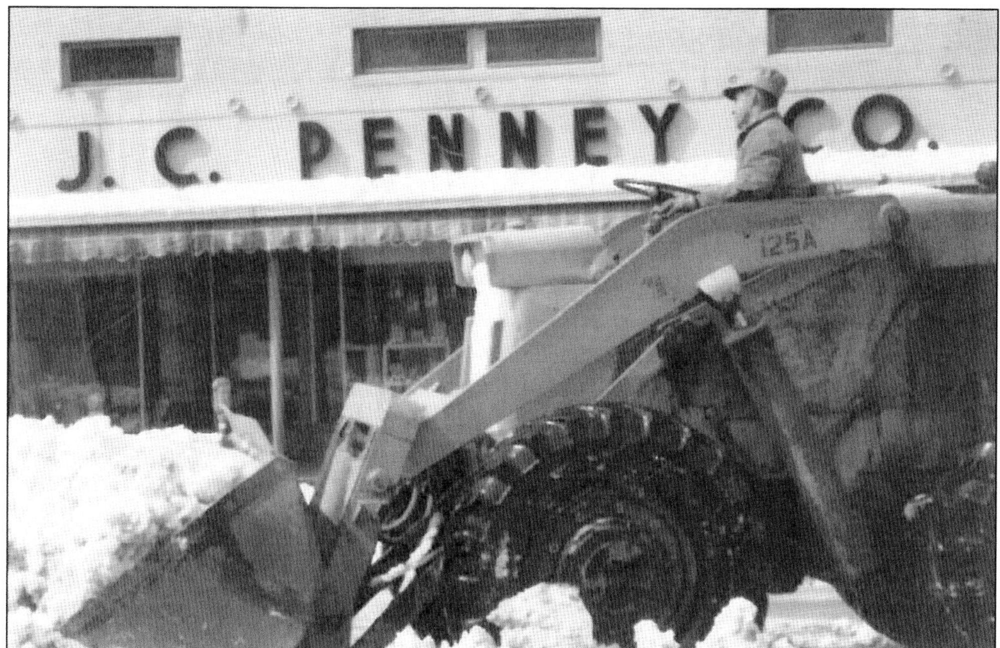

A spring blizzard in 1959 brought heavy wet snow and icy winds. Temperatures fell from a high of 54 degrees to 18 degrees in less than four hours. The snow coated and froze the telephone lines, snapping between 700 and 1,000 lines. Local calls could be made, but there was no direct service for long-distance calls between Fort Morgan and Denver.

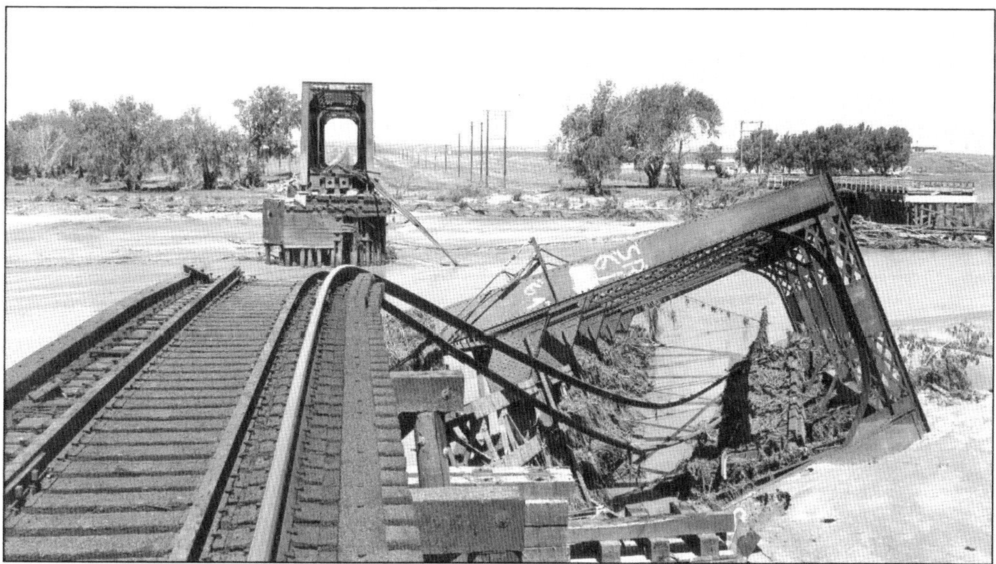

On June 18, 1965, raging floodwater from the Bijou Creek tore out several Highway 80 S (I-76) bridges. The town of Wiggins was evacuated. When the water backed up against the Chicago, Burlington & Quincy Railroad's bridge, huge waves crested and twisted the tracks east of Wiggins. Then the roiling waters converged with the South Platte River. Fort Morgan was cut off on three sides. Riverside Park and the city's community swimming pool were submerged. Water rose waist high in the city power plant. Dikes at the public-service substation held. The Big Beaver Creek flooded portions of Brush and all downtown businesses were sandbagged.

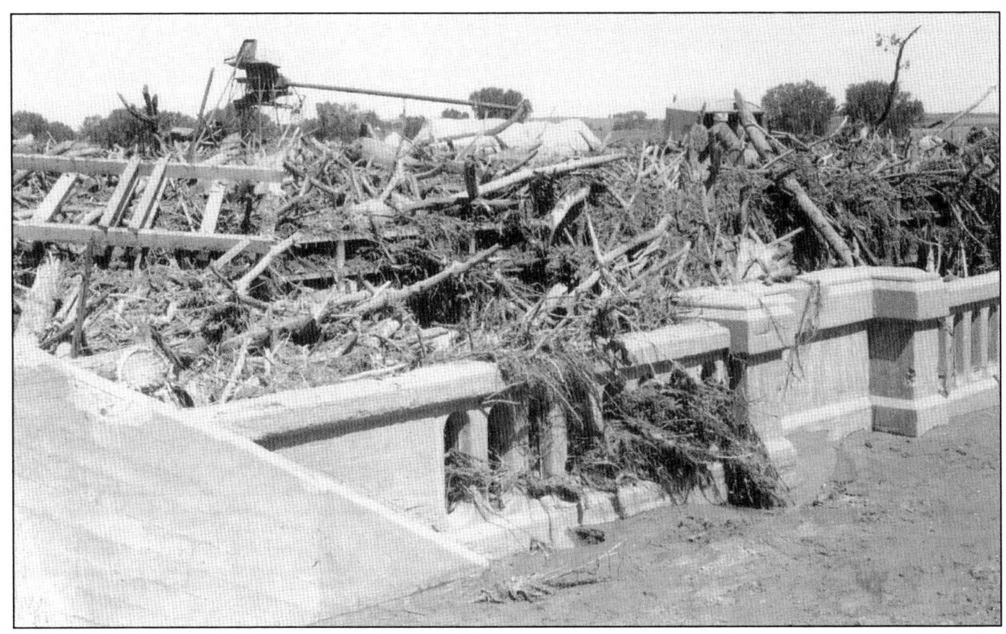

During the 1965 flood, the Bijou Creek was running three miles wide when it joined with the South Platte River. The new bridge, which was built in 1963, was taken out by the floodwaters. Yet the Rainbow Bridge, located next to the new bridge, held, just as it had during the flood of 1935. This 11-arch concrete bridge was built in 1923 and is the only rainbow arch bridge in Colorado. In 1984, the bridge was placed in the National Register of Historic Places, and in 1992, it was designated a Colorado Civil Engineering Landmark.

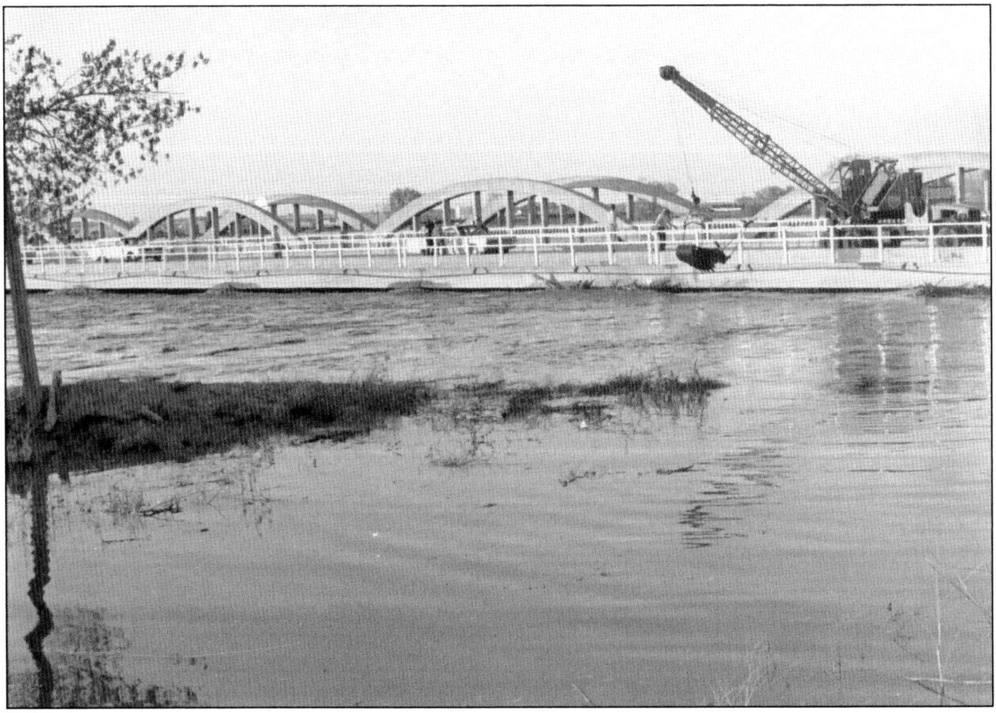

Pictured here is a crane lifting debris from the front of the bridges after the 1965 flood.

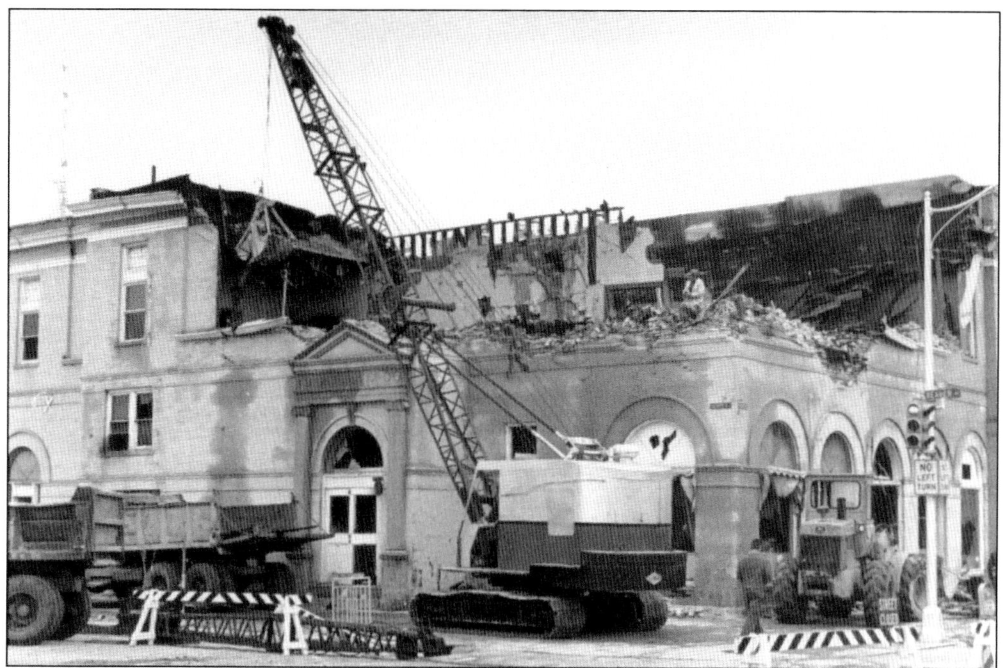

Some 40 firemen battled a blaze for nine hours in the Masonic temple in Fort Morgan on April 20, 1971. The fire started in the barbershop on the first floor and destroyed the original half of the building, which had been constructed in 1923. The newer north end of the building, where the lodge room had been moved, was saved, along with records and photographs of past lodge masters.

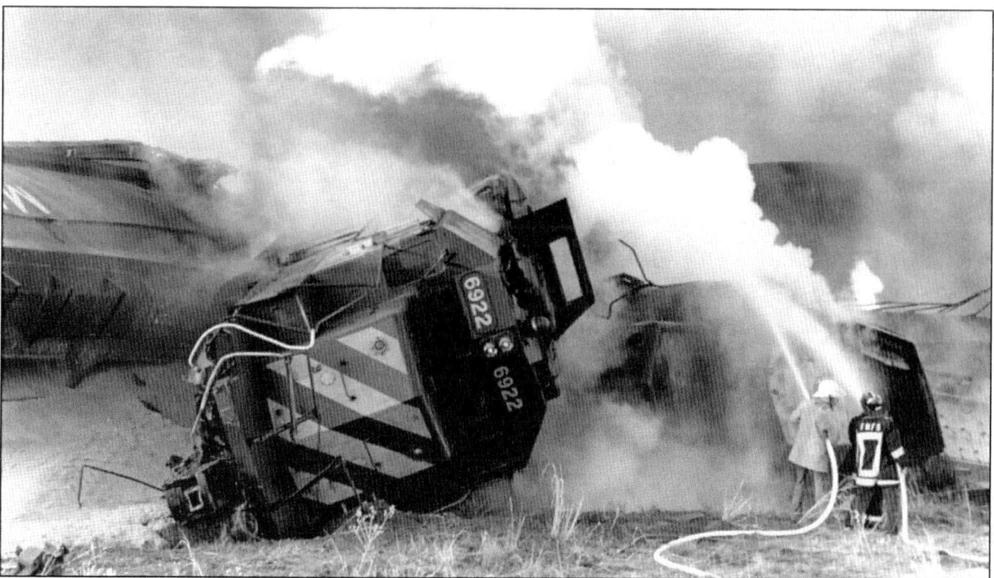

At 3:55 a.m. on April 13, 1984, two Burlington Northern trains collided, resulting in a fiery train wreck outside of Wiggins. When engineer Richard Sponsel saw the headlights of another train coming toward him, he ordered his crewmen to jump. Then he leaped, landing on top of them. They miraculously escaped with their lives. Others were not as fortunate; five crewmen died in the crash.

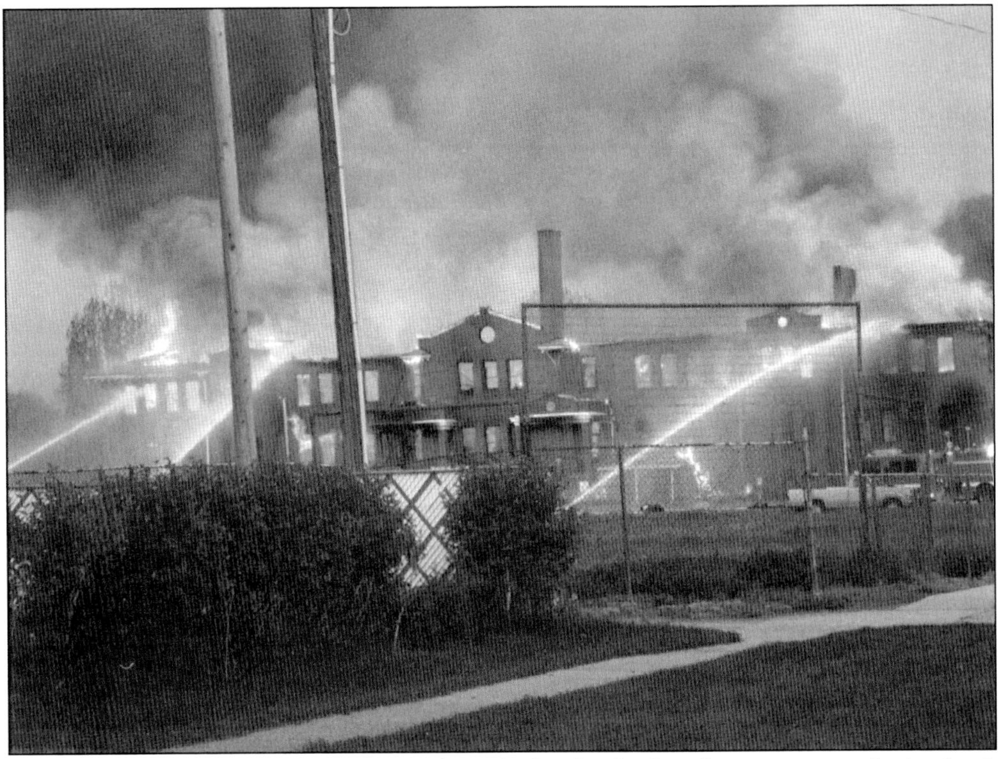

Baker School burned on May 22, 1995. Built as a high school, it later became a junior high school. The buildings burned to the ground. The building was razed and replaced by the new Baker School. The fire was determined to be arson—set to cover up a burglary.

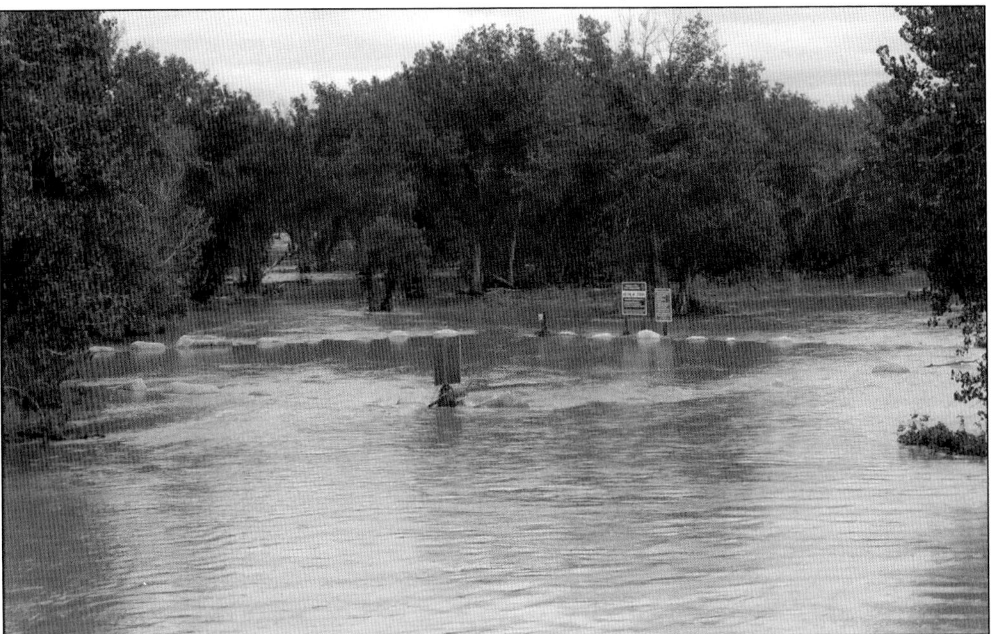

Floodwaters of the South Platte flow through Riverside Park in the fall flood of 2013. High water usually comes in June, but there are other fall floods on record.

Nine

MILITARY HISTORY

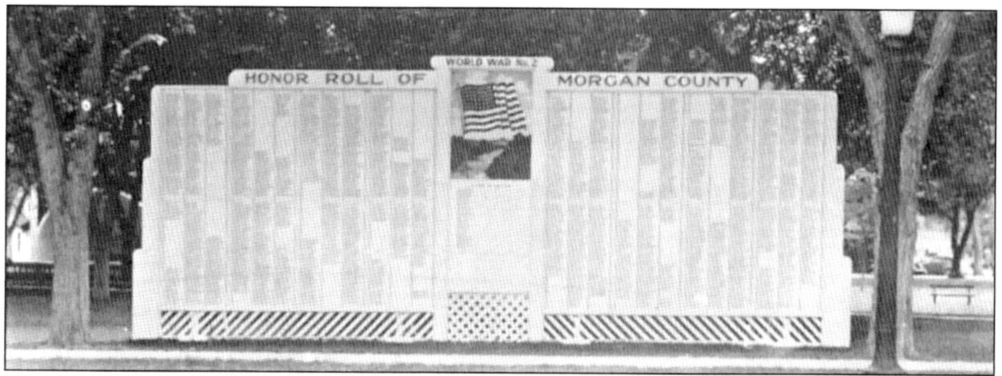

Pictured here is the honor roll of Morgan County veterans. This service record was sponsored by VFW Post No. 2551, assisted by the Fort Morgan and Community Business Men.

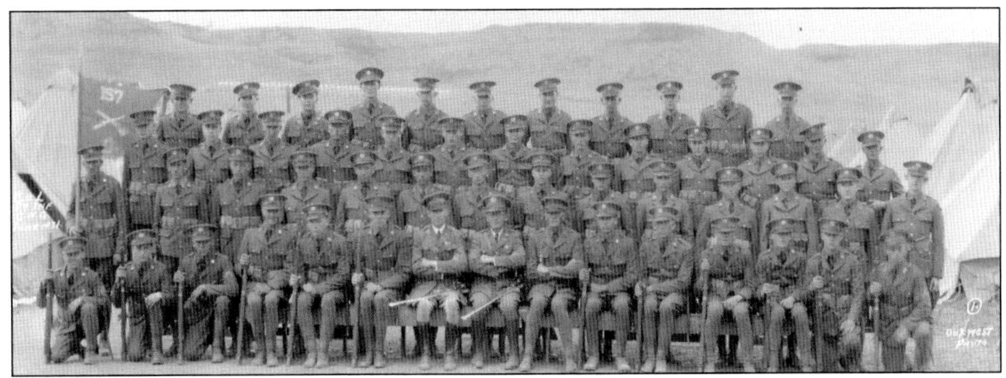

Pictured here in June 1930 is Company L, 157th Infantry of the Colorado National Guard. This unit was located in Brush, Colorado. The photograph was probably taken at Camp Carson, Colorado.

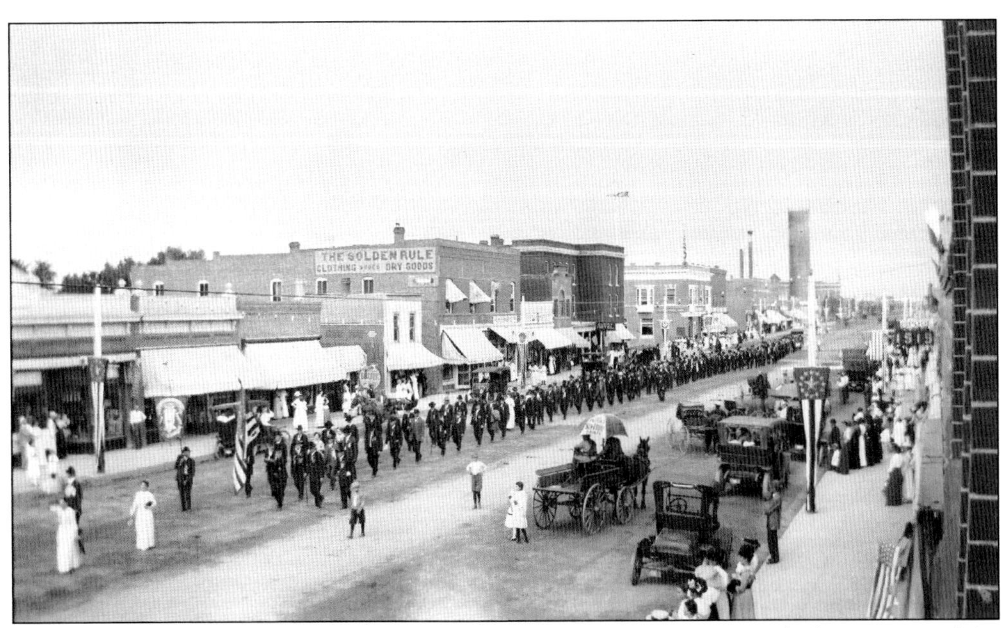

Pictured here in 1918 is a Grand Army of the Republic homecoming parade for veterans of the Civil War.

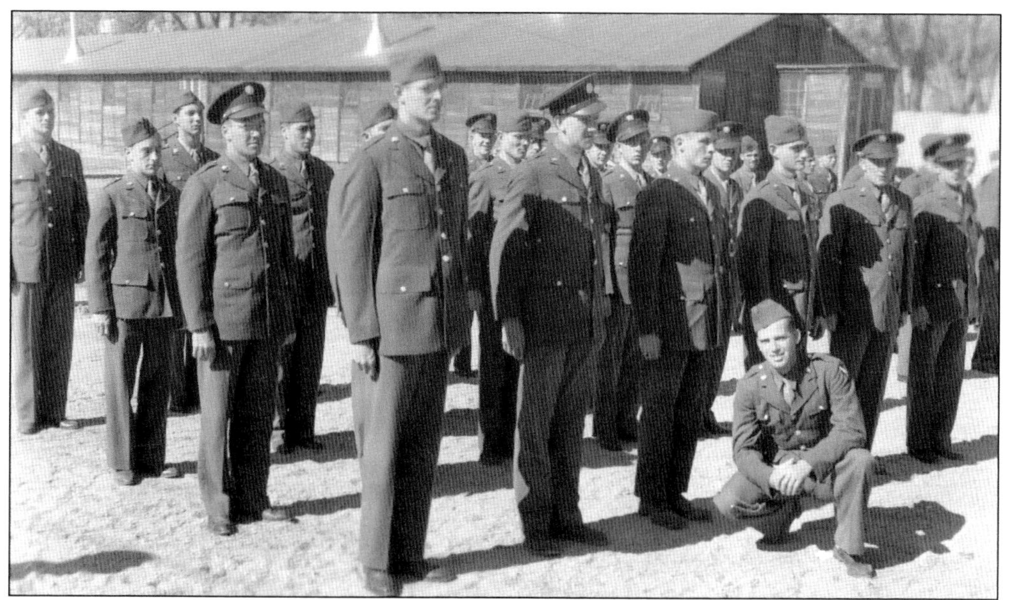

During World War II, no actual gliders were flown in Fort Morgan. The school flew small aircraft and students then went on to glider-pilot training in Texas.

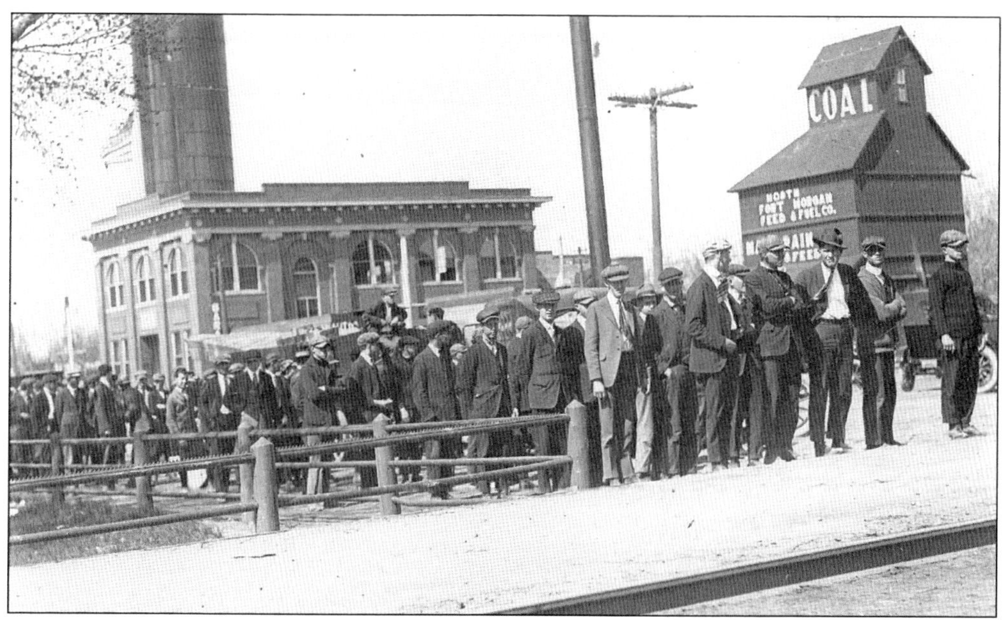

Pictured here in 1918 are local boys leaving to fight in World War I. The men are lined up next to the yard of the Fort Morgan depot. In the background is the Fort Morgan City Hall.

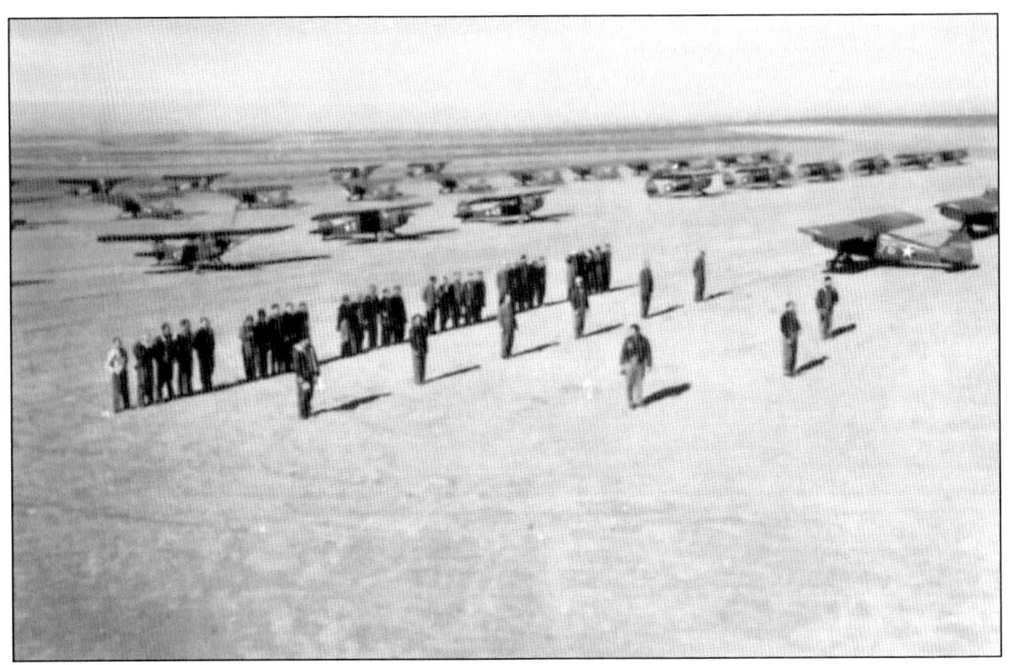

The Fort Morgan Municipal Airport played host to a six-week training school for military glider planes during World War II from 1942 to June 1943.

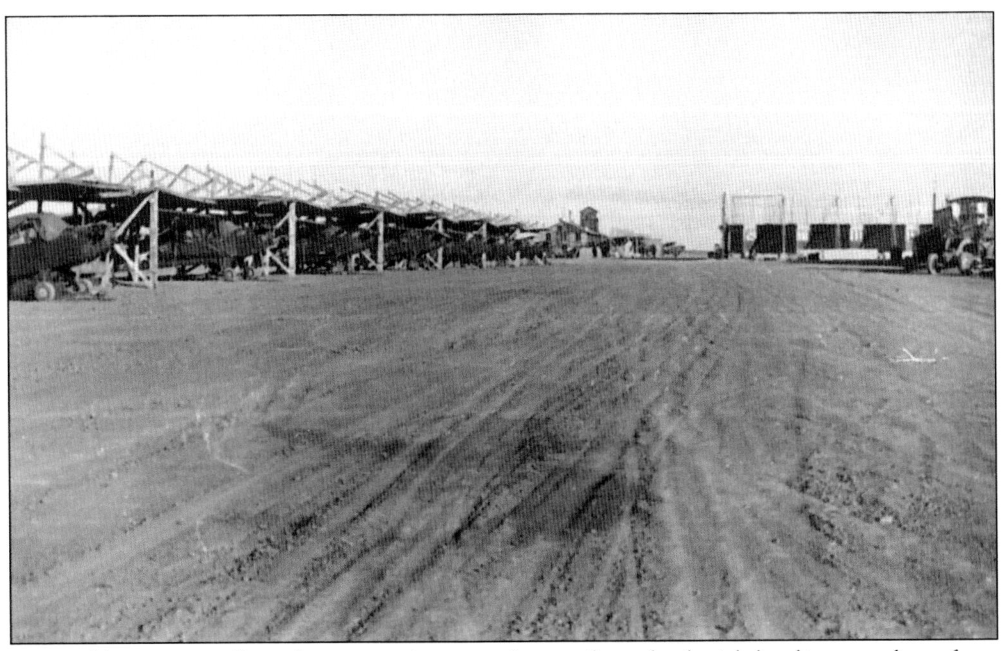

Pictured here are small single-engine planes used to perform dead stick landings; students from across the nation called Fort Morgan their temporary home.

Flagpoles and monuments mark the veterans' section of Riverside Cemetery. The larger monument is dedicated to the veterans of the Civil War. The modern monument was moved to the site upon the closing of the Fort Morgan Military Museum, a privately owned museum.

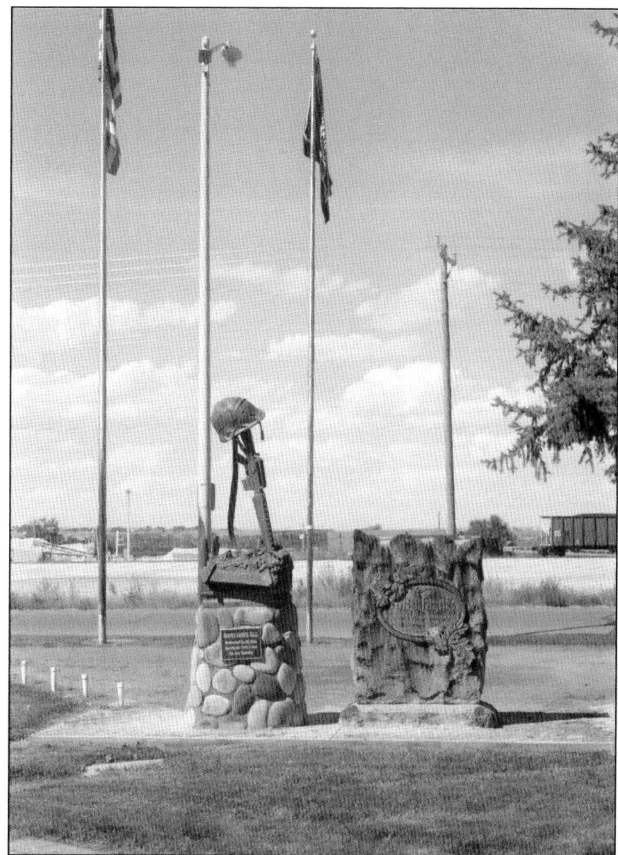

Pictured here are 10 members of the Army Air Corps Band putting on a performance; in the right center is Glenn Miller, in profile playing a trombone.

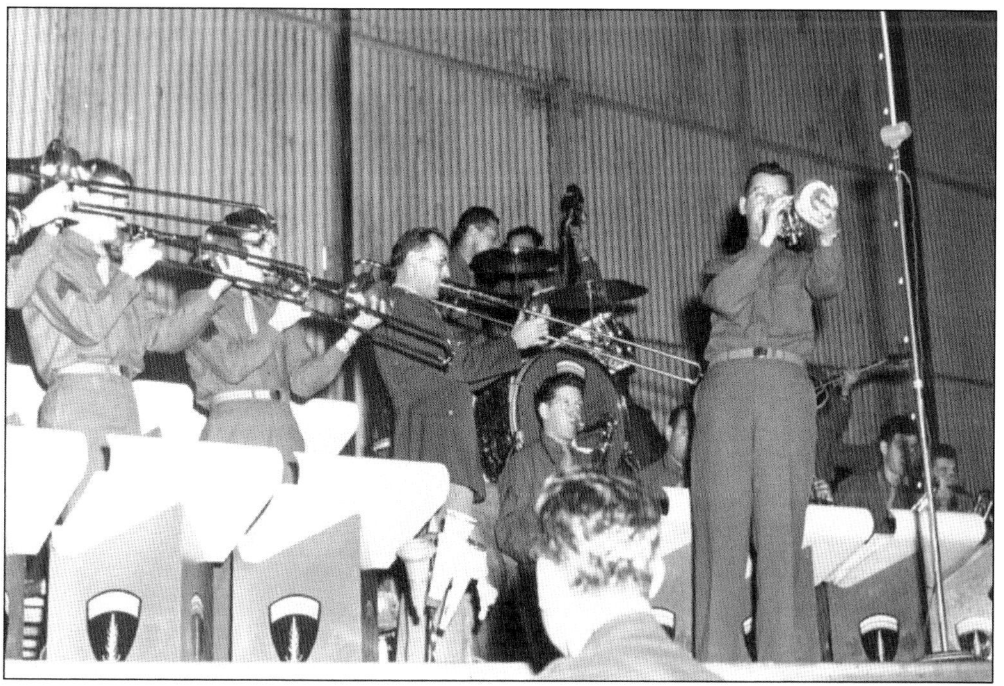

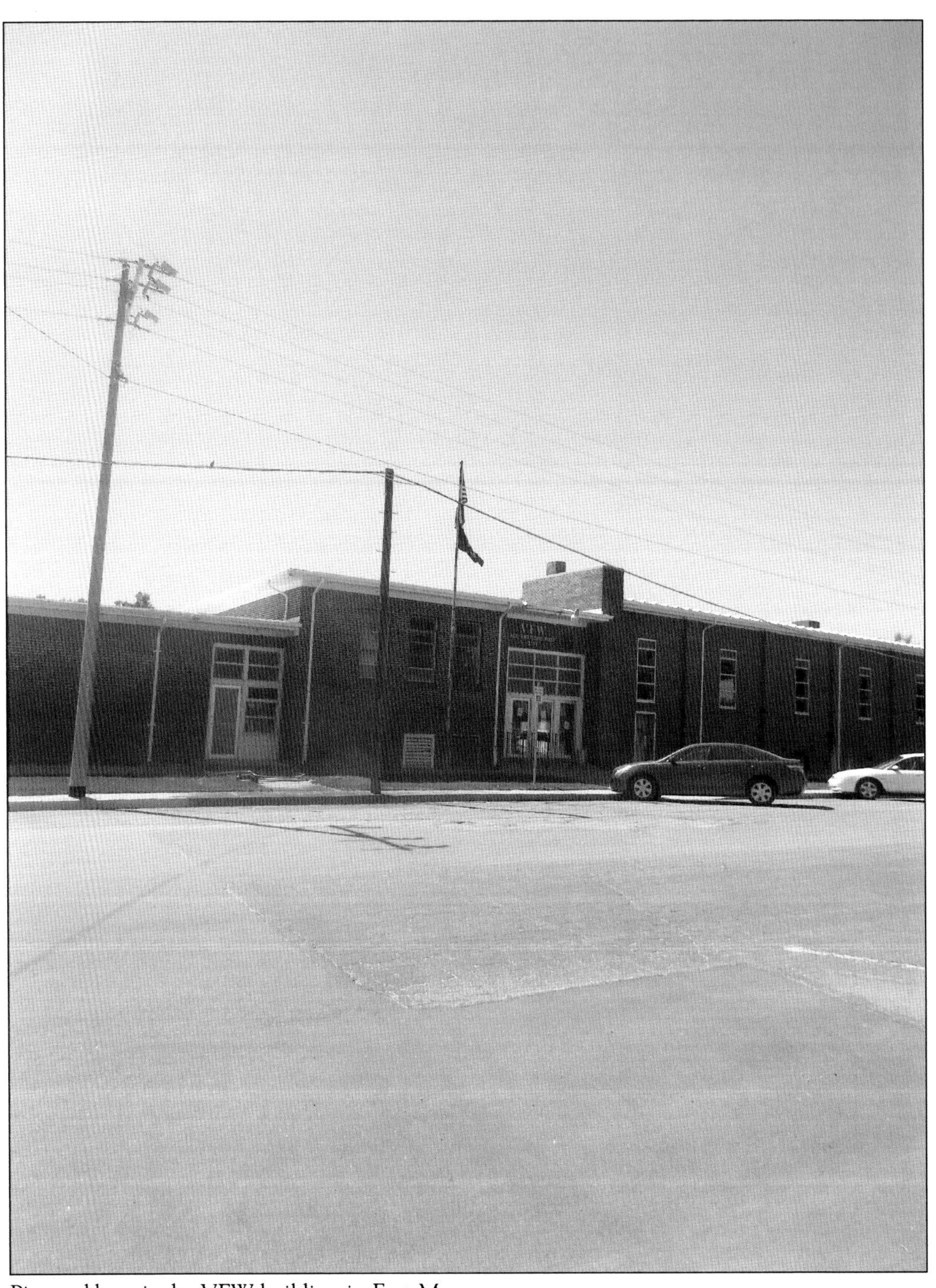

Pictured here is the VFW building in Fort Morgan.

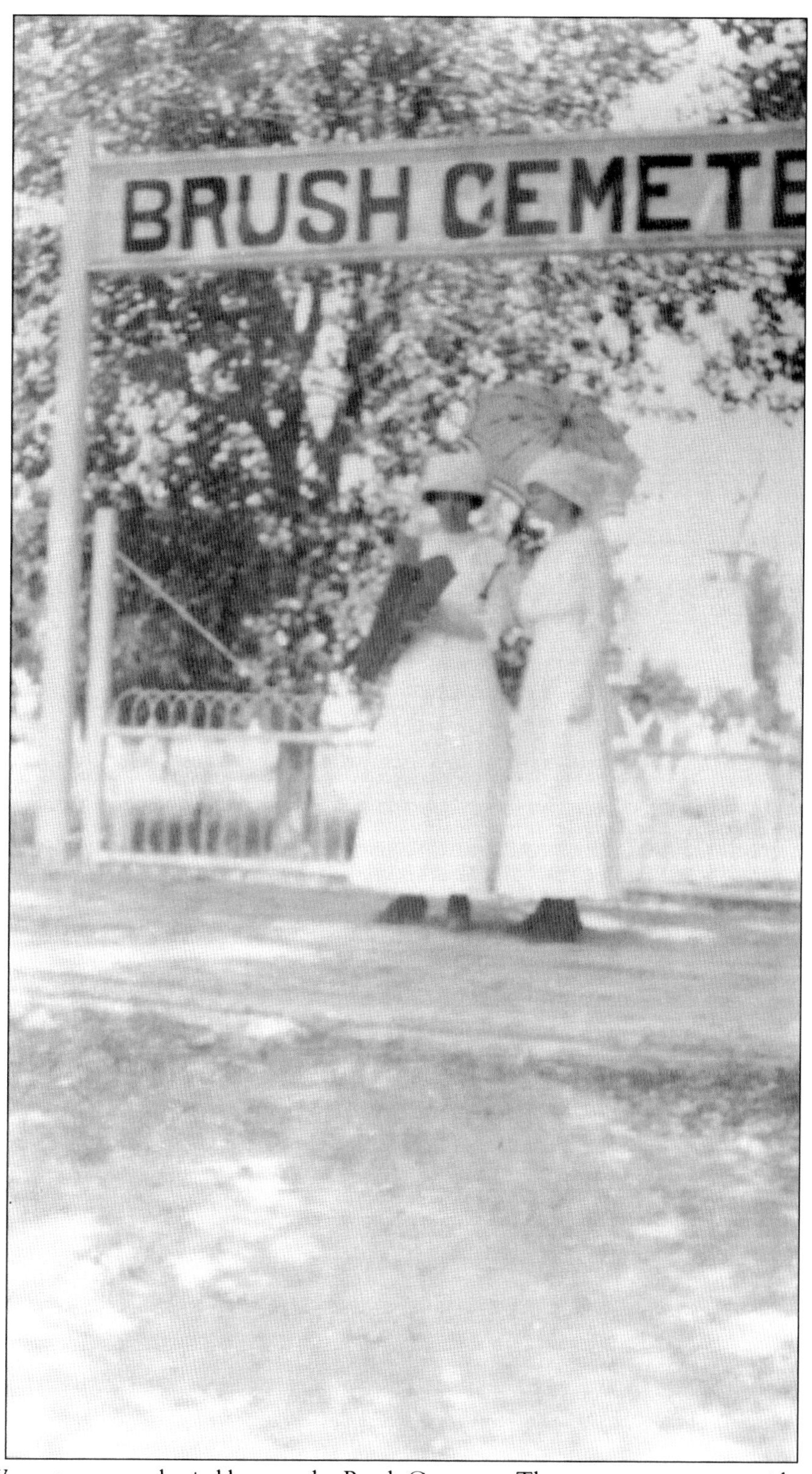

Civil War veterans are buried here at the Brush Cemetery. These two women are unidentified.